Tramps, Workmates
and Revolutionaries

Tramps, Workmates and Revolutionaries

Working-class Stories of the 1920s

Edited by
H. Gustav Klaus

Journeyman Press
LONDON • BOULDER, COLORADO

First published 1993 by Journeyman Press
345 Archway Road, London N6 5AA
and 5500 Central Avenue,
Boulder, Colorado 80301, USA

A catalogue record for this book is available
from the British Library

ISBN 1 85172 030 8 hb
ISBN 1 85172 031 6 pb

Library of Congress Cataloging in Publication Data
Tramps, workmates and revolutionaries : working-class stories of the
    1920s / edited by H. Gustav Klaus.
    192 p. 22 cm.
    Includes bibliographic references.
    ISBN 1–85172–030–8
    1. Working class–Great Britain–Fiction. 2. Working class
writings, English. 3. English fiction–20th century. 4. Short
stories, English. I. Klaus, H. Gustav, 1944–
PR1309.L3T73 1993
823' .0108920623–dc20   92–7332
                                                          CIP

Designed and produced for Journeyman by
Chase Production Services, Chipping Norton
Typeset from authors' disks by
Stanford Desktop Publishing Services, Milton Keynes
Printed in Finland by WSOY

Contents

Acknowledgements

The editor and publishers gratefully acknowledge permission to reprint copyright material in the book as follows:

Liam O'Flaherty, 'The Tramp', reprinted by permission of Jonathan Cape Ltd.
Joe Corrie, "The Day Before the Pay', reprinted by permission of Morag Corrie.
Harold Heslop, 'Compensation', reprinted by permission of Phyllis Heslop.
James Hanley, 'The Last Voyage', reprinted by permission of David Higham Associates.
Ethel Carnie Holdsworth, 'The Sheep', reprinted by permission of Mrs Quinn.
Hannah Mitchell, 'May Day', reprinted by permission of Geoffrey Mitchell.
James C. Welsh, 'The Meeting', reprinted by permission of J.L. Irvine.

Every effort has been made to trace copyright holders, but in a few cases this has proved impossible. The publishers would be interested to hear from any copyright holders not here acknowledged.

Introduction

The existence of a body of short fiction in the 1920s that can be called working-class is as yet unrecognised. Given the absence of anthologies, then as now, this will come as no real surprise. But compilations past or present can never be more than a first clue for the historian of working-class literature. If there is to be a recovery of forgotten or neglected texts, this necessitates a process of searching, sifting, discriminating and re-circulating. In our case it means browsing through the labour press of the decade, and consulting tiny avantgarde magazines. For it was in such media that these stories were published, not in anthologies and only exceptionally in collections.

Authors

Compared to the standard profile of the English writer up to about 1950 our authors are in an anomalous position.[1] A look at their social origins reveals that they do not come from the professional classes (v. the biographical notes). None of them received a public school education or went to Oxbridge. With Maxim Gorky they could say that life was their university. And the world, for most of them travelled widely. Beech, Hanley and O'Flaherty went to sea. Others who roamed far and wide include Davies, Alfred Holdsworth, Lawrence and James Leslie Mitchell. Beech and Fox in the early 1920s, Corrie, Heslop and O'Flaherty towards the close of the decade, visited Soviet Russia. Welsh at one point emigrated to New Zealand, where Mansfield came from to Europe.

There is, as one would expect, another anomaly, and that is the political affiliations or sympathies of these writers. With very few exceptions they would in the 1920s have regarded themselves as socialists or communists. And prior to that, many of them were known and some persecuted for their opposition to the War (Ashton, Beech, Carnie Holdsworth, Fox, Lawrence, Hannah Mitchell, Siffleet and Welsh).

Some readers might be surprised, or alarmed, to find D.H. Lawrence and Katherine Mansfield in this company. Yet it may be refreshing and

instructive to read them in a context different from the one in which
they are usually placed. What Lawrence shares with the rest is not only
his social background and consequent first-hand knowledge of working
people but a capacity to write from within a working-class community,
superbly evoking an atmosphere, a 'spirit of the place' with a few
sentences, though it is true that in his stories from the 1920s he rarely
returns to the working-class themes of his early phase. Mansfield's
power of empathy is similarly impressive, though, again, it has to be
granted that the choice of a working-class protagonist is fairly untypical
of the bulk of her work. To have these two writers here brings out their
strengths as well as their limitations, e.g. the danger of patronisation in
'Life of Ma Parker' or the obsession with the hideousness of industrialism in 'Fanny and Annie' (and elsewhere in Lawrence).

To emphasise such common factors among the authors of this
anthology is, of course, not to blind oneself to the essential differences
between them. The singular position of the friends, expatriates and established literati Lawrence and Mansfield needs no exposition.

Next there are the three or four other names that might be familiar
(Davies, Hanley, James Leslie Mitchell and O'Flaherty), all incidentally
of Celtic origins and young men struggling in the twenties to become
professional writers, who in pursuing this aim drifted from a proletarian or rural environment felt increasingly to be stifling, to a metropoli-
tan bohemian milieu, even though in their writings they would often
return to their original social and regional background.

We then have the older working-class writers (Ashton, Carnie
Holdsworth, Corrie, Fox and Welsh), who had quite a reputation and
public in their time, whom patronage and temporary success enabled
to 'escape' from their traditional community and to move for some time
on the fringe of literary circles, but who have dropped again into
obscurity. This group of writers, despite settling for a less precarious,
perhaps less monotonous or less exhausting job, never really severed their
working-class ties.

This is also true to some extent of the younger working-class authors,
people like Greenwood, Heslop and Hyde, who would achieve fame
– often shortlived – only in the following decade. Some of them first
took to writing during the enforced leisure of unemployment, thus fore-
shadowing a significant feature of the 1930s.

Finally, there are those occasional short-story writers – trade unionists
and other workers for the Cause, such as Beech, Alfred Holdsworth,
Hannah Mitchell and Siffleet – who never had a book to their credit,[2]
yet always took an active interest in the promotion of working-class

literature and intermittently made their own modest contribution to it by producing sketches and stories for a trade-union or political paper.

Women are under-represented in this anthology, with regard to both authorship and portraiture. *Tramps, workmates, revolutionaries* — the title indicates that this is very much a man's world. The female textile and leather workers, the clerks and shop assistants do not figure in these stories. Nor do the female trade unionists and fighters for women's rights, except for a very brief appearance in Hannah Mitchell's 'May Day'. The main reason for this absence is that so very few working-class stories were published by women, working or former working women in particular. Ethel Carnie Holdsworth is by all accounts an exceptional figure, and the inclusion of Katherine Mansfield's story at least reminds us of the multitudes engaged in domestic service throughout the inter-war period.

Hence that only three of the twenty stories are by women writers reflects the real history of published working-class short fiction in our period. Those interested in working-women's writing are referred to other genres: the documentary sketch, the diary or autobiography.[3]

Tramps

Not the tramping artisan of the old days but the modern vagrant makes an appearance in these stories, a tramp as often from choice as from necessity and, interestingly, by no means an abject or sullen figure but a person capable of enjoying life to the full. Perhaps at a time when the factory system, and its concomitant discipline and routine, has at last come to regulate the lives of the majority of the working population, the man who eschews work and rambles through the country acquires an aura of freedom and a touch of romanticism which serve as an antidote to the treadmill and dead-end prospects of factory life. Fox's booklet *Factory Echoes* (1919) contains a sketch of a worker who one morning hesitates at the factory gate and then, instead of clocking on, strolls out of town, exchanging for one day the smell and clamour of the workshop for the calm and clear air of the fields and returning wholly rejuvenated in the evening.[4] It is a yearning for a life not exclusively ruled by economic necessity and social constraints, which finds its epitome in O'Flaherty's 'The Tramp':

> I said to myself that it was a foolish game trying to do anything in this world but sleep and eat and enjoy the sun and the earth and the sea and the rain. That was twenty-two years ago. And I'm proud to

say that I never did a day's work since and never did a fellow-man
an injury. That's my religion and it's a good one.

Pauper in appearance, king in spirit. However idealised such an
image may be, there can be no doubt about the real-life quality of some
of the portraits that we find in these pieces. Witness Fox's two extraordinary characters: Jack Smith, also known as the Westminster Demosthenes for his very accomplished oratory, and his mate Clement
Bonham, a no less gifted talker who counts in his repertoire hilarious
tirades against old age and teetotalism. Jack has his own way of com-
memorating the Workers' Day or, for that matter, of celebrating
springtime: 'On the first day of May he always left whatever job he might
have, and struck out for the open country.'

The sympathy and understanding with which these characters are
drawn suggest that for Fox, O'Flaherty, Alfred Holdsworth and Hanley,
whose tale of a tramp has not been included here,[5] there exists no
unbridgeable moral and social gap between the *lumpen* and the proletariat proper.

All that seems a long way from George Orwell's description of 'the
regular character of a tramp – abject, envious, a jackal's character',[6]
though in his individual character-sketches Orwell was more generous.
The major difference between the working-class stories that treat of
vagrancy and Orwell's reportage is, of course, that Orwell mixed with
the down-and-out in order to shed some of his class prejudices and, from
a certain point onward, to gather the material for his factual account,
whereas our authors did not have to go slumming in order to come into
physical contact with vagrants. It is, for example, illuminating to see that
Orwell, even when he disclaims that tramps are a filthy race, cannot help
continually displaying his revulsion at squalor and sordidness, whereas
in Fox, Hanley, Alfred Holdsworth and O'Flaherty one will look in vain
for such references. Orwell's position as an outsider, if participant
observer and social explorer, as well as his intended audience, led him
almost by necessity to adopt the documentary form. The working-class
story-tellers, by contrast, could concentrate their attention on the
fictional exploration of a not unfamiliar feature of their environment.

The interest in the tramp,[7] and in the experience of a rootless life that
lacks the warmth but also the inevitable restrictions of continuous
employment, a tightly-knit community and a regular family life – all
aspects which are central to the dominant type of inter-war working-
class fiction – support the view that there is a different, if minor strand

of working-class narratives 'based not on place and continuity but on dislocation and transience'.[8]

The Workplace

It is, however, in the thematisation of work, in all its particulars and consequences, that the central tradition of proletarian story-telling finds its most frequent and common expression. Work as necessity, as ethos, as toil, but also in numerous concrete concerns such as the physical side of the labour process (Hanley), the permanent risks for life and health in many exacting jobs (Carnie Holdsworth, Corrie, Hanley, Heslop), the workplace facilities (Beech), the relationship between management or foreman and workforce (Corrie, Siffleet, Venner), the mood of, and relations amongst, the workers (Hanley, Hyde).

What these glimpses of the working day offer, is, most importantly, an inside view of the engineering works, the mine or the ship – not, as in the classic nineteenth-century middle-class perspectives of industry, merely a factory building that issues smoke, or a liner that moves as if of its own accord. That is, we see all these workplaces through the eyes of the people themselves – not through the lenses of some outside observer or temporary visitor, however sympathetic and well-meaning – and hence are invited to partake of their preoccupations and concerns, their dreams and nightmares, their anger and humour, in brief their humanity.

A good example of this is Stacey W. Hyde's 'The Turner' which is set entirely in a metallurgical plant. The story depicts a group of men during their lunch break, as they gather around a stove, prepare their food and tea, read a newspaper and talk about things until a particular subject is reached. It is the most ordinary of situations happening many times every week, and yet the author succeeds in engaging the reader's attention through one of his great strengths, the careful, unadulterated reproduction of the dialect, habits of speech, idioms and jokes of his 'shopmates' – hence the title of his collection. Once the conversation between the workmen is under way, no self-conscious narrator intrudes to qualify or mock this mode of speech. The brisk and vigorous language, which old Charlie uses in his yarn about a presumed parson, brings the characters to life – the story-teller no less than the objects of his yarn. And in doing so, it reveals the individuality of the turners, thus calmly disposing of the assumption, still widely held in the twenties, that the industrial proletariat is an undifferentiated mass of amorphous beings.

However, there is also a risk involved in lending an attentive ear and eye to the people if the findings, when transposed into literature, are not controlled and shaped by some sagacious mind. For all its fun and liveliness, the episode on which Hyde has chosen to dwell is ultimately of no consequence. Just how impressionistic and aimless his overall conception is, can be gauged when 'The Turner' is set against the lunch or tea breaks in *The Ragged Trousered Philanthropists,* where Tressell excels in driving home a particular message.

But we might as well take one of our authors as a contrasting example. In Joe Corrie's story 'The Day Before the Pay' three miners are likewise shown conversing during their 'piece'. And the representation of the Scottish vernacular in this story appears no less faithful than Hyde's. But the author is clearly not content to let the matter rest there. He assails an industrial system which makes it impossible for an honest working man to support his family. As with the figure of Tam here, Corrie often singles out the hard-working, a-political, non-union miner who is exposed as a victim of conditions beyond his understanding, and yet which he in his political dullness unwittingly helps to perpetuate. As one of the more aware colliers comments: 'It's a hell of a job when men can only see daylicht through an empty belly.' If there is a trace of irony is this treatment, it is not of the savage attacking kind that we find, for example, in Tressell, but rather one tainted with bitterness and a sense of tragedy, as in another of the author's stories, 'The Last Day',[9] in which an old miner, again a working-class Tory, hangs himself after having been given notice.

Work is a commanding presence in these stories even when the focus shifts from the point of production to the home. In James Hanley's 'The Last Voyage' the extension of the work process into what is nominally leisure time takes on a truly obsessive character, when at night the old sailor Johnny Reilly, instead of falling asleep, continuously and nightmarishly re-lives the ordeal of his just completed voyage. Johnny's plight results not only from the general fatigue of old age, further aggravated by a recent accident, but from his exposure to the most callous and brutal taunts and humiliations by the younger crew for being old.

In the other sea story of this collection, by Dick Beech, the protagonist actually dreams of a packet-boat, though the real working and living conditions on board have miraculously been substituted for splendidly equipped cabins complete with bathrooms and a library. It is a seaman's utopia, as the reader realises when the dreamer wakes up at the end of the tale to find himself lying on the sofa at home.

At Home

As these stories demonstrate, the home is a separate sphere and yet connected with, and penetrated by, the world of labour in various ways. It is thus not possible to draw a clear demarcation line between the two areas. For even where the ostensible locale is the home or an open space, work may loom in the background. It does so ominously in the stories of D.H. Lawrence and Rhys Davies. The opening scene, indeed the very first word of 'Fanny and Annie' pictures the male protagonist waiting on the platform, 'flame-lurid' from the iron-foundry in which he is employed. In 'A Bed of Feathers', though this is primarily an exploration of religious dogmatism coupled with lechery and possessiveness, we cannot be oblivious either of the labour of Jacob and his brother Emlyn, as we see them set off in the morning for the mine, or follow Rebecca, the young bride whom Jacob has lured with his savings into an unconsummated marriage, adapting to the duties of a collier's wife. Only once do we actually get a glimpse of the pit, in the climactic scene in which Jacob brings about a roof-fall in order to rid himself of his brother. But this deadly incident only epitomises the atmosphere of claustrophobia – associated with the occupation of the men – which encumbers these invariably base characters.

An oppressive mood permeates also Ethel Carnie Holdworth's 'The Sheep'. Work here has in effect entered the home and is ever-present in the world of a young child. For Peter's mother has, one gathers, to earn a living as a washerwoman after her husband's death in a quarry accident. But work is also present in the performance of the slaughterer whom Peter watches in the backyard going about his bloody and ugly business. In the troubled mind of this child, so disturbed by the loss of his father, work and killing appear somehow connected, and the author suggests that the child's sensitiveness and intuitive insight are greater than those of the hardened adults.

Together with 'Life of Ma Parker' the three afore-mentioned stories are also notable in so far as women rank among the protagonists, whereas in the other stories they are either absent or lead only a subordinate existence as housewives. Thus this section somewhat alleviates the general impression given by the anthology that this is exclusively a man's world.

Moments of Struggle

Comparatively few stories cover moments of social or industrial strife. This is striking in view of the fact that in most socialist novels of the period, often by the same authors,[10] such scenes are given prominent treatment. Perhaps the genre was deemed unsuitable for this kind of theme. It may have been felt that in order to portray a strike, violent demonstration or battle with police a slow build-up and epic canvas were needed for them to be successfully rendered.

When one reads some of the actual stories that depict militant struggles, such caution on the part of the more conscientious practitioners of short fiction appears well-founded. In Arthur Siffleet's 'The Broken Baton', for example, which was written during the miners' lockout of 1926 and deals with a police assault on colliers who are trying to prevent a shift of blacklegs entering a pit, we are shown the growing resentment of a newly-recruited constable, from miners' stock himself, at the preparations for his first mission. No doubt such feelings existed among individual members of the police force, but the solution adopted by the author seems rather contrived: 'In a flash Jim's Working class instincts blazed up',[11] and in the middle of the turmoil he cracks his baton on the Inspector's head – without even being detected.

The same improbabilities mar one of Hyde's *Shopmates* stories that treats of an apprentices' strike. Here, however, the wishful thinking goes in the other direction. After a prolonged and bitter fight, victory for the lads comes not through the solidarity of the other workers, or the pressure of public opinion which the young strike leader has sought to influence through skilfully launched interviews. The happy outcome is rather the result of a personal intervention by the factory owner, Lord Murray, who has read about the disagreeable affair in the papers. This gentleman, or rather *deus ex machina*, (con)descends to visit the factory and to personally reinstate the victimised apprentices' leader, praising him for his 'initiative' and 'character' while admonishing the baffled manager.[12]

Rather than reprinting these scarcely satisfying stories, which would not have done their authors justice, I have selected two fairly self-contained episodes from novels of the decade, even though such a procedure may invite criticism. But H.R. Barbor's 'Sabotage' has really the shape and tone of a short story. It traces the awakening to action of an old and lonely, hitherto a-political railway worker, from an initial restlessness, as he sees the young men of his village depart in order to join the revolutionary forces, to a harrowing uneasiness, when the village is occupied by the reactionary troops, and finally to his resolve to give his all to the revolution. Neither the place nor the protagonist of this story had before been introduced in the novel, nor does the author return to them thereafter. The insertion of such an isolated episode certainly fulfils a function for the novel, but there is no denying that it can be read without loss outside the context of the novel.

Not quite the same can be said of the excerpt from James C. Welsh's *The Morlocks*. However, the tense atmosphere created in this narrative and (as in Barbor) the final tragic note are so rare in the political short fiction of the period – O'Flaherty's 'The Sniper' is the only other example I can think of[13] – that once again formal considerations had to come second.

Where Welsh leads us into the thick of the struggle, Hannah Mitchell offers a multiply mediated view of a demonstration and meeting. The choice of a reporting narrative, the point of view of a political apathetic and the comic mode all serve to distance the incident, though such a method, supported as it is by the Lancashire dialect, need not prove less effective, as Teddy Ashton, Hannah Mitchell's acknowledged source of inspiration, was only too aware.[14]

This section, and the anthology, closes with a dramatisation of the contemporaneous struggles going on elsewhere in the world against British imperialism.

Technique

Grouping these stories by their settings and subjects brings out the attention that most of our authors pay to real places. A slice of real life is presented, not in the naturalist sense (for such crucial tenets of Naturalism as the overpowering impact of the environment and the depiction of passive suffering are clearly missing here), but in the concentration on an incident, situation or character which, despite their apparent ordinariness, are shown to have an interest.

This recreation and exploration of various aspects of the multi-faceted world of working-class experience does not in my view necessarily require dramatisation. The inclusion of a number of sketches such as those by Fox or Hannah Mitchell, are evidence that I have taken a liberal view on genre boundaries.

The actual techniques used in these stories are so manifold that no unified picture emerges. A wide range of narrative procedures and effects is employed: from the chronological ordering of the narrative to the retrospective glance; from the direct reporting stance to the free indirect speech and interior monologue of a character; from the suggested meaning to the clear lesson; from the framing device (the story within the story) to the surprise-ending. The authors of the miniature pieces must have found the latter type particularly congenial for their purposes, so often do they have recourse to it. (On the economy of the short-story production see the next section.)

Where a number of these stories might be said to differ from mainstream short fiction is in the extensive and powerful reproduction of dialect, which goes much further than anything Kipling had attempted. These are at the same time the stories that are conspicuous for their humour (excepting the piece by Corrie). It would, I think, lead nowhere to try to trace literary influences of this mode. The stories in question are so much rooted in everyday working-class life that something of the original situation of oral story-telling, as it survived perhaps in the pub, is preserved here.

Distribution

During the whole of the decade only two collections of stories by individual worker-writers seem to have gone to the press, Stacey Hyde's *Shopmates* (1924) and Joe Corrie's *The Last Day* (1928). And in each case the imprint was a non-commercial, socialist one, the Labour Publishing Co. and the Forward Publishing Co. respectively. (Hanley's first collection *Men in Darkness* followed somewhat later, in 1931; his earlier stories, including 'The Last Voyage', were all privately printed and published in limited editions. Walter Greenwood's stories, though written between 1928 and 1931, did not appear until 1937.)[15] This illustrates how heavily dependent on a sympathetic labour press the working-class tale was in these years for its distribution. Large-scale patronage from politically committed middle-class intellectuals with an access to the publishing business, as we find it in the thirties, was simply non-existent.

Of the working-class newspapers which played a vital role in the promotion of the proletarian tale the communist-oriented *Sunday Worker* (1925–9) has probably the best record. From its inception, this paper made a habit of encouraging its readers to submit sketches and stories, and for a time offered a prize each week 'for the best article or story *illustrative* of Workers' life'.[16] An expressly documentary and representative angle was urged upon prospective contributors, which shows in such early titles as 'A Day in the Life of a Building Trade Worker' (14.6.1925), 'A Pit Boy's Story' (28.6.1925) or 'A Weaver's Life' (5.7.1925) though later this trend to shop-floor themes subsided somewhat and the writing competition was abandoned. A whole number of worker-writers had their stories printed in this way, authors who with very few exceptions would remain obscure figures.

The *Worker* (1918–31), which started as the organ of the workers' committees in Scotland and subsequently became the paper of the National Minority Movement, also opened its pages to working-class authors who would never have found an outlet in the middle-class press. Under John S. Clarke's editorship literature became an integral part of this militant weekly. When in 1926 the paper moved from Glasgow to London, the driving force behind the sketches and tales 'From Real Life' (thus the heading of the column) may have been Robert Ellis. As a delegate to the First International Conference of Revolutionary and Pro-letarian Writers held in Moscow in the wake of the Tenth Anniversary of the October Revolution, Ellis would have been familiar with the move to build up proletarian literature through the creation of workers' correspondents movements in all countries. On one of his frequent visits to the Soviet Union, Ellis probably became acquainted with Heslop's first novel, issued in 1926 in Leningrad under the most unusual cir-cumstances.[17] Heslop started contributing to the *Worker*, first short stories, then regular reviews well before any of his novels were published in Britain. Ellis later invited Heslop to do some part-time editing for the *Worker*, and they went jointly to Kharkov in 1930 to attend the Second International Conference of Revolutionary and Proletarian Writers.

A third weekly which displayed an occasional interest in working-class literature was the Scottish *Forward* (1906–1960) edited from Glasgow. This ILP paper limited its attention almost exclusively to Scottish writers. John S. Clarke, after his resignation from the *Worker*, had for years a regular 'Views and Reviews' column in it, and Joe Corrie's short stories as well as a novel were first serialised here.

This mode of distribution also reveals something about the original readership of the stories. On the negative side, however, we have to note the inevitable restrictions imposed on the contributors. As almost no literary editor of a paper seemed inclined to reserve an entire page for a story, authors could expect to be offered no more than 600–900 words. Theoretically the periodicals of the labour movement could have intervened to provide greater space. This, however, was not the case. In the *Labour Monthly*, the *Plebs*, the *Communist Review* and the *Socialist Review*, art and literature are not accorded any significant status. Though book reviews feature in some, by no means all of them, the thing itself – the short story, serialised novel, literary reportage or dramatic sketch – remained barred. It is a situation which contrasts poorly with earlier periods in the history of the British labour movement. The Chartist press, it is as well to remember, had made it a virtue to house politics, history, criticism and literature under the same roof. And in the 1880s *Justice* and *Commonweal* did not hesitate to open their pages to socialist fiction.

If there was one single point of succour in the late twenties, to which several of our more ambitious young authors turned for assistance, it was Charles Lahr's Progressive Bookshop in Holborn, with its Bohemian and radical clientèle. Of German origin and Anarchist-Syndicalist leanings, Charlie Lahr had, along with the London Wobblies, joined the CP at the time of its foundation in 1920, but had left it again in disgust shortly after the announcement of the New Economic Policy in Soviet Russia. Lahr became the publisher of the *New Coterie* (1925–7) which included D.H. Lawrence, Liam O'Flaherty and Rhys Davies among its contributors. He also brought out the latter's first collection of stories, *The Song of Songs* (1927). And it was in Lahr's home that James Hanley found temporary accommodation in order to write the stories that make up *Men in Darkness*.[18] It must have been here, too, that the slightly earlier 'Last Voyage' was completed, for it carries a dedication to Lahr's daughter Oonagh. Other progressive writers that would make regular appearances in the Bookshop included R.M. Fox, Hugh MacDiarmid and Jack Lindsay, co-editor of the *London Aphrodite* (1928–9), in which Davies's 'A Bed of Feathers' first appeared.

Lahr's stimulating personality and entourage, his warm encouragement and practical aid remained an exception. For most working-class authors, story writing, like the composition of poetry, came to be seen as an initial or transitional stage in a writing career in which the crowning achievement was the publication of a novel, since by itself the genre appeared to offer little recompense, commercially or critically. Thus Welsh in his introduction to Hyde's *Shopmates* immediately recommended that the author 'try his hand at larger things'.[19] Welsh himself had, like Ethel Carnie Holdsworth before or Joe Corrie after him, made his entry into literature with a volume of poems, of which several pieces had, characteristically, first appeared in working-class papers. He had then proceeded to short stories (never published in book format) and finally tackled the novel.

A consequence of this widespread uncritical acceptance of a hierarchy of literary forms in which the novel was privileged, is that rather less creative energy went into the production of sketches and tales than might have been possible or desirable. The harvest of these years, as gathered in this anthology, is thus all the more impressive.

P.S.

It remains for me to thank Andy Croft, Carole Ferrier and Paul Salveson for their advice on some sections of this book.

Notes

1. For the standard patterns see Raymond Williams, *The Long Revolution* (Harmondsworth, 1965 [1961]), pp. 255–70, and Malcolm Bradbury, *The Social Context of Modern English Literature* (Oxford, 1971), pp. 129–43.

2. Hannah Mitchell's autobiography *The Hard Way Up* (London, 1968) was not published during her lifetime.

3. See, for example, Margaret A. Pollock ed., *Working Days: Being the Personal Records of Sixteen Men and Women written by Themselves* (London, 1926); Margaret Llewellyn Davies ed., *Life as We Have Known It: By Co-operative Working Women* (London, 1931); Annie Kenney, *Memories of a Militant* (London, 1924); Kathleen Woodward, *Jipping Street: Childhood in a London Slum* (London, 1928). Davies's collection and Woodward's autobiography were reprinted by Virago in 1977 and 1983 respectively.

4. R.M. Fox, 'The Slacker' in his *Factory Echoes and Other Sketches* (London, n.d. [1919]), pp. 17–21.

5. James Hanley, 'Rubbish' in his *Men in Darkness* (London, 1931). The first published story of Leslie Halward, a short-story writer who rose to prominence in the 1930s, also deals with a tramp, 'The Devil's Bait', *Everyman*, 18 April 1929.

6. George Orwell, *Down and Out in Paris and London* (Harmondsworth, 1966 [1933]), p. 136.

7. Part of the interest in the figure of the tramp may also derive from W.H. Davies's *The Autobiography of a Super Tramp* (1907) which by 1920 had gone through five impressions.

8. Ken Worpole, 'Expressionism and Working-Class Fiction' in his *Dockers and Detectives* (London, 1983), p. 77. Worpole identifies this strand, in the 1930s, in the sea stories of James Hanley, George Garrett and Jim Phelan.

9. Joe Corrie, *The Last Day and Other Stories* (Glasgow, n.d. [1928]), pp. 3–5.

10. For a discussion of some of these novels see my article 'Silhouettes of Revolution: Some Neglected Novels of the Early 1920s'

in H. Gustav Klaus ed., *The Socialist Novel in Britain* (Brighton, 1982), pp. 89–109.

11. Arthur Siffleet, 'The Broken Baton', *Sunday Worker*, 28 November 1926.

12. Stacey W. Hyde, 'The Apprentice' in his *Shopmates* (London, 1924), pp. 89–116.

13. Liam O'Flaherty, 'The Sniper', *New Leader*, 12 January 1923; later incorporated in his *Spring Sowing* (London, 1924), from which 'The Tramp' is also taken.

14. Since Teddy Ashton (alias Allen Clarke) often reprinted his stories without usually indicating the date of first publication, it cannot be ruled out that 'The Great Chowbent Football Match' saw the light before the 1920s.

15. Walter Greenwood, *The Cleft Stick, or 'It's the same the whole world over'* (London, 1937).

16. *Sunday Worker*, 13 September 1925.

17. *Pod Vlastu Uglya* (Under the Sway of Coal), which was later published in English under the title of *Goaf* (London, 1934). For an account of the author's life and work see H. Gustav Klaus, 'Harold Heslop: Miner Novelist' in *The Literature of Labour* (Brighton, 1985), pp. 89–105.

18. Cf. David Goodway, 'Charles Lahr: Anarchist, bookseller, publisher', *London Magazine* (June–July 1977), pp. 46–55.

19. James C. Welsh, 'Introduction' to *Shopmates*, op. cit., p. viii.

Liam O'Flaherty The Tramp

There were eight paupers in the convalescent yard of the workhouse hospital. The yard was an oblong patch of cement with the dining-room on one side and a high red-brick wall on the other. At one end was the urinal and at the other a little tarred wooden shed where there was a bathroom and a wash-house. It was very cold, for the sun had not yet risen over the buildings that crowded out the yard almost from the sky. It was a raw bleak February morning, about eight o'clock.

The paupers had just come out from breakfast and stood about uncertain what to do. What they had eaten only made them hungry and they stood shivering, making muffs of their coat sleeves, their little black woollen caps perched on their heads, some still chewing a last mouthful of bread, others scowling savagely at the ground as they conjured up memories of hearty meals eaten some time in the past.

As usual Michael Deignan and John Finnerty slouched off into the wash-house and leaned against the sink, while they banged their boots on the floor to keep warm. Deignan was very tall and lean. He had a pale melancholy face and there was something the matter with the iris of his right eye. It was not blue like the other eye, but of an uncertain yellowish colour that made one think, somehow, that he was a sly, cunning, deceitful fellow, a totally wrong impression. His hair was very grey around the temples and fair elsewhere. The fingers of his hands were ever so long and thin and he was always chewing at the nails and looking at the ground, wrapped in thought.

'It's very cold,' he said in a thin, weak, listless voice. It was almost inaudible.

'Yes,' replied Finnerty gruffly, as he started up and heaved a loud sigh. 'Ah —' he began and then he stopped, snorted twice to clear his nose, and let his head fall on his chest. He was a middle-sized, thick-set fellow, still in good condition and fat in the face, which was round and rosy, with grey eyes and very white teeth. His black hair was grown long and curled about his ears. His hands were round, soft and white, like a schoolmaster's.

15

The two of them stood leaning their backs against the washstand and stamped their feet in a moody silence for several minutes and then the tramp, who had been admitted to the hospital the previous night, wandered into the wash-house. He appeared silently at the entrance of the shed and paused there for a moment while his tiny blue eyes darted around piercingly yet softly, just like a graceful wild animal might look through a clump of trees in a forest. His squat low body, standing between the tarred doorposts of the shed with the concrete wall behind and the grey sky overhead, was after a fashion menacing with the power and vitality it seemed to exude. So it seemed at least to the two dejected, listless paupers within the shed. They looked at the tramp with a mournful vexed expression and an envious gleam in their eyes and a furrowing of their foreheads and a shrinking of their flesh from this fresh dominant coarse lump of aggressive wandering life, so different to their own jaded, terror-stricken lives. Each thought, 'Look at the red fat face of that vile tramp. Look at his fierce insulting eyes, that stare you in the face as boldly as a lion, or a child, and are impudent enough to have a gentle expression at the back of them, unconscious of malice. Look at that huge black beard that covers all his face and neck except the eyes and the nose and a narrow red slit for the mouth. My God, what throat muscles and what hair on his chest, on a day like this too, when I would die of cold to expose my chest that way!'

So each thought and neither spoke. As the tramp grinned foolishly – he just opened his beard, exposed red lips and red gums with stray blackened teeth scattered about them and then closed the beard again – the two paupers made no response. The two of them were educated men, and without meaning it they shrank from associating with the unseemly dirty tramp on terms of equality, just as they spent the day in the wash-house in the cold, so as to keep away from the other paupers.

The tramp took no further notice of them. He went to the back of the shed and stood there looking out of the door and chewing tobacco. The other two men, conscious of his presence and irritated by it, fidgeted about and scowled. At last the tramp looked at Deignan, grinned, fumbled in his coat pocket, took out a crumpled cigarette and handed it to Deignan with another grin and a nodding of his head. But he did not speak.

Deignan had not smoked a cigarette for a week. As he looked at it for a moment in wonder, his bowels ached with desire for the little thin, crumpled, dirt-stained roll of tobacco held between the thumb and forefinger of the tramp's gnarled and mud-caked hand. Then with a contortion of his face as he tried to swallow his breath he muttered,

'You're a brick,' and stretched out a trembling hand. In three seconds the cigarette was lit and he was inhaling the first delicious puff of drug-laden smoke. His face lit up with a kind of delicious happiness. His eyes sparkled. He took three puffs and was handing the cigarette to his friend when the tramp spoke.

'No, keep it yerself, towny,' he said in his even, effortless, soft voice. 'I've got another for him.'

And then when the two paupers were smoking, their listlessness vanished and they became cheerful and talkative. The two cigarettes broke down the barriers of distrust and contempt between themselves and the tramp. His unexpected act of generosity had counteracted his beard and the degraded condition of his clothes. He was not wearing a pauper's uniform, but a patched corduroy trousers and numbers of waistcoats and tattered coats of all colours, piled indiscriminately on his body and held together not by buttons but by a cord tied around his waist. They accepted him as a friend. They began to talk to him.

'You just came in for the night?' asked Deignan. There was still a con-descending tone in the cultured accents.

The tramp nodded. Then after several seconds he rolled his tobacco to the other cheek, spat on the floor and hitched up his trousers.

'Yes,' he said, 'I walked from Drogheda yesterday and I landed in Dublin as tired as a dog. I said to myself that the only place to go was in here. I needed a wash, a good bed and a rest, and I had only ninepence, a piece of steak, a few spuds and an onion. If I bought a bed they'd be all gone and now I've had a good sleep, a warm bath, and I still have my ninepence and my grub. I'll start off as soon as I get out at eleven o'clock and maybe walk fifteen miles before I put up for the night somewhere.'

'But how did you get into the hospital ward?' asked Finnerty, eyeing the tramp with a jealous look. The cigarette had accentuated Finnerty's feeling of hunger, and he was irritated at the confident way the tramp talked of walking fifteen miles that day and putting up somewhere afterwards.

'How did I get in?' said the tramp. 'That's easy. I got a rash on my right leg this three years. It always gets me into hospital when I strike a workhouse. It's easy.'

Again there was a silence. The tramp shuffled to the door and looked out into the yard. The sky overhead was still grey and bleak. The water that had been poured over the concrete yard to wash it two hours before, still glistened in drops and lay in little pools here and there. There was no heat in the air to dry it.

The other six paupers, three old men with sticks, two young men and a youth whose pale face was covered with pimples, were all going about uncertainly, talking in a tired way and peering greedily in through the windows of the dining-room, where old Neddy, the pauper in charge of the dining-room, was preparing the bread and milk for the dinner ration. The tramp glanced around at all this and then shrugged his shoulders and shuffled back to the end of the wash-house.

'How long have you been in here?' he asked Deignan.

Deignan stubbed the remainder of his cigarette against his boot, put the quenched piece in the lining of his cap and then said, 'I've been here six months.' 'Educated man?' said the tramp. Deignan nodded. The tramp looked at him, went to the door and spat and then came back to his former position:

'I'll say you're a fool,' he said quite coolly. 'There doesn't look to be anything the matter with you. In spite of your hair, I bet you're no more than thirty-five. Eh?'

'That's just right about my age, but –'

'Hold on,' said the tramp. 'You are as fit as a fiddle, this is a spring morning, and yer loafing in here and eating yer heart out with hunger and misery instead of taking to the roads. What man! You're mad. That's all there's to it.' He made a noise with his tongue as if driving a horse and began to clap his hands on his bare chest. Every time he hit his chest there was a dull heavy sound like distant thunder. The noise was so loud that Deignan could not speak until the tramp stopped beating his chest. He stood wriggling his lips and winking his right eye in irritation against what the tramp had said and jealousy of the man's strength and endurance, beating his bare hairy chest that way on such a perishing day. The blows would crush Deignan's ribs and the exposure would give him pneumonia.

'It's all very well for you to talk,' he began querulously. Then he stopped and looked at the tramp. It occurred to him that it would be ridiculous to talk to a tramp about personal matters. But there was something aggressive and dominant and yet absolutely unemotional in the tramp's fierce stare that drove out that feeling of contempt. Instead Deignan felt spurred to defend himself. 'How could you understand me?' he continued. 'As far as you can see I am all right. I have no disease but a slight rash on my back and that comes from underfeeding, from hunger and … and depression. My mind is sick. But of course you don't understand that.'

'Quite right,' said Finnerty, blowing cigarette smoke through his nostrils moodily. 'I often envy those who don't think. I wish I were a farm labourer.'

'Huh.' The tramp uttered the exclamation in a heavy roar. Then he laughed loudly and deeply, stamped his feet and banged his chest. His black beard shook with laughter. 'Mother of Mercy,' he cried, 'I'll be damned but you make me laugh, the two of you.'

The two shuffled with their feet and coughed and said nothing. They became instantly ashamed of their contemptuous thoughts for the tramp, he who a few minutes before had given them cigarettes. They suddenly realized that they were paupers, degraded people, and contemptible people for feeling superior to a fellow man because he was a tramp. They said nothing. The tramp stopped laughing and became serious.

'Now look here,' he said to Deignan, 'what were you in civilian life, as they say to soldiers, what did you do before you came in here?'

'Oh the last job I had was a solicitor's clerk,' murmured Deignan, biting his nails. 'But that was only a stopgap, I can't say that I ever had anything permanent. Somehow I always seemed to drift. When I left college I tried for the Consular Service and failed. Then I stayed at home for a year at my mother's place in Tyrone. She has a little estate there. Then I came to Dublin here. I got disgusted hanging around at home. I fancied everybody was pitying me. I saw everybody getting married or doing something while I only loafed about, living on my mother. So I left. Landed here with two portmanteaux and eighty-one pounds. It's six years ago next fifteenth of May. A beautiful sunny day it was too.'

Deignan's plaintive voice drifted away into silence and he gnawed his nails and stared at the ground. Finnerty was trying to get a last puff from the end of his cigarette. He was trying to hold the end between his thumbs and puckered up his lips as if he were trying to drink boiling milk. The tramp silently handed him another cigarette and then he turned to Deignan.

'What did ye do with the eighty-one quid?' he said. 'Did ye drink it or give it to the women?'

Finnerty, cheered by the second cigarette which he had just lit, uttered a deep guffaw and said, 'Ha, the women blast them, they're the curse of many a man's life,' but Deignan started up and his face paled and his lips twitched.

'I can assure you,' he said, 'that I never touched a woman in my life.' He paused as if to clear his mind of the horror that the tramp's suggestion had aroused in him. 'No, I can't say I drank it. I can't say I did anything at all. I just drifted from one job to another. Somehow, it seemed to me that nothing big could come my way and that it didn't matter very much how I spent my life, because I would be a failure anyway. Maybe I did drink too much once in a while, or dropped a few pounds at a race meeting, but nothing of any account. No, I came down just because I seemed naturally to drift downwards and I couldn't muster up courage to stop myself. I … I've been here six months … I suppose I'll die here.'

'Well I'll be damned,' said the tramp. He folded his arms on his chest, and his chest heaved in and out with his excited breathing. He kept looking at Deignan and nodding his head. Finnerty who had heard Deignan's story hundreds of times with numberless details shrugged his shoulders, sniffed and said: 'Begob, it's a funny world. Though I'm damn sure that I wouldn't be here only for women and drink.'

'No?' said the tramp. 'How do you make that out?'

'No, by Jiminy,' said Finnerty, blowing out a cloud of blue smoke through his mouth as he talked. 'I'd be a rich man to-day only for drink and women.' He crossed his feet and leaned jauntily back against the washstand, with his hands held in front of him, the fingers of the right hand tapping the back of the left. His fat round face, with the heavy jaw, turned sideways towards the doorway, looked selfish, stupid and cruel. He laughed and said in an undertone, 'Oh boys, oh boys, when I come to think of it.' Then he coughed and shrugged his shoulders. 'Would you believe it,' he said turning to the tramp, 'I've spent five thousand pounds within the last twelve months? It's a fact. Upon my soul I have. I curse the day I got hold of that money. Until two years ago I was a happy man, I had one of the best schools in the south of Ireland. Then an aunt of mine came home from America and stayed in the house with my mother and myself. She died within six months and left mother five thousand pounds. I got it out of the old woman's hands, God forgive me, and then… Oh well,' Finnerty shook his head solemnly, raised his eyebrows and sighed.

'I'm not sorry,' he continued, leering at a black spot on the concrete floor of the wash-house. 'I could count the number of days I was sober on my fingers and thumbs. And now I'd give a month of my life for a cup of tea and a hunk of bread.' He stamped about clapping his hands and laughing raucously. His bull neck shook when he laughed. Then he scowled again and said, 'Wish I had a penny. That's nine o'clock striking. I'm starving with the hunger.'

'Eh? Hungry?' The tramp had fallen into a kind of doze while Finnerty had been talking. He started up, scratched his bare neck and then rummaged within his upper garments mumbling to himself. At last he drew forth a little bag from which he took three pennies. He handed the pennies to Finnerty. 'Get chuck for the three of us,' he said.

Finnerty's eyes gleamed, he licked his lower lip with his tongue and then he darted out without saying a word.

In the workhouse hospital a custom had grown up, since goodness knows when, that the pauper in charge of the dining-room was allowed to filch a little from the hospital rations, of tea, bread and soup, and then sell them to the paupers again as extras at nine o'clock in the morning for a penny a portion. This fraudulent practice was overlooked by the ward-master; for he himself filched all his rations from the paupers' hospital supply and he did it with the connivance of the workhouse master, who was himself culpable in other ways and was therefore prevented by fear from checking his subordinates. But Finnerty did not concern himself with these things. He dived into the dining-room, held up the three pennies before old Neddy's face and whispered 'Three.' Neddy, a lean wrinkled old pauper with a very thick red under-lip like a negro, was standing in front of the fire with his hands folded under his dirty check apron. He counted the three pennies, mumbling, and then put them in his pocket. During twenty years he had collected ninety-three pounds in that manner. He had no relatives to whom he could bequeath the money, he never spent any and he never would leave the workhouse until his death, but he kept on collecting the money. It was his only pleasure in life. When he had collected a shilling in pennies he changed it into silver and the silver in due course into banknotes.

'They say he has a hundred pounds,' thought Finnerty, his mouth dry with greed, as he watched Neddy put away the pennies. 'Wish I knew where it was. I'd strangle him here and now and make a run for it. A hundred pounds. I'd eat and eat and eat and then I'd drink and drink.'

The tramp and Deignan never spoke a word until Finnerty came back, carrying three bowls of tea and three hunks of bread on a white deal board. Deignan and Finnerty immediately began to gulp their tea and tear at the bread, but the tramp merely took a little sip at the tea and then took up his piece of bread, broke it in two, and gave a piece to each of the paupers.

'I'm not hungry,' he said. 'I've got my dinner with me, and as soon as I get out along the road in the open country I'm going to sit down and cook it. And it's going to be a real spring day, too. Look at that sun.'

The sun had at last mounted the wall. It was streaming into the yard lighting up everything. It was not yet warm, but it was cheering and invigorating. And the sky had become a clear pure blue colour.

'Doesn't it make ye want to jump and shout,' cried the tramp, joyously stamping about. He had become very excited, seeing the sun.

'I'm afraid I'd rather see a good dinner in front of me,' muttered Finnerty with his mouth full of bread.

'What about you, towny?' said the tramp, standing in front of Deignan. 'Wouldn't ye like to be walking along a mountain road now with a river flowing under yer feet in a valley and the sun tearing at yer spine?'

Deignan looked out wistfully, smiled for a moment dreamily and then sighed and shook his head. He sipped his tea and said nothing. The tramp went to the back of the shed. Nobody spoke until they had finished the bread and tea. Finnerty collected the bowls.

'I'll take these back,' he said, 'and maybe I might get sent over to the cookhouse for something.'

He went away and didn't come back. The tramp and Deignan fell into a contemplative doze. Neither spoke until the clock struck ten. The tramp shrugged himself and coming over to Deignan, tapped him on the arm.

'I was thinking of what you said about … about how you spent your life, and I thought to myself, 'Well, that poor man is telling the truth and he's a decent fellow, and it's a pity to see him wasting his life in here.' That's just what I said to myself. As for that other fellow. He's no good. He's a liar. He'll go back again to his school or maybe somewhere else. But neither you nor I are fit to be respectable citizens. The two of us were born for the road, towny. Only you never had the courage of your convictions.'

The tramp went to the door and spat. Deignan had been looking at him in wonder while he was talking and now he shifted his position restlessly and furrowed his forehead.

'I can't follow you,' he said nervously and he opened his mouth to continue, when again he suddenly remembered that the man was a tramp and that it would not be good form to argue with him on matters of moral conduct.

'Of course ye can't,' said the tramp, shuffling back to his position. Then he stuck his hands within his sleeves and shifted his tobacco to his other cheek. 'I know why you can't follow me. You're a Catholic, you believe in Jesus Christ and the Blessed Virgin and the priests and a heaven hereafter. You like to be called respectable and to pay your debts. You were born a free man like myself, but you didn't have the courage …'

'Look here, man,' cried Deignan in a shocked and angry voice, 'stop talking that rubbish. You have been very kind about – er –

cigarettes and food, but I can't allow you to blaspheme our holy religion in my presence. Horrid. Ugh.'

The tramp laughed noiselessly. There was silence for several moments. Then the tramp went to Deignan, shook him fiercely by the right arm and shouted in his ear, 'You're the biggest fool I ever met.' Then he laughed aloud and went back to his place. Deignan began to think that the tramp was mad and grew calm and said nothing.

'Listen here,' said the tramp. 'I was born disreputable. My mother was a fisherman's daughter and my lawful father was a farm labourer, but my real father was a nobleman and I knew it when I was ten years old. That's what gave me a disreputable outlook on life. My father gave mother money to educate me, and of course she wanted to make me a priest. I said to myself, I might as well be one thing as another. But at the age of twenty-three when I was within two years of ordination a servant girl had a child and I got expelled. She followed me, but I deserted her after six months. She lost her looks after the birth of the child. I never clapped eyes on her or the child since.' He paused and giggled. Deignan bit his lips and his face contorted with disgust.

'I took to the road then,' said the tramp. 'I said to myself that it was a foolish game trying to do anything in this world but sleep and eat and enjoy the sun and the earth and the sea and the rain. That was twenty-two years ago. And I'm proud to say that I never did a day's work since and never did a fellow-man an injury. That's my religion and it's a good one. Live like the birds, free. That's the only way for a free man to live. Look at yourself in a looking-glass. I'm ten years older than you and yet you look old enough to be my father. Come, man, take to the road with me to-day. I know you're a decent fellow, so I'll show you the ropes. In six months from now you'll forget you were ever a pauper or a clerk. What d'ye say?'

Deignan mused, looking at the ground.

'Anything would be better than this,' he muttered. 'But … Good Lord, becoming a tramp! I may have some chance of getting back to respectable life from here, but once I became a tramp I should be lost.'

'Lost? What would you lose?'

Deignan shrugged his shoulders. 'I might get a job. Somebody might discover me here. Somebody might die. Anything might happen. But if I went on the road…' He shrugged his shoulders again.

'So you prefer to remain a pauper?' said the tramp with an impudent, half-contemptuous grin. Deignan winced and he felt a sudden mad longing grow within his head to do something mad and reckless.

'You're a fine fellow,' continued the tramp, 'you prefer to rot in idleness here with old men and useless wrecks to coming out into the free air. What man! Pull yourself together and come over now with me and apply for yer discharge. We'll foot it out together down south. What d'ye say?'

'By Jove, I think I will!' cried Deignan with a gleam in his eyes. He began to trot excitedly around the shed, going to the door and looking up at the sky, and coming back again and looking at the ground, fidgeting with his hands and feet. 'D'ye think, would it be all right?' he kept saying to the tramp.

'Sure it will be all right,' the tramp kept answering. 'Come on with me to the ward master and ask for your discharge.'

But Deignan would not leave the shed. He had never in all his life been able to come to a decision on an important matter.

'Do you think, would it be all right?' he kept saying.

'Oh damn it and curse it for a story,' said the tramp at last, 'stay where you are and good day to you. I'm off.'

He shuffled out of the shed and across the yard. Deignan put out his hand and took a few steps forward.

'I say –' he began and then stopped again. His brain was in a whirl thinking of green fields, mountain rivers, hills clad in blue mists, larks singing over clover fields, but something made him unable to loosen his legs, so that they could run after the tramp.

'I say –' he began again, and then he stopped and his face shivered and beads of sweat came out on his forehead.

He could not make up his mind.

R.M. Fox   Casuals of the City

Among the rootless vagabonds I have known, Jack Smith stands out as the most satisfying. Many would enjoy tramping in the summer – a lovely summer evening on a white country road, with perhaps the faint sickle of a moon above it. But on a winter's night when the howling wind cuts notches in your spine, Jack Smith would be just as gay. He was a great walker, with arched feet like a ballet dancer – of which he was very vain – and he loved the vagrant wind and the wild night. Necessity often drove him on the road, for he was usually penniless. But he was a tramp from choice as well. Many a time when he had a good job he would throw it up at a moment's notice, spend all his money before he left town, and set out on his travels. Spending his money first was a ritual with him. I have known him start out on a racketing evening round the London public-houses with a group of friends, with no other purpose than to begin his tramp with empty pockets the next day. Later he would emerge ready for what he would call 'travelling light.'

On the first of May he always left whatever job he might have, and struck out for the open country.

'Why do you want to go?' his foreman once asked, uncomprehendingly, for Jack was an excellent workman. 'Isn't the job good enough? Have you got another to go to? Do you want more money?'

'It's too good!' groaned Jack. 'Three meals a day and a bed every night. I can't stand it!'

He spoke of his rambles over England as the one part of his life that was really worth living. 'All the rest,' he declared, reflectively, 'are just dirty grey patches!'

He was a hoarse little cockney, with a toothbrush moustache and a stubbly chin, an untidy, likeable little man. He had a talent for public exhortation, varying from railings in Hyde Park to pill-selling and tie-selling in different market-places. He made blacking and sold it in the gutter, though he would never demean himself to the extent of using any. His friends called him the Westminster Demosthenes.

As soon as he entered a town or a village his cracked voice and quaint humour assured him a welcome. People competed to give him food and

25

shelter, while the local cobbler usually regarded it as a privilege to mend his boots free of charge. He knew where to call in any village on his route, just where he was most likely to secure that hobo trinity – a bed, good boots, and a meal.

His close companion on his travels was Clement Bonham, a dark, curly-haired, pale-faced young man. Slim, neat and and clean-shaven, with his hair carefully oiled, he contrasted strangely with Smith's rough, unkempt, stocky build. Jack was shabby and untidy, but Clement's garments were always neatly pressed and brushed. The two were great friends. Smith's rude energy acted as a foil to the aristocratic languor of the other. Clement recited Oscar Wilde's *Ballad of Reading Gaol* outside the local public-houses with polished elegance, his pale face expressing agony no less than his anguished tone. Oratory and pill-selling were his accomplishments, too. Among his speeches was one against old age, which he usually delivered wherever he could find an audience to listen. On arriving at a village they would proceed to the village cross, obtain a ginger-beer box, gather a crowd, and Bonham would solemnly begin his indictment of the aged. I can see him standing in a scornful attitude, with a hushed, bewildered audience before him.

'These men,' he declaimed, 'have lived to an indecent old age. They dodder about and persist in getting in everybody's way. They must not be tolerated any longer. Some of them,' he proceeded, dropping his voice to a whisper, and wagging his finger impressively, 'even have whiskers – whiskers, mark you, whiskers!' he repeated darkly, leaving his village audience mystified but impressed. They gave coppers to the collection, especially if an old veteran, with a fringe of whiskers and a waving stick, could be provoked to come forward and defend his side.

Bonham had an anti-temperance speech, too, which used to drive teetotal enthusiasts to frenzy. 'People talk of the waste of money in drink!' he exclaimed. 'What nonsense! Think of how much more is wasted in rent and in food. The tragedy of my life is food! I would like to wear splendid clothes, to live in a splendid house, to save money. But if I get two shillings or half-a-crown, or even five shillings, it all goes in food! Eating is a far greater vice than drinking. Then we have to consider the moderate drinker. The moderate drinker is far worse than the teetotaler. If you drink at all you should drink a lot. What is the use of fiddling about with a drink here and a drink there! If a man can't drink plenty he had far better leave it alone altogether!' Turning to his audience, he flung out the challenging question: 'Can you point to a single man of genius who did not drink? Without exception they have all been drunkards. Look at the poets – Shelley, Byron, Swinburne; the dramatists

– Kit Marlowe, the great Elizabethan dramatist, died in a drunken brawl, through being hit over the head with a quart pot – what a glorious death!'

Bonham would do anything to create a sensation. On one occasion he procured an old tall hat, which he wore at a dockside meeting, sending it round afterwards for the collection. But this was an error, for the dock labourers and riverside loafers, in mufflers and caps, had never seen the inside of a tall hat before. They peered so long and curiously into its depths that they had no time to think of giving anything at all. An even more impressive appearance was at a street corner meeting in the West End of London, where he appeared in a billowing black cloak and an opera hat, with an attendant in a gorgeous chocolate-and-gold uniform. Stepping on to the rostrum he took off the hat with a flourish, shut it, divested himself of the cloak, and handed both to his servitor, who stood stiff and attentive. For half an hour or so he preached the wildest anarchy. Then his attendant handed him his hat and cloak and he left the meeting followed respectfully by the uniformed man. The clothes were borrowed, and the attendant was a friend employed at a neigh-bouring cinema. His appearance created a sensation all the same. Flamboyant performances of this kind were indulged in out of pure joy of life. But when he was really hard up I have known him engage a taxi and spend the whole day visiting wealthy men and interesting them on his own behalf. After paying the taxi man out of the proceeds he has been left with anything from £20 to £50 as a reward for his initiative and enterprise.

Smith's style of oratory was altogether different. He was ruder and cruder. I saw him one night standing on the edge of that oasis of cheerful bustle and friendly lights called Woolwich Market Place. In the centre were gay flower stalls, flanked by gleaming fruit but, in the half-light, nothing could be clearly seen. He held up a small object that looked like a wire puzzle, wrapped with rag.

'Ladies and gentlemen,' he cried. 'Look at this! Here you have the invention of the age!'

He leaned forward, speaking hoarsely and confidentially.

'Come closer and I'll show you how it works! Here,' – pointing with his finger – 'is the wire frame. Now, observe!' He picked up a strip of stuff and twisted it round the wire. 'With these you can make ties equal to any sold at seven-and-six in the West End shops. I give you the frame and one – two – three different ties, all for sixpence!'

Suddenly he grabbed a mallet and beat it on a tin with a deafening noise.

'Who wouldn't be a credit to his boss for sixpence!' he roared. 'If you wear one of these every one will think he gives you enough to live on. Of course, in a civilised society we shan't wear pieces of rag tied round our collars. But we must do it today to keep up appearances. Think of the advantages,' he went on. 'No more dragging at your tie when the alarm goes in the morning. No more quarters lost! All you've got to do when you hear the buzzer go is to grab this, hook it on and run – run like hell! I used to do it! Don't I know!'

He broke into a trot round the ring, hooking the wire arrangement firmly in his collar, while the audience moodily looked on.

These two tramped the roads together, meeting many adventures. One day, as they neared a village, two girls who were cycling came up and asked the way. They talked for a while, and Smith suggested going to a wayside tea-garden, where they sat in a shady arbour and drank glasses of lemonade. The vagabonds had exactly fourpence, which Bonham wanted to save for emergencies. Smith was nervous till he made sure that the lemonade was only a penny a glass, when he flung the money down with an air and walked out. The girls said good-bye and rode off. The two walked along side by side, penniless.

'You were a fool, Jack!' said Bonham, bitterly.

'Fellowship is life; lack of fellowship is death!' returned Jack, sententiously, and strode on satisfied.

Smith had all the inconsequence of the true hobo – the sort of man who, in America, will risk his life jumping a train to get to a place only to wander away when he reaches it. Once he set out from London on a ramble planned to last three months or more. I was surprised to see him in the city again in a week.

'What made you come back so soon?' I asked.

'Well, I was standing by a railway station in Kent,' he answered. 'I had just passed some hop fields and saw the light green hops trailing over the sticks. They made me feel thirsty. Then I saw a poster advertising a Wagner season in London. It came to me suddenly that I hadn't heard a Wagner opera for months, so I just tramped back.'

Alfred Holdsworth   **The Jungle**

Early one October morning, Bill and I dropped off a slow freight train that had pulled up at one of the small townships in the mountain section of British Columbia. We had passed the night in an empty box-car, and were powdered from head to foot with cement, but had the satisfaction of knowing that the distance between us and the Pacific coast was now less by about 150 miles. It was the time of the year when men who know the winter East of the Big Divide begin to think of warmer climes, and go. The thought had come to us on a frosty morning in North Saskatchewan, beyond Prince Albert. We had done the usual cheap stunts that men in Canada soon tumble to – and act upon, however much the Law be 'agin it'. From Saskatoon, we were 'extra-gang' men, going free-fare to the Yellowhead Pass to work we never intended to do. At Edmonton, a few hundred miles in the direction we wanted to go, we gave Yellowhead the jump, and proceeded South by buffer to Calgary. Here we struck the mainline to the Coast, and a kindly oil-tank carried us over the backbone of the Rockies on a brilliant, moonlit night. In our evasion of the Railroad Police at - - - we had been obliged to dump the bulk of our belongings, and now carried only a potato sack with but little in it. Consequently, we appeared a rough-and-ready two as a gentleman in 'civies' approached us when we disclosed our presence in that little township of British Columbia.

'You'd better get out of here, quick,' said the aforementioned gentleman, not too unkindly.

'And why?' retorted Bill, 'Are the "bulls" too thick around?'

'I'm the Chief myself,' said the other, 'but it's all right so long as you don't hang around. You get a train out tonight or there'll be something doing. You'll find the jungle yonder,' pointing up the track.

Wherever trains are accustomed to stop, at water-tanks or at sidings, the tramps or 'hoboes' have their camps or 'jungles'. Here the men await and board the trains, some taking the buffers, others the tender, some climb the tops of the carriages, others ride the rods underneath – any old place a man can creep into or hang on to; and away they go East or West, many caring little which direction so long as they be on the road somewhere.

This particular jungle was ideally situated – trust the hobo to know a good thing when he sees it! Beyond a secluding fringe of scrub, a clump of gigantic cedars, widespreading, afforded shelter for many small groups of men from the worst the rain could do. Nearby, a stream of clear mountain water rindled through rushes and ferns to a fordable river, alive with fish, across which was an Indian encampment where deer-meat could be had for the asking.

Each little group of men had a fire where fish and flesh were being cooked, and all around, on the rocks, or stuck between branches of trees, were tins and wide-necked bottles for drinking.

We had tea and sugar in our sacks, and, having paid toll of both, joined a group of about ten men under the biggest of the cedars. You give no greeting, and get none. The fire was there for them when they arrived: in fact, countless men contributed to the ashes of it – maybe the site had never cooled since the first hobo hit the ties of the mountain section. You do well, though, to hunt for wood, and forage for food; which done, you are one of them, and begin to understand each other.

Two or three of the men were sleeping, the rest smoking, and a yarn was afoot. The speaker was a bony-built man, with a fine face on him, hard, resolute, and as reckless as the life could make him.

'There was a time,' he said, pausing to light his pipe with a blazing stick, 'when I'd board a freight, an' didn't give a damn where I'd wake next morn'n'. But there's nuthin' to it. 'Ere am I, one o' the mugs who blasted out that same track, waitin' fer the glorious privilege of hangin' on to a slow freight, an' got to, or rot 'ere in this neck o' the woods. I'm a rebel, boys, an' all the thugs under the Star Strangled Banana 'll never club me to nuthin' different. As old One-Leg remarked last time I struck 'im patchin' 'is pine-foot down the Arrow-Head, "I am, for the reason as I ain't". Look at that 'ere kid! 'E ain't more'n got the smell o' mother's milk off 'im yet, lyin' there dreamin', dreamin' mebbe as I did, at 'is age, of a garden an' somebody in it gatherin' Mornin' Glories. An' there 'e is, forgotten in a country the Big Boss cussed when 'e made it. Hush! Train East, boys!'

Only one of the whole company made it, and as he disappeared through the little side door of a box-car, the rebel remarked.

'Goin' East – well, it's up to him, anyway, he's the doctor. That 'ere aforementioned One-Leg lost 'is prop – leastways, so 'e put it – in the hintrests of bosses, an' 'e's been after the hide o' them contractors ever since. "Another strike like this," said 'e, when the Two Valley crowd won out, "an' we'll knock the props from under the foundations o' this 'ere rotten system." An' off they went to raise 'ell in the next camp, but the galoots would give 'em nary a hand, so –'

'Is this t'jungle?'

It was a broad Lancashire voice that interrupted, and its owner was a short, loosely-set chap with a grimy, woebegone face surmounted by a hat that a basket of pups might have been squabbling over, by the looks of it. Evidently, he had just dropped off the Eastbound train. His long overcoat was wet, and glistened with coal-dust. He looked so very miserable as he stood awaiting some response to his query. His legs had a semi-reverential kink in them, and his face showed signs of slipping. No one spoke. The catastrophe to his features appeared imminent. He continued, however, with a sigh.

'Cos if it is, aw wish aw were dead. It were t'hobby, aw think, 'at telled mi abeaut t'jungle; aw thowt aw met get hanged if aw stopped up yon. Somebry telled mi this were a free country, but aw'd niver 'a' guessed it misel. Aw'm sick o' t' seet o' Christmas trees, an' aw've noa faith i' paper brass – aw wish aw were awhoam. Con aw come an' sit mi deaun?'

'Sure!' said Bill, who was a Lancashire lad himself, once.

'Ah dear, this is a country,' he said with another sigh, as he sat down by the fire, sheepishly, 'aw've niver done ony wark, it isn't in mi, an' it meks mi fair sick to think abeaut it. All aw iver did were help t'wife, but 'oo deed an' left mi destitute, soa aw coom ower 'ere. Aw can't reckon these Canada foak up. When aw went into yon shop fer a bit o' baggin', they looked at mi as they mud 'a' thowt aw weren't wick or a hanimal or summut. Aw'm reight ruined neaw, look at mi coit! Aw con fair feel misel gooin' to t'dogs. Aw niver ...'

The clanging bell of a Westbound freight brought Bill and myself to attention, so we left the man of sorrows, and ten minutes later we were snugly hidden in a car of hay headed for the Dry Belt.

Stacey W. Hyde   The Turner

The farm worker is aroused in the morning by the crowing of cocks, and dresses and breaks his fast to the chorus of the wild birds. His day is ruled by the sun. By its inclination he knows just when to take his 'elevenses,' his dinner and his tea. When it slopes down to the West and spreads a golden glory over the earth, he realises that the night cometh when no man can work, and returns home to rest and slumber. When it is raining he presumably works on until the call of the inner man makes itself heard – or he guesses.

Modern engineering science has determined that its devotees shall have surer and more emphatic alarums than those of gentle Nature; so it has evolved the steam hooter and the electric syren. They do not call. 'Blare' most inadequately describes their ear and soul-shattering voices. The trumpets of Joshua felled the walls of Jericho, but Babylon itself would have succumbed to a choir of steam hooters; Nineveh would have fallen before the terror of a battery of electrical syrens. They are the soul of industrialism made articulate, the spirit of the factory bursting into song. But people have 'got used to 'em.'

Not only so, but eager, at the right time, for the sound of them. The men in the turning shop at Murrays, Ltd, looked up at the big clock on the end wall, and, wiping their hands on cotton waste that only smoothed down the dirt instead of removing it, thought that, after going at a fair speed all the morning, the hands must suddenly have come to a dead stop at a quarter of a minute to one. While they ruminated bitterly thus, the preliminary whisper of the hooter insinuated itself into their thoughts, and their hands automatically reached out and shut off their machines. The electric motors that drove the shafting ran quickly down the octaves, their tenor becoming baritone, bass, until the breath left their bodies and they expired with a grunt. The only noise remaining in the shop was the tramp of feet hurrying their owners home for the midday meal; and that rapidly died away in its turn, leaving a silence almost oppressive in a place whose life was bustle and activity.

A little group of men, whose homes lay too far off for them to be able to get there for dinner, assembled with their packages and tea cans around the coke stove that stood proud and erect in the middle of the shop. It was a convenient stove. It was round and the height of a tall man, and its breadth was the breadth of a man. Through it ran three or four wide pipes, sloping slightly upwards, that drew the air through them and heated it in the passage. The whole thing, as a matter of fact, might have been designed for the sole purpose of baking potatoes in the shortest possible time; and the men, as they placed their raw tubers carefully inside the pipes, were grateful that that aspect had not struck the works management. If it had, the stove would have been immediately removed.

Empty drawers were dragged from benches near and turned sides up to act as seats. A small apprentice was despatched with half a dozen cans, threaded carefully on a stick, to the far end of the shop to make the tea. Going was a fairly easy matter, but the return journey would have taxed the powers of a Blondin himself. However, any especially depleted can could always be explained by the fact that the hot water supply had run out. They stretched feet and hands towards the warmth and prepared luxuriously for an hour's refreshment and rest.

For a while mouths were too full and minds too interested in newspapers to admit of conversation. But it does not take long to eat a packet of sandwiches or to absorb all the really interesting paragraphs in a paper. The silence was suddenly broken.

'Boy, 'ave a look at them 'taters!'

''Ave a look yerself!' retorted the boy, deep in the adventures of Sexton Blake.

The speaker, one Charlie Stubbs by name and the oldest man there, shot lightning at the lad from his eyes. The apprentice read on, utterly unmoved, and, as he was farther away than the potatoes, Charlie contented himself with threats of bodily vengeance. The potatoes, too, proved to be just right, and the royal odour of the floury mass, as he broke the skin, compensated for his wounded dignity.

'I see,' said Curly Harper, so called on account of his baldness, from the other side of the stove, as he gulped down a hot mouthful – 'I see there's to be an open-air meeting at the half-hour at the Main Gate, with a real, live parson to address it.'

'Oh, well,' commented one, glancing up at the glass roof, on which the rain was noisily pattering, 'he's got a nice fine day for it.'

'Who said cats?' called out old Charlie, catching up a lump of steel.

'Cats?' replied Curly, staring.

'Ah! You said something about cats, didn't you?'

'Never mentioned 'em. You're gettin' a bit 'ard of 'earin'!'

'No, I ain't,' said the old man, stung. 'I know you said something about cats.'

'Wot I said was,' Curly repeated the words slowly and emphatically, 'that a parson is 'olding an open air meeting at the Main Gate.'

'That's it, is it?' Old Charlie chuckled. 'Funny thing, cats and parsons always 'ave affected me the same all me life. Soon as ever I see a cat, I must chuck something at it. Soon as ever I see a parson, blow me if I don't want to do the same.'

'And yet,' put in a youth sitting by him, 'when that parson came round with old Murray the other day and started talking to you, there you was kow-towing and "sir"-ing 'im and nearly choking yourself, you was so polite.'

'Kow-towing be damned! O' course, you must 'ave a bit o' distance between yer to make any sport out of it. If a cat comes up and rubs its 'ead against my leg, I tickles its ears for it. And if a parson comes up and begins soft-soaping me, I tickle 'is ears for 'im. But that don't mean I like either of 'em.'

'Can't say I'm over-fond o' parsons meself,' contributed Curly Harper. 'They're too fond o' talkin'.'

'And tea, and women,' growled Charlie. 'I don't blame 'em. They want their evenings off as much as possible, like the rest of us. So they 'ave to do their calling in the afternoon when there's nobody but the women at 'ome. But it don't 'elp them to understand men.'

'Really, y'know,' mused Curly, 'a parson's got to be a bit of a sport to make anything of 'imself. 'E's bred up on a lot o' special college theology — stuff that don't matter a tinker's cuss whether it's true or not — and told if 'e believes it and gets other people to believe it, everything in the garden will be lovely. And then, when 'e comes across a fellow knocking 'is wife about or swearing hard or making a beast of 'imself, 'e don't know what the deuce to make of it. Calls the fellow a sinner and puts 'is back up at once.'

'That sort ain't so bad,' argued Charlie; 'they're willing, though soft like. There's another crowd go in for it just for what they can make out of it. That's the sort I can't stand.' He made a gesture of despair.

'It don't seem to me either of you two have met any modern parsons,' said a young man.

'I ain't bin to church since I was a boy,' boasted Charlie.

'Nor me,' said Curly.

'Well, I met a few in the trenches. Some of 'em were rank, but the others were fine chaps. Seemed to tumble to what a man was and what he wanted. None o' this ancient Jewish stunt with dead Sundays and silly yarns. I got on with 'em all right.'

He fell silent, rather astonished at his own loquacity. The others pondered.

'That's as may be,' said old Charlie at last, stuffing his briar with 'Battle Axe.' 'That's as may be. I ain't going to contradict you. All I say is that when I see a parson – Got a match? Thanks! – When I see a parson I want to 'eave something at 'im; and it was born in me and I can't 'elp it. P'r'aps it's their collars and p'r'aps it's their 'ats. I don't know.'

He puffed vigorously at his pipe, took it out of his mouth and gazed at it affectionately. The edge of the bowl was all burnt away, and it was abominably foul. As he replaced it the nicotine bubbled in the stem. He spat in the fire and then burst out laughing. The smoke caught his breath, but the resulting cough was powerless to stop him, and cough and laughter mingled in a strange cacophony.

''E's got 'em again,' said his neighbour despairingly. ''Ere, 'old still and let me slap yer on the back.'

'Ow! 'Old on, I ain't so young as you!' Charlie wriggled his back under his coat to disperse the sting. 'You didn't ought to be'ave like that,' he said reproachfully.

'And you ought to know better than to go chokin' yourself at your time o' life.'

Old Charlie nodded and chuckled again.

'I was just thinking of an 'oly man I once knew. Talk about a coughdrop! 'E was the fair limit.'

'Spit it up,' remarked Curly. 'It's a rotten day, and we can't go out, so we may as well 'ave the yarn.'

'All right,' said old Charlie, 'and I 'ope it'll be a warnin' to you!'

He puffed a mouthful of smoke into the air and watched it disappear.

'I was working in a little place in Soho, Birmingham, at the time. Do you know Birmingham, any of you? Some of it ain't so black as it's painted, and some of it ain't painted nearly as black as it is. Specially this part o' Soho. Talk about Lime'ouse on a foggy morning; it's a city of 'eavenly light compared to Soho.

This place I was at was a repair shop – non-union shop, though I was gettin' the rate – one o' these places with about a dozen machines and a dozen fitters. Wasn't much in the work – pretty rough stuff most of it – but there was a good bit of it, and we was kept pretty busy. This was a long time before the War, o' course, before the Boer War, I believe it was. Yes, it was! because I remember our boss was one of the leaders of the mob that tried to do in old Lloyd George. 'E was 'ad up for it,

and we all 'ad a day off to go and 'ear the case. Let off with a caution,
'e was, and the fat old magistrate said 'e admired 'is spirit. Suppose if it
was to 'appen now 'e'd be called a blackguard and sent to quod for six
months. Rare patriot our boss was; made a fortune during the war, so
I've 'eard.

Any'ow, we was fairly 'appy and comfy there, spite of it bein' non-
union, except for one bloke – Dirty Dick we used to call 'im. 'Andsome
feller 'e was, with 'is eyes tryin' to look at each other across 'is nose.
But they couldn't; it was a darn sight too big. 'E wore one o' these nice,
oily quiffs skewed down over 'is forehead, as if 'e was ashamed to show
it. It wasn't much to write 'ome to mother about. 'E wouldn't 'ave 'ad
to tilt 'is 'ead back far to balance an apple on it.

I don't think I'm what you'd call a particular kind o' chap. I've
smoked, and in my time I've chewed and 'ad a pint or two and eaten
onions. I've also, on a few occasions, got pretty smarmed up with oil,
but I ain't never come across any one like Dirty Dick. 'E lived on whisky
and onions, and chewed tobacco to take the smell away. When 'e put
a shirt on, 'e put it on for keeps. It didn't come off again until it
dropped off. If anybody 'ad mentioned the word "bath" to 'im, 'e'd 'ave
'ad 'ydrophobia on the spot. Stink? Workin' next to 'im was like
working over a cesspool. 'E was a surly devil, too. Couldn't answer you
polite if 'e tried. Sort o' feller 'ood give you a bash over the jaw if you
asked 'im 'ow 'e was, and then tell you 'e felt better than you did. Swear?
As I say, I ain't particular, but to listen to 'im conducting an ordinary
conversation with a mate of 'is would make me blush up to me bald
spot.

'E worked an old millin' machine they 'ad there, and 'e 'ad one 'obby
– collectin' tools. All the money 'e 'ad over from buyin' beer and onions
and baccy, 'e used to spend on tools. Wonderful collection 'e 'ad. 'E
'ad a small chest made and stood it in the corner next to 'is machine,
with a chain round a pillar and a padlock on it. You can't mention a
tool 'e didn't 'ave. About a dozen micrometers o' different sizes, all
brand-new. As soon as one got a bit worn out 'e'd sell it to a second-
hand man and buy another. Squares, protractors, rules, scribin' blocks,
'ack-saws, verniers, every bloomin' thing you can think of. Fair crazy
'e was over 'em. If 'e saw some new patent gadget advertised, 'e must
'ave it. I don't know that I was right in saying 'e spent what money 'e
'ad left over on tools. I think 'e bought them and spent what 'e'd got
left on beer and baccy and onions. 'E must 'ave 'ad a 'undred quids'
worth or more in that chest.

One of our turners got fed up one day and pushed off, and a week or so later a new man came in to take 'is place. Short chap 'e was and fat. Very fat and very refined. Brand-new overalls 'e 'ad on, and 'is finger nails were kept as neat as you please. 'E'd stop 'is lathe sometimes to touch up 'is finger nails, and I expect 'e 'ad a go at 'is toe nails as soon as 'e got 'ome. Kept a cake of oatmeal soap in 'is drawer to wash 'is 'ands with. 'E 'ad one o' these pink faces, you know, the kind that don't look as if they ever 'ave to shave, though I s'pose 'e 'ad to every night, really. Clean collar every morning and shiny boots. Kept some boot polish in 'is drawer, too, to give 'em a rub every night before 'e went 'ome.

'E was a nice chap, though, for all that, and we got on with 'im first-rate. Always cheerful, 'e was. Most fat chaps don't like 'ard work, but 'e revelled in it. Slogged in all day as if 'e'd be ill if 'e left you off a minute. Not but what 'e wouldn't answer you civil enough if you went up and spoke to 'im. But mostly 'e kept 'imself aloof and just smiled at yer when 'e came in and when 'e went out. The boss used to rub 'is 'ands as 'e looked at 'im and 'old 'im up as an example. But you couldn't take offence at 'im, 'e 'ad such funny little ways and such a 'appy smile.

When 'e'd bin there a fortnight or so the rumour got about that 'e was a parson, come into the works to find out exactly 'ow the workin' man lived during the day. We first thought there was somethin' rummy about 'im when we found 'e didn't swear. Some people put a lot too much emphasis on swearing, but it don't seem 'ardly natural for a bloke not to swear at all. Little Jack Parker came up to me one day and says, "What do you think? I just dropped a lump o' steel on Fatty's foot – by accident, of course – right bang on it, and 'e didn't say a word. Not a single, solitary, feeble little 'Damn.' Just smiled at me and, when I said, 'I'm sorry,' said 'That's all right, old chap.' Must 'ave 'urt 'im, too."

Well, that set us thinking. And then one day a few of us was 'aving a little game o' banker in the corner just before work. Fatty came in and stood watching us for a while. Little Jack Parker 'ad just dusted me out o' me last copper, when 'e says in 'is little thin, squeaky voice, like so many fat men 'ave, 'e says: "What is it you men are playing? It seems to be some sort of gambling game."

That put the tin 'at on it. "It's a game called banker, sir," I says at once. Slipped out without me thinking. Seemed the only thing to do, call 'im "sir" after that.'

"Banker?" says 'e. "How interesting. And how do you play it?" So the four of us showed 'im 'ow to play it, and 'e picked it up at once.

So we asked 'im if 'e'd like a game. "Oh, no, no, no, thank you," he said, "I'm afraid I don't gamble." Quite apologetic about it, 'e was.

That seemed to fit in all right with the theory. If 'e really wanted to know 'ow the workin' man lived, it was only right that 'e should learn all about gambling. Though, on lookin' back, it seems 'ardly likely that a parson would watch us and not tell us off at all. 'Owever, it seemed very fit and proper just then.

When the rumour reached the ears of Dirty Dick – it took a long time to get anything into 'is 'ead through 'is ears, they was that filthy and there wasn't much room inside – 'e got 'is wool off about it.

"Wot the 'ell does a parson want in 'ere?" 'e says.

We explained to 'im what we thought about it.

"All right," 'e says, "if 'e wants to know all about the workin' man, I'll learn 'im a thing or two!"

So a day or two later Fatty was standin' quietly at 'is lathe working away as usual, when Dirty Dick sent the labourer over to the other corner of the shop to fetch 'im a pile of castin's what were lyin' there. As 'e came across with 'em on a barrow Dirty went to meet 'im and come up with 'im just be'ind Fatty's back. Dirty lurched up against the labourer and knocked 'im off 'is balance, so that the castin's all fell off the barrow on to the floor. Dirty winked at 'im and then began to carry on at 'im. All the filth and the blasphemies 'e'd ever 'eard of came pouring out – and 'e'd heard a few. The labourer was that shocked 'e 'ad to stop 'is ears up. 'E told me afterwards it made 'im feel like a ruddy amateur, and 'e 'ad a pretty flow o' language 'imself. Presently Fatty turned round and looked at him.

"Oh, I beg your pardon, sir," says Dirty, stoppin' short. "I didn't notice you was there."

"Now don't you spoil yourself by telling lies," says Fatty, smiling.

"Wot?" says Dirty, taken aback.

"I repeat, don't spoil yourself by telling lies," says Fatty. To listen to 'im you'd 'a' thought 'e was addressin' a girls' Sunday school. "You knew perfectly I was there, and you arranged the whole thing in order to give me the opportunity of listening to your tongue. Now, didn't you?"

Dirty could do nothin' but stare. Fatty beamed at him and went on.

"It shows what an innocent and childlike mind you really possess. Nobody but a child would have conceived such a scheme. You thought to yourself: 'Now here's a man who doesn't know what swearing is, and I'll give him a little information on the subject.' Just as a boy throws a snowball at a silk hat. The scheme, I say, was that of a child. The matter, the mere accidental acquisition of experience. That's why I said, 'Don't spoil yourself by telling lies.'"

Dirty was too dazed to reply. 'E just mumbled something under 'is breath and sloped off. But the laugh was against 'im, and we felt more pleased with the parson than ever. 'E was a new kind. If Dirty 'ad bin anything of a man, 'e'd 'ave seen the joke and shook 'ands on the spot and bin friends. But, as I said, 'e was a surly devil, and 'adn't got the brains of a pigeon.

'E brooded over this little affair, and wanted to get 'is own back. 'E wasn't exactly a coward; 'e'd go for a fellow all right, but 'e 'adn't got the necessary moral courage to tackle Fatty. 'E thought and thought about it, and the only way 'e could see was the good old joke of the water-can fixed to the strikin' gear. You know, you can fix a can full o' water up at the top of the startin' lever so as, when the fellow comes along and pulls it over to start 'is machine, down comes the water on 'is head. O' course, if 'e' appens to look up before 'e starts it, the joke's off.

This time it came off all right. Dirty got a can and filled it with a filthy mixture o' soapsuds and oil and dirty water and put it up during the dinner-hour one day, while we was all away. I don't know that we should 'ave stopped 'im doing it if we'd seen 'im; we might 'a' made 'im use clean water, or tried to. But, after all, 'e 'ad bin scored off in a way, and Fatty was big enough to look after 'imself.

Fatty came in and never glanced up, but pulled over 'is lever like billy-oh. Then 'e gave a squeal, and Jack Parker, 'oo was near 'im, said a week or two afterwards that 'is face was murderous for a moment. At the time, though, 'e didn't notice it. Fatty looked a picture. Green oil spread all over 'is 'air and streamin' down 'is face; saturated with water, 'is collar going all limp and 'is clothes wet through. Dirty stood a few yards away and put 'is 'ands on 'is knees and laughed till the tears ran down 'is cheeks. Left grooves on 'is face they did. Wasn't often it felt water.

Fatty turned round to 'im. "Are you responsible for this?" 'e said.

Dirty couldn't say a word, 'e was laughin' that 'ard, but there wasn't much doubt about it. 'E was the only one laughing. The rest of us were standing round feeling a bit scared.

All of a sudden we was surprised to see Fatty begin smiling, and then 'e burst out laughing and smackin' 'is knee, same as Dirty. "I told you before you were a child," 'e says, spitting out a mouthful of oil, "and this clearly confirms it. How many a booby trap did I rig up for my elders when I was a boy. Ah baby, baby!" and 'e shook 'is finger at 'im, laughing all the time.

That set us all off. We all laughed, too, partly at him, but a damn sight more at Dirty. And Dirty knew it. The more Fatty laughed the straighter Dirty got, till in the end 'e was glarin' blue murder and stalked off to 'is machine as 'ot as 'ell. Fatty put 'is coat on, and went off 'ome to change, still laughing.

The other fellows all agreed that that settled it. 'E definitely was a parson. Nobody but a parson could laugh at a jape like that, meant so vindictive as it was, too. But I didn't feel so sure. It didn't seem in 'uman nature, parson or no parson, not to say a word of anger or tell 'im off in the least. To tell the truth, I felt a wee bit afraid. But Dirty Dick was known ever after that as Baby Dirty.

The end o' the next week, the boss 'ad a special job 'e wanted finished, a turning job it was. Fatty 'ad been workin' at it all day, but it wasn't 'alf done, so the boss told 'im 'e'd better work all night on it. It meant costing a bit – running the shaft and light all night for one man. But the boss said – it was a Friday – that the job absolutely must be finished by the week-end, so there was no 'elp for it. 'E gave Fatty the key of the shop door and told 'im if 'e got done before the morning, to switch the juice off and leave the key with the caretaker in 'is little office. There was two or three parts to the works – the machine shop, the fitters' shop, the stores and one or two other places. Everybody 'oo worked overtime 'ad to go out through the caretaker's office to make sure they wasn't taking anything away with 'em.

Well, Fatty said "Good-night" to us all, and as I was passing 'im 'e called me. I went up to 'im, and 'e says, in 'is refined way, "I am about to attempt something I have never attempted before. I sincerely trust I shall come through all right."

"'Corse you will," says I; "why shouldn't you?"

"I have an ominous foreboding," says 'e. "Good-night, my friend, good-night!" and 'e shook my 'and nearly off.

I came in next morning 'alf expectin' to see 'is body lyin' stretched out on the floor. But I couldn't see 'im anywhere; nor could anybody else, though the job in 'is lathe was nowhere near finished. 'E was gone, completely vanished. And so was Dirty's kit of tools!'

Old Charlie chuckled and knocked the ashes out of his pipe.

'When Dirty came in and found 'is chest broken open and 'is tools gone, 'is face was a study. 'E stared at it for a moment and then threw 'imself down on 'is 'ands and knees and began searching all over the floor. When the boss came in, 'e was still searching. But all 'e ever found was two or three nice, well-stuffed cushions of feathers be'ind 'is chest and a note written in neat, round 'andwritin' pinned to one of 'em.

"Dear Baby Dirty," it said, "Exchange is no robbery, is it? You are quite welcome to these cushions, because I'm sick and tired of wearing them. You've no idea how hot they are – except when they're wet. Believe me, dear friend, to be,

Your loving,

Rev. Fatty.'"

'And did they ever catch 'im?' asked the youth next to Charlie, breathlessly.

'Never set eyes on 'im from that day to this.'

The hooter blared forth across the shop again, and they rose to resume their labours.

'Ah!' said Curly, gravely, 'these parsons! They're all alike.'

'Strikes me,' said Bill, wiping his hands on a piece of cotton waste, 'that if we sort of fitted a bit of a whatyoumaycallit on that there sprocket and run up a bit of a shelf, like, it'd be an improvement. Save labour, if you asks me.'

'Nobody asked you,' said the gang foreman. 'You mind your job. Leave them things to them as knows 'em.'

'Oh. All right,' said Bill. 'I was only thinking.'

'You ain't paid to think,' said the gang foreman.

'I was thinking the other day,' said the gang foreman to the overseer, 'that we could save a job of work on that machine. It only needs an extension on that sprocket and a bit of a shelf under the feed.'

'Hardly worth bothering about,' said the overseer.

'Save a bit of labour,' said the gang foreman.

'Won't save ours,' said the overseer.

'Like this,' said the overseer to the works' manager. 'A B is the existing sprocket. C is the proposed double stummied gimble projection, D E is the limferated cross wiffler to be furbled into No. 9. Output differential remains constant. Labour costs go down 37 on maximum load. What about it?'

'I'll speak about it,' said the works' manager. 'Of course, it's not strictly new; I've been trying to get the same idea put up for years. Still, it won't do any harm to have another shot.'

'Well, don't forget me when the doings are given out.'

'Come and have one now,' said the works' manager. 'There's still time. No. I'll take the drawing. You don't want it back, of course?'

'No. It's only a rough sketch. I'll leave it with you.'

'The proposal is, gentlemen, that the machines in No. 11 shop be overhauled and fitted with this new contrivance. I have had the matter thoroughly looked into, and I find that quite apart from an improved efficiency and a reduced fuel cost, the new device which I have patented will bring an appreciable saving in overhead expenses, because of the reduction in labour costs. I have here some figures which the members of the board might like to see,' said the works' manager.

'The board is very much pleased with this further evidence of your diligence, Mr Penny,' said the President. 'Your proposal means a further capital outlay, but that will soon be set off by the increased output and reduced expenses.'

'That is so,' said the works' manager.

'Excellent,' said the President. 'The extra capital we can get from the public. The new machines will come from one of our subsidiary companies. Any objections, gentlemen? Moved, then, that the works' manager be empowered to carry on with the arrangements.'

'In recognition of your services,' said the President, 'the board has decided to appoint you to the position of general manager. As some sort of honorarium for your efforts over the new device, which has so materially improved the prosperity of the firm, the board has unanimously decided to ask you to accept this cheque for £1,000, along with their most whole-hearted expressions of admiration and regard.'

'Thank you, sir,' said the works' manager. 'I try to give satisfaction. Any ideas I may have are at the service of the company.'

'That's the spirit,' said the President.

'How'd you like to be works' manager?' said the new general manager to the overseer. 'I mentioned that idea of mine to the board and they were very keen. I told them you had a hand in it and they've left me a free hand to do something for you. You won't get the salary I was getting at first. But I think we can manage another hundred a year, what?'

'You're a good friend to me, Mr Penny.'

'That's all right, then. Any more ideas like that you just bring to me. I'll look after your interests.'

'Someone's getting busy with that machine improvement you spoke of,' said the new works' manager to the gang foreman. 'I'll put in a word for you as overseer. You ought to get some of the credit.'

'That's very good of you,' said the gang foreman.

'And I'll see if I can wangle another ten bob a week for you, one of these days. Dash it all, the company ought to encourage ideas.'

'I'd like that overseer's job,' said the gang foreman.

'And one of these days you shall have it. You trust me. I'll not let you down. You haven't any more tips that might be useful, I suppose? No? Well, you pass them on to me when you have.'

'Bill,' said the gang foreman, 'Got a bit of bad news for you. You won't be wanted after pay day. Cutting down expenses a bit, you know. Now we've got the new machines in here, we can't carry passengers, you know. I'll give you a damned good reference, and if I hear of anything going, I'll let you know. But we shan't want you after pay day.'

'Blimey!' said Bill, contemplating the new machines, 'I never thought of that. Strike me pink!'

Arthur Siffleet Joe Crabbe's Christmas Dinner

Joe Crabbe, head foreman to Messrs Barlow & Co., engineers, seemed for once to be doing a little work. He had cleared up his wooden office, with its spy-hole into the workshop, and was carefully covering his desk, shelves, and a part of the floor with sheets of newspaper. This task finished, a sharp rap on the door made him bawl out: 'All right! Bring 'em in!'

A deliveryman from the poulterer's began to drag in big baskets full of ducks. The ducks were laid out closely, side by side, first upon the desk, then on the shelves, and finally upon the floor till the foreman's office resembled a poulterer's shop.

It was Christmas Eve; and the ducks were the firm's annual Christmas gifts to their employees.

Some years before the workers had received, not ducks, but turkeys, and in addition the fruit necessary for the Christmas puddings and cakes. Now they only got ducks, and the fruit had been replaced by a pretty card that breathed benevolent yule tide sentiments betwixt man and man.

But not everyone got a duck. Bad timekeepers, agitators, or such as were caught smoking, larking, or lingering unduly in lavatories were liable to go duckless at Christmas.

Left alone, Joe Crabbe began to pick up the ducks and weigh them in his hand. The big plump ducks formed a select company on the shelves, the medium-sized birds lay on the table, whilst the more doubtful specimens he laid on the floor. And from the largest ducks on the shelves he selected four whoppers; from which again he picked one that was enormous. This monster he carefully wrapped in brown paper and pushed it behind some lumber out of sight.

Needless to say this treasure was for Joe Crabbe himself.

Every year as Christmas approached it was noticeable that some workers became exceptionally civil to the head foreman. His health came to be, for a few days before Christmas, a subject of acute interest. 'Good mornings' and 'Good nights' took on a strange tone of courtesy.

Even caps were raised to him. By some peculiar coincidence these men invariably got the bigger ducks.

On the other hand there were men who seemed proof against the genial spirit of Christmas. Such men even at the season of goodwill would grumble about low wages, piece rates, factory rules, and so on. Such men, while grudgingly accepting the ducks, would consign them verbally to all manner of places. These sullen fellows by some obscure workings of justice invariably took home the invalids, the undernourished, the weaklings of the duck-pond.

The bell sounded. The day's work was done. The men peeled off their overalls, received their pay-tins, and lined up, bags in hand, outside Crabbe's office for their ducks.

In each case, the foreman peeped out of his spy-hole. He saw the particular man outside and picked him out a particular duck.

The recipients of plump birds were effusive and in quavering tones wished the foreman a happy Christmas. The eyes of some were moist with gratitude. And strange to say even some who got small birds were visibly moved by such generosity.

'What the hell do you call this?' asked one man, holding out his duck contemptuously, and staring at the large birds on the shelf.

'What's wrong with it, Morgan?' asked Crabbe.

'For three years now you've given me one of these C3 b——s. This year I want a duck. What about one from that shelf?'

'I take them as they come. That's yours. Take it or leave it.'

'Then you can ...' Morgan expressed in his peculiar way his non-requirement of the bird and walked out.

So to the accompaniment of tears of gratitude, or scowls of ingratitude, the foreman distributed the birds.

Three alone, three mighty birds, remained on the shelf. Then entered the three under-foremen to claim these three monsters.

'Going round to the 'Flowerpot' for a wet?' they asked.

'I'll meet you outside in ten seconds,' replied Crabbe.

In a few minutes he staggered out under the weight of a poulterer's bag, and with his three companions entered the 'Flowerpot.'

Several rounds of drinks were consumed amid smoke, laughter, and gossip. In the bar were several of the workmen who begged Crabbe to accept a drink which that worthy obligingly did. At last his eyes began to glisten. He began to sway. He became incoherent and sentimental.

'Queer chap that Morgan! Nothing ever pleases him. Cut up rough over the duck. Queer chap!'

The other foremen were preparing to give their opinions of Morgan when the discussed man entered the bar. He called for beer and then catching sight of Crabbe walked up to him.

'Sorry I was a bit awkward this afternoon,' said Morgan, 'Have a drink?'

The foreman looked awkward and would have probably refused had not Morgan instantly ordered the drink. 'Christmas comes but once a year,' he said jovially. 'May we all get the luck we deserve!'

The company was undoubtedly strained. Conversation stopped dead, for all four foremen had fallen foul of Morgan many times during the year. The man to their relief, however, wished them the compliments of the season, took himself off, and mingled amongst the others in the bar.

'Queer chap that Morgan,' repeated Crabbe uneasily.

As Crabbe drank he seemed to mount upon a cloud higher and higher. He could no longer concentrate upon the conversation, his tongue felt tied, and through the haze he began to see two of everything. Instinctively he began to think about getting home.

'Now this must be the last,' he stammered.

But there was yet another – two more in fact.

Outside the 'Flowerpot' the men shook hands with maudlin ceremony.

'Christ! That's some duck you've got there,' said an under-foreman to Crabbe. And truly the weight of the basket pulled the foreman right out of the perpendicular.

'Well, and what if it is?' snarled Crabbe. 'You've not done so bad any of you,' and then, 'Well good night! Happy Christmas!'

As the foreman staggered homeward, the image rose in his brain of the splendidly forgiving Morgan. For three years he had picked out Morgan the very worst of the birds. And yet at the bottom of his heart Morgan seemed to bear him no malice. 'Queer chap, Morgan,' he muttered drunkenly.

'A pretty time to get home,' snapped Mrs Crabbe. 'And drunk as usual.'

'Well, here's tomorrow's dinner anyhow,' said Crabbe buoyantly, slinging the basket upon the table with a bang. 'You've got something good there, ma, I can tell you.'

His wife scowled at him, took from the dresser a large dish which she wiped carefully. Then from the basket she pulled a parcel and opening it found a sack, and inside – a brick!

Joe Corrie The Day before the Pay

They sat at their 'piece' at the head of the run. Jock, Tam and Wullie, who worked in adjoining places in the 'Slaughter-house Run'.

'Aweel,' said Jock, dumping his piece-box on the 'pavement', 'if that's it I've got it.'

'Ham and eggs the day again, Jock?' asked Wullie.

'Aye, but bashed intae jeely as usual,' replied Jock.

The joke was passed without a smile. It is an old one, growing a beard, as we say. Our fathers passed the same joke many a time. Ham and eggs bashed into jelly — bashed into margarine is more topical now-a-days.

Tam had not begun his piece.

'Are ye no' for ony piece the day, Tam?' asked Jock as he withdrew a short clay pipe from the inside of his cap and put the flame of his lamp to it.

'No,' answered Tam, 'I'm no' hungry this morn.'

'Are ye weel enough?'

'Aye.'

'There's something wrang wi' a man that canna tak' his piece.'

'That's yin thing aboot me, I've aye been able tae tak' my piece, nae maiter where I was workin', aye, and could hae taen mair than I got mony a time.'

'The same here,' said Wullie with his mouth full.

Then it suddenly dawned on Jock that it was the day before the pay.

'Hae ye nae piece?' he asked abruptly.

'Aye,' answered Tam awkwardly, 'but I'm no' hungry.'

'Where's yir piece-box?'

'I left it doon at the "face",' answered Tam, but he could not hide the lie.

'What wey did ye no' say ye had nae piece wi' ye,' said Jock angrily, 'I could hae gi'en ye half o' mine.'

Wullie stopped eating.

'Here, Tam!' He held out his piece-box containing a slice of bread.

'Never bother, Wullie, I'm no' hungry onywey.'

49

'Tak' the bloody thing,' said Jock, 'and don't be silly. You're no' the first man that has had tae come tae the pit withoot a piece on the day before the pey. Hae ye ony tea?'

'Aye,' answered Tam. 'I left it doon at the face.' He took the slice of bread from Wullie and crawled down the 'wall' to his place.

'Britons never, never shall be slaves,' was Jock's remark.

'Aye,' answered Wullie, 'rule Britannia. Tam's a great Liberal tae, non-political Union man, peace in industry and a' rest o't.'

'Aye,' said Jock, 'it's a hell o' a job when men can only see daylicht through an empty belly.'

'It's hopeless, Jock, we're livin' in a world o' mugs. It's no gaun tae be easy gettin' six home winners the morn. I spent three oors at the coopon last nicht, and I'm damned if I can get six likely things ata'.'

'I had a while at it mysel' last nicht, Wullie, and seen it was gey stiff. But hope springs eternal in the human breast.'

'Aye,' laughed Wullie, 'six good home teams and anither bob goes west – but never say die, Jock, never say die.'

'Listen! – Is that thae pans started, Wullie?'

'That's them started, sir. They're shairly in a hurry this mornin'. What time is it?'

Jock looked at his watch. 'It wants five meenits tae startin' time yet.'

'Aweel, we're hain oor five meenits, tae hell wi' them!' and he lighted another Woodbine.

'Here's a licht comin' up. It's his "Nabs".'

It was Robert, the section gaffer.

'Are you chaps gaun tae sit here a' day? Did ye no' hear the pans startin'? The manager's doon there.'

The sweat stood on Robert's brow, the sweat of fear, for gaffers are as much afraid of the manager as a rabbit is of a weasel.

'Come back in five meenits,' was Jock's answer, and he puffed harder at his pipe.

'The pans are started, and the manager's doon,' repeated Robert.

He was in a bonnie funk.

'Tell the manager tae look his watch. We'll be at oor wark when piece time's feenished.'

'If he comes up he'll gi'e ye the seck on the spot, mind ye,' was Robert's warning.

'Rin doon, Robert, and tell him,' said Wullie, 'But dinna let on tae him that we'd be better on the "dole".'

Robert was one of the type that was misplaced as a gaffer. He did not swear and could not bully. And he crawled away down the 'run', threatening to tell the manager.

But ere he arrived at the next place a yell of agony was heard above the noise of the machinery.

Jock jumped. 'That's Tam's voice, Wullie!' He rushed down the 'wall', Wullie following hard on his heels.

They were met by Robert. 'Hurry up, boys!' he shouted, 'Tam's pinned wi' a big stane.'

'For Christ sake get thae pans stoppit,' roared Jock, yet scarcely heard above the noise of the machinery.

'We canna stop the pans,' said Robert, 'the manager's doon there.'

'Get thae pans stoppit ye silly bas…!' And Robert rushed away.

Tam was pinned by the leg. They wrenched the stone away and carried him clear of the pans. No sooner was he clear than the signal was given to start them away again, for the manager was down.

Word was sent to the manager of the accident, but he did not trouble when he heard it was only a broken leg.

It was half an hour before the stretchers arrived, and another half hour elapsed ere Tam reached the pithead.

Coal! Coal! Coal! is the cry. Break yesterday's record!

'What's wrang the haulage is stoppit?'

'They're cairryin' up that man that has got his leg broken.'

'Hurry up, boys, the manager's doon.'

The ambulance was waiting, and Jock and Wullie went with Tam to the hospital.

On the way home Jock was suspicious of the weight of Tam's piece-box, which he was bringing home. They opened it and found the slice of bread which Wullie had given him.

He had done without it himself to take home to the bairns.

Harold Heslop   Compensation

Shot Douglas said nothing, for the simple reason that he never had very much to say. But he understood, and that is far better than talking a great deal. His inner sense told him that the place was going to 'work,' and there was no need to advertise the fact.

When a place, in the deep seams, begins to 'work' there is the devil to pay. Of course, the miners have no high falutin names for a place which is working. They simply say that it 'has taken the creep.' Apart from a first-line trench during a bombardment there is nothing so awe-inspiring as a place that has taken the creep. It is the roof in action. It speaks with a million voices. It thumps, it howls, it whimpers, it yells, it weeps. Men like Shot Douglas know all these voices, all the tones of those voices; they have a quick sympathy. 'Hush, little lady!' they generally say. Sometimes it does hush; more often than not it doesn't. Yet that is not all. The sides also lift up their voices. They crush and crackle and moan. All the time the roof, with its millions of tons, is pressing upon them, forcing them down through the floor. It is awful, painful, shameful. The floor begins to heave and wrench, until finally there is neither floor nor roof left. They almost jam together overnight. In the West District it did this once.

It was Monday, a dreary, miserable morning. Shot felt it very much to have to waken poor Johnny and take him, for the first time, to the pit; but the claims of the family came first. Seven mouths take a lot of feeding, especially when there are only two to do the providing. Shot shook him, 'Come on,' he growled.

After breakfast they set out for the pit head ...

They sat at the pit top waiting until the six o'clock buzzer should blow and give the signal for them all to get a move on. It blew. The bells clanged out their messages and the ropes began to move. The huge, slimy cage glided slowly into view and came to rest at the appointed place. The banksman flung open the gates and closed them after the scanty few had stepped inside.

When Shot had successfully scrambled into a tub he attached the pony to it, climbed on to the limbers, between the pony and the tub, and set off for home. The pony broke into a trot.

The pony trotted on. Johnny whistled serenely ...

They came to a low part. The top of the tub scraped monotonously against the roof supports. Shot fell to wondering why they never thought of repairing that part of the road.

'Expense!' he grunted contemptuously.

The pony stopped with a jerk. The tub jerked. Shot wondered what had happened. He sat waiting. He became anxious.

'Johnny!' he shouted.

Johnny did not reply. Shot began to wonder. What was the matter? What had happended to the lad?

'Johnny!' he yelled, 'Johnny!'

Shot was at a disadvantage. The tub itself was scarcely big enough to hold him comfortably. He could hardly move. As the tub was scrubbing against the top he could not get out. He raised his light, but he could not get it high enough to see the top of the tub. He could see nothing. A great fear struck his heart.

'Johnny! Johnny!' he yelled. 'Johnny! W'at's the matter?'

He held his light sideways in a vain endeavour to cast his light at the roof, but he just managed to save his light from going out. Then he began to grope about the top of the tub. His groping hand came into contact with something soft. It was Johnny's cloth cap. He felt closer ... hair. Yes, it was hair. He could feel Johnny's head. He felt it lovingly, fondly. With difficulty he drew his hand away. Somehow a great fear held him in thrall. It was a new Shot Douglas, a stranger, a child, a relic of a man ...

Wednesday came. The coroner wrote down a verdict of accidental death. Thursday came. The miners gathered about Shot's home, a poor, broken-down hovel. They erected their banner, gathered together their instrumentalists, struck up the Dead March in Saul, and headed the pathetic procession to the cemetery.

Poor Shot. He was mad. He could not be restrained. He raved at one moment and laughed at another. Strong men wept with him in his sorrow. Men who had never known what imagination was lived with the poor, stricken fellow during his awful three hours in his cage, knowing his boy was dead and unable to render him any aid, unable to succour him. Women shuddered in their sorrow.

The coal-owners and the coal-miners sat in council the next week. Compensation cases always call for a great deal of deliberation. As Johnny Douglas was not the main support of the family, his father being alive and able-bodied, it was decided to pay the costs of the funeral. The coal-owners are always sticklers for the Compensation Act ...

Six weeks later Shot died. The shock had been too great. The blow had felled him, had brought him to his knees. It was a happy release.

Out of sheer sympathy the miners once again raised their banner and formed up their brass band and struck up the Dead March in Saul and headed the pathetic funeral procession. They all shared Shot's widow's great grief.

But Shot had not been killed in the mine, neither had he died of injuries received while following his employment in the mine. There was no need for a coroner. Shot had simply died.

The coal-owners paid no compensation ...

Dick Beech   A Home from Home

'I see the old "Hardorio" is down to sign at eleven o'clock,' said Bill Gordon, addressing his remarks to a small group of seamen outside the shipping office in Wells Street. 'She is well named. I made a trip on her twelve months ago to the West Indies, and you can take it from me there's nothing easy on her. What you miss in food and accommodation, you make up for in work.'

'I'm hanged if I see much difference in any of them,' chipped in one of the group. 'Anyway, I don't care what sort of a packet she is, if there's a job going I'm taking it.'

'As far as that goes I suppose we all will,' replied Bill, looking at his watch. 'Gee, its gone eleven, they should be coming out now to pick the crew,' he added.

As he spoke, the mate and second engineer came out of the shipping office. Immediately they were surrounded by about two hundred men, each one trying to hand in his discharge book. Only about thirty were required, and in less than fifteen minutes they were taken. Bill found himself one of the number.

The crew signed on, and were ordered aboard at midnight. Bill cashed his advanced note, which cost him a pound, and proceeded home. During the afternoon he was busy buying the various items he would require to take away. By seven o'clock he had his bag packed and was ready.

It was a bitterly cold night, and he was undecided whether he would go out or have a lie down on the sofa. Ultimately, he decided on the latter. He went off to sleep, and didn't wake up till ten o'clock. He then made up his mind to get aboard and claim his bunk. Saying goodbye to his wife and family he picked up his bag and proceeded in the direction of the ship.

At ten-thirty he arrived alongside. For a few minutes he stood gazing at her. Suddenly he noticed that all amidships was lit up. He thought this was very unusual, from what he remembered of his previous trip the strictest economy always prevailed. Lifting his bag on to his shoulder

55

he walked up the gangway. Reaching the deck he turned to go aft, where the fo'c'sle was, when a voice said, 'Where are you going mate?'

Bill turned and saw a young man coming towards him. He had noticed him leaning over the rail as he came up.

'I'm one of the firemen,' answered Bill. 'We signed on today. I'm going along to the fo'c'sle. I suppose you are the watchman?'

'Yes,' was the reply, 'but the firemen's quarters are no longer aft; all the crew's accommodation is now amidships.'

Bill nearly dropped his bag in astonishment. 'Firemen's quarters amidships,' he repeated. 'How long has that been?'

'Oh, just lately,' continued the watchman. 'A new company has recently bought this packet, and they have had her reconstructed.'

Bill noticed as he followed his guide that all the amidships seemed rather strange. There appeared to be an extra deck. As they reached a long alleyway, the watchman said:

'These cabins along here are the crew's quarters. Firemen are at this end, stewards in the centre, and the sailors are at the far end. Two berths are in each cabin, as you can see.' He opened one of the doors. 'There's a wardrobe to hang your clothes in, and that's a closed-in washstand. In these drawers you can keep your other gear. You will notice the earphones, hanging on each bunk; a listen-in to the wireless between the watches will be a welcome change, eh?'

'Over here is the bath house,' he continued, opening another door. There was a row of baths in cubicles with showers fixed over each. Opposite was a number of lockers in which to hang up clothes.

'Well,' exclaimed Bill, 'this is some ship now. What a difference to the trip I made in her twelve months ago. We had a bucket issued between the two of us and we had to wash in the stokehold.'

'Oh, all that's changed now,' the watchman replied. 'This room here is the general mess room. You will notice it's a good size. No more eating and sleeping in the one room. The officers have their meals at that small table, and the rest of the crew have this long one. In the evening, it is intended that this place will be used as a recreation room. There's the piano in the corner, also a gramophone, so we shall be able to have a sing song occasionally.

'Should you be fond of book-reading, just gaze at those shelves. I'm one of the sailors, I've been working by and believe me this ship is going to be a 'Home from Home.' Since they have converted her into an oilburner she will be a good job down below for the firemen. Well, I must be getting back to the gangway, you had better pick your berth.'

Bill made for one of the cabins and claimed a bunk. He thought what a difference there was going to be between this voyage and the last he had made. He took a glass of water from a stone filter that hung in the corner on the cabin, and sat down on the settee opposite the bunks. His mind drifted back on various ships he had been on. Slowly he dozed off.

Suddenly someone shook him by the shoulder saying, 'Hi, hi, get up or you'll be too late, it's nearly eleven now.' Bill opened his eyes to find himself lying on the sofa, and his wife telling him she had been quite five minutes trying to get him to wake up.

James Hanley The Last Voyage

The eight to twelve watch had just come up. The foc'sle was full. The four to eight crowd were awake now. Some were already getting out of bed.

'Where is she now?' asked a man named Brady.

'She's home, mate. Look through the bloody porthole. Why she's past the Rock-light.'

And more of the four to eight watch began climbing out of bed. They commenced packing their bags. The air was full of smoke from cigarettes and black shag. A greaser came in.

'Reilly here?' he asked gruffly.

A chorus of voices shouted: 'Reilly! Reilly! Come on, you bloody old sod.'

A figure emerged from a bottom bunk in the darkest corner of the foc'sle.

'Who wants me?' he growled.

'Second wants you right away. Put a bloody move on.'

The man put on his dungaree jacket, a sweat-rag round his neck, and went out of the foc'sle.

'His goose is cooked, anyhow,' said a voice.

'Nearly time too,' said another.

'These old sods think they rule the roost,' said another.

'He's just too old for Rag-Annie,' said yet another.

And suddenly a voice, louder than the other, exclaimed: 'What the hell's wrong with him, anyhow? If some of you bastards knew your work as well as he does you'd be all right. Who says his goose is cooked?'

'The doctor.'

'The second.'

'Everybody knows it.'

'That fall down the ladder fixed him all right.'

'The old fool'l get gaol. D'you know he's sailin' under false colours?'

'False colours?'

'Yes. False colours. The b——'s sixty-six, and he's altered his birth-date. They've got him down on the papers as fifty-six.'

'Has he been found out?'

'I don't know.'

'Some lousy sucker must have cribbed.'

'Give us a rest, for Christ's sake,' shouted a Black Pan man. 'You'd think it was sailin' day to hear you talkin'. Don't you know it's dockin' day? We'll all be home for dinner.'

'And a pint of the best, eh?'

The packing of the bags continued, whilst the flow of conversation seemed unceasing.

'This ship is the hottest and lousiest I ever sailed in,' growled a trimmer. 'A real furnace, by Jesus.'

'Oh, listen to that,' said a voice. 'You want to sail on the *Teutonic* if you like the heat.'

Suddenly the man Reilly appeared in the foc'sle. He walked back to his bunk past the crowd of men, who were now so occupied with bag-packing that they hardly noticed his return. Suddenly a voice exclaimed:

'Well, Christ! Here he is back again.'

'Who?'

'Old Reilly.'

All the faces turned then. All the eyes were focussed upon the man Reilly.

'Did you get your ticket, mate?' asked one.

'Did he kiss you behind the boiler?' asked another.

'Are you sacked then?' asked another.

Everybody laughed.

'He went down to kiss the second's ——,' growled one.

The man Reilly was tall and thin. His eyes, once blue, were black. Heavy rings formed beneath them. His skin was pasty looking, his hair was grey. He was very thin indeed. When he took off his singlet, they shouted:

'His fifth rib's like a lady's.'

'His arms would make good furnace slices.'

'He's like a blood rake.'

'The soft old b——. Why doesn't he go in the blasted workhouse.'

Suddenly Reilly said: 'Go to hell.'

Then he commenced to roll up his dirty clothes.

'Here, you! Shut your bloody mouth and leave Reilly alone,' exclaimed a man named John Duffy. 'If half you suckers knew your job as well as he does, you'd get on a lot better.'

'He's an insolent old sod, anyhow,' said a deep voice in the corner.

'I've been twenty years in this ship,' said Reilly.

'Aye. And by Christ, the ship knows it too. I'll bet you must have been growlin' for that twenty years.'

'Who's growlin'?' shouted Reilly. 'You young fellers think you can do as you like,' he went on. 'Half of you don't know your job, but you can come up to us old b— and get the information though. Who the hell told you I was sacked? Don't you believe it. You'll have me here next trip whether you like it or not.'

'Oh Christ!'

'By God! I'll look for another packet, anyhow.'

'So will I.'

'Why in the name of Jesus don't they let you take the ship home with you? Anyhow we don't all kiss the second's —.'

'That's enough,' shouted Duffy.

A silence fell amongst the group in the foc'sle. Reilly, having packed his bag, went out on the deck. He sat down on No. 1 hatch. The ship already had the tugs, and was being pulled through the lock. He walked across to the rails and leaned over. He glared into the dark muddy waters of the river. He thought:

'Good God! All my life's been like that. Muddy.'

Duffy came out and joined him. He spoke to him. 'Hello, Johnny,' he said. 'How did you get on with Finch?'

Finch was the second engineer, a huge man with black hair and blue eyes, and a chin with determination written all over it. It was known that he was the only second engineer who had ever tamed a Glasgow gang from the Govan road.

'This next trip,' said Reilly, 'is my last. It's no use. I tried to kid them all along. But it wouldn't come off. I just come up from the second's room now.'

'What did he say?'

'"Reilly," he said, "I'm afraid you've got to make one more trip, and one only. You'll have to retire."

'"Retire, Mr Finch," I said.

'"Yes. You're too old. I'll admit I like you, for I think you're a good worker, a steady man. You know your job. What I have always liked about you is your honesty and your punctuality. I have never known you fail a job yet. That's why I've hung on to you all this time. You're a man who can always be trusted to be on the job. I'm sorry, but you know, Reilly, I'm not God Almighty. The Superintendent Engineer had you fixed last trip. But I asked him a favour and he did me one."

'"D'you mean that, Mr Finch?" I asked him.

"Yes, I do. Look here, Reilly. What have you been doing with that book of yours? You're down as being ten years younger than you are."

"Can't I do my job?" I asked him.

"Of course you can, Reilly, but that's not the point. You're turned the age now. Once you become sixty-five the company expect you to retire."

"On ten shillings a week," I said to him.

"That's not my business, Reilly," he said: "I repeat that I'm sorry, very sorry, but I'm not very much higher than you, and if I disobeyed the Super, I wouldn't be here five minutes."

"By Christ!" I said.

"Look here, Reilly," he said, "it's your last trip this time. I can't stand here talking to you all day. I'm sorry, very sorry. It might have been worse. You ran a chance of getting gaol, altering the age in your book. Here. Take this.'"

'He gave me a pound note,' said Reilly to Duffy.

'He did?' Duffy wiped his mouth with his sweat-rag. 'He's not a bad sort himself, isn't the second. Not bad at all.'

'Not much consolation to me though,' said Reilly, 'after thirty-nine years at sea. By Jesus! I tell you straight I don't know how to face home this time. It's awful. I've been expecting it, of course, but not all of a sudden like this. But d'you know what I think caused it?'

'What?' asked Duffy, and he spat a quid of tobacco juice into the river.

'Falling down the engine room ladder three trips ago.'

'But that was an accident,' remarked Duffy.

'Accident. Yes,' said Reilly. 'But don't you see, if I'd been a younger man I'd have been all right in a few days. But I'm not young, though I can do my work with the best of them. I was laid up in the ship's hospital all the run home.'

'Ah, well. Never mind,' said Duffy.

'S'help me,' exclaimed Reilly, 'but those young fellers fairly have an easy time. Nothing to do only part their hair in the middle, and go off to French Annie's or some other place. By God! They should have sailed in the old ships. D'you remember the *Lucania*?'

'Yes.'

'And the *Etruria*?'

'Yes.'

'D'you remember that trip in the big ship when she set out to capture the Liverpool to York speed record?'

'Aye.'

'D'you remember Kenny?'

'I do,' said Duffy. 'The bloody sod! All he thought about was his medal and money gift from the bosses, but us poor b—! Everytime we stuck our faces up to the fiddley grating to get a breath of air, there he was standing with a spanner, knocking you down again:

'"Get down there. Get down there."'

'Half boozed too,' said Reilly. 'I'll swear he was.'

'He was that,' remarked Duffy. 'All in all, nobody gives a damn for us. Work, work, work, and then – '

'You're a sack of rubbish,' said Reilly. 'And by Christ I know it. I know it. All my life. All my life. I've worked, worked, worked, and now –'

'Will you have a pint at Higgenson's when we get ashore,' asked Duffy.

'No. I won't. Thanks all the same,' said Reilly, and he suddenly turned and walked away towards the alloway amidships.

'It's hard lines,' said Duffy to himself, as he returned to the foc'sle. All the men were now dressed in their go-ashore clothes. Duffy began to dress.

'Where's the old boy?' they asked in chorus.

'I don't know,' replied Duffy, and he put on his coat and cap. Overhead they could hear the first officer shouting orders through the megaphone; the roar of the winches as they took the ropes; the shouts of the boatswain as he gave orders to the portwatch on the foc'sle head. The men went out on to the deck.

'She's in at last. Thank God.'

She was made fast now. The shore-gang were running the long gangway down the shed. A crowd of people stood in the shed, waiting. Customs officers, relatives of the crew, the dockers waiting to strip the hatches off and get the cargo out. All kinds of people. The gangway was up. The crew began to file down with their bags upon their backs.

'There he is!' shouted a woman. 'Hello Andy!'

'Here's Teddy!' shouted a boy excitedly.

And as each member of the crew stepped on to dry land once more, some relative or other embraced him. The men commenced handing in their bags to a boy who gave each man a receipt for it. He placed each one in his cart. Now all the crew were ashore. The shore gang went on board. An old woman stood at the bottom of the gangway. She questioned an engineer coming down the gangway.

'Has Mr Reilly come off yet, sir?' she asked.

'All the crew are ashore,' he replied gruffly.

But they were not. For Reilly was in the foc'sle. He was sitting at the table, his head in his hands. His eyes were full of tears.

'What a time you've been, Johnny,' exclaimed Mrs Reilly, when eventually her husband made his appearance. 'The others came down long ago.'

'I had something to do,' said Reilly, and there was a huskiness in his voice. Near the end of the shed he suddenly stopped and put his bag down. 'Have all those fellers cleared?' he asked. 'I wanted to send this bag home with Daly.'

'I'll carry it, Johnny,' said his wife.

'How the hell can you carry it?' he said angrily. 'I'll carry it myself. Only for this here rheumatism. I've never been the same since that there fall down the stokehole.'

He picked up the bag and put it on his shoulder. They walked on. At the dockgates they had to stop again, whilst the policeman examined his pass.

'I haven't got it,' exclaimed Reilly, all of a flutter now, for he suddenly remembered that he had left it on the table in the foc'sle.

'You're a caution,' said his wife. 'Indeed you are.'

'If you haven't a pass, mister, I'll have to search your bag. Are you off the *Oranian*?'

'Yes. I am. You ought to know me, anyhow. I've been on her for years.'

'I don't know you,' said the policeman gruffly. 'Let's have a look at it.' He picked the bag up and took it into the hut.

'Good heavens,' said Mrs Reilly. 'How long will he be in there? I'm perished with the cold.'

'Serve you right,' said her husband angrily. 'Haven't I told you time after time not to come down here, meetin' me? It's not a place for a woman at all.'

'There were other women here as well as me,' said Mrs Reilly.

'The other women are not you,' said Reilly, more angry than ever. 'Anyhow, here's the bloody bag.'

The policeman said: 'Everything's all right. Good night.'

Mrs and Mr Reilly walked away without replying. They passed through the dock gates. The road was deserted. Suddenly the woman exclaimed: 'Did you take those Blaud's pills while you were away, Johnny? I've been wondering. How d'you feel now?'

'Rotten,' he replied.

They walked on in silence.

'Shall I get you a glass of beer for your supper?' asked his wife.

'No.'

Again silence.

'Mary's husband got washed overboard,' said Mrs Reilly quite casually. 'Of course, I wrote to you about it.'

'Jesus Christ! Andy? Andy gone?'

'Yes. Poor feller. He was coming down the rigging after making the ratlines fast.'

'My God!'

They reached the end of the road. Turned up Juniper Street. Reilly spoke. 'How's Harry? Did he get any compensation?'

Mrs Reilly looked at her husband.

'He got twenty pounds. Lovely, isn't it? And him with his jaw gone.'

'Poor Andy, poor Andy,' Reilly kept saying to himself. 'Poor Andy.' And then suddenly he said aloud: 'Holy Christ! What a life! What a lousy bloody life!'

'It's God's Holy will,' said his wife. 'You shouldn't swear like that, Johnny.'

'I dare say I shouldn't,' he said, and he stopped to spit savagely into the road. They reached the house. The three children, twelve, fifteen, and sixteen, all embraced him.

To the boy, Anthony, who was sixteen, he said: 'Well, are you workin' yet, Anthony?'

'No, dad. Not yet.'

The father sighed. He turned to Clara, twelve years of age, and took her upon his knee. 'How's Clara?' he asked her.

She smiled up at him, and he smothered her in a passionate embrace.

When the children had gone to bed, Mrs Reilly made the supper. They both sat down.

'Eileen has to go into hospital on Wednesday,' said Mrs Reilly.

'What for?'

'Remember her gettin' her arm caught in the tobacco cutting machine?'

'Yes. But I thought it healed up?'

Mrs Reilly leaned across and whispered into his ear: 'Don't say anything, John.'

'I'm sorry I came home. By God, I am. Coming and going. Coming and going. Always the same, trouble, trouble, trouble.'

He put down his knife and fork. He could not eat any more, he said, in reply to his wife's question. He drew a chair to the fire and sat down.

Mrs Reilly began clearing the table. She talked as she gathered up the dishes.

'Trouble. God love us, you don't know what trouble is, man. How could you know? Sure you're all right, aren't you? Away from it all. You have your work to do. And when you've done it you can go to bed and sleep comfortable. You have your papers and your pipe. You have your food and your bed. Trouble. God bless me, Johnny, but you don't know what the word means. The rent's gone up, and then Anthony not working, and Eileen's costing me money all the while. And she'll end up by being a drag on me. How can the poor girl work? I get on all right for a while and then something happens. You see nothing. Nothing at all.'

Reilly jumped up and almost flew at his wife. She dropped her hands to her side. She looked full into his face.

'See nothing! Jesus Christ Almighty! You don't know what I see. You don't know what I have to do. What worry I have. You don't know what I think, how I feel. No. No. God's truth, you don't. Me! ME! An old man. And I have to hop, skip, and jump just like the young men, and if I don't, I'm kicked out. And where would you be then? And all the children. In the bloody workhouse. I have to put up with insults, humiliations, everything. I have to kiss the engineer's behind to keep my job. By heavens, you're talking through your hat, woman!'

'Am I? How do you know I'm talking through my hat? Was I talking through my hat that time you fell twenty-five feet down the iron ladder into the engine room? Was I? Was I? Was I talking through my hat when I made you come away from the doctor who examined you? Was I daft? You with a piece of your skull sticking in your brain, and no jaw, and all your teeth knocked out, and three ribs broken. And you actually wanted to take a lousy twenty-three pounds from the shipping company's compensation doctor. The dirty blackguards! You tried to kiss *his* behind. That I do know.'

'Look here, woman. I'll cut your throat if you torment me much longer. You don't know what I have on my mind. God! you don't. Kiss his backside. I had to. Supposing I had done as you say. Asked for a £100 compensation. I know it would have been all right if we had got it, but we didn't get it, did we? And I knew we couldn't. So I took what they offered – twenty-three pounds, and my job back.'

'Did that pay the doctor's bill and rent and food, for all the eleven weeks you were ill in bed on me? Did it? No. You had a right to ask for the hundred pounds. It's too late now.'

'I had no right.'

'You had. Good God! You know you had.'

'Damn and blast you, I tell you I had no right. I could never have got it. Didn't the union try? Didn't everybody try? It was no use. I got off lucky. I got my job back anyhow, didn't I?'

'Your job,' said Mrs Reilly, sarcastically.

'My job! My job! My job!' he screamed down the woman's ear. 'My job.'

'The people next door are in bed,' she said.

'I don't care a damn where they are.'

'I do,' said his wife.

'Christ, you'd aggravate a saint out of heaven. I feel like chokin' you.'

'Go ahead then. You hard-faced pig. That's what you are.'

'Oh, go to hell,' said Reilly. He walked out of the kitchen. Went upstairs. He undressed and got into bed. He lay for a while. Suddenly he got up again. He went into the children's room. They were sleeping. He went up to each one. He kissed them upon the forehead and upon the lips. He kissed Clara, murmuring: 'Oh, dear little Clara. Dear little Clara. I wonder what you'll do. I wonder how you'll manage.' Then he kissed Eileen.

'Poor Eileen. Poor darlin'. Losing your little arm. Your poor little arm. And nothing – NOTHING can save it.'

He kissed Anthony and murmured: 'Poor lad. God help you. I don't know how you'll face life. No, I don't know. Poor boy.'

Then he tip-toed out of the room and returned to his bed. All was silent in that house now. Below, Mrs Reilly was sitting in the chair just vacated by her husband. She was weeping into her apron. Above – he lay.

He thought. 'First night home. Good Lord. Always trouble. Always something. And me – me defending my job, and I haven't got one after this trip. Finished now. All ended now.'

Mrs Reilly came up to bed. Neither spoke. She got into bed. Lay silent. No stir in that room. All dark outside. Roars of winches and shouting of men they could hear through the window. Mrs Reilly slept. The husband could not sleep. He got out of bed again, and went into the children's room. Anthony was in one bed. Clara and Eileen in the other. He lay down on the edge of the boy's bed.

'Nothing. Nothing now,' he said. 'Things I've done. All these years. Nothing now. How useless I am. Poor children. If only I had been all right. Oh, I wonder where you'll all be this time next year. I wonder.' He closed his eyes but could not sleep. Was nothing now, he felt. Nuisance. And young men coming along all the time. Young men from same street. Street that was narrow, and at the back high walls so that sun could not come in. 'No sun in one's life,' he thought.

Mrs Reilly woke. Felt for her husband. Not there.

'O Lord!' she exclaimed. 'Where is he? Surely he hasn't gone.'

She called. And her voice was thin and cracked and outraged silence of that room. 'Johnny, are you there?' she called.

He heard. He would not reply. Was crying quietly, and one long arm like piece of dried stick was across Anthony's neck. She called again.

'Oh my God! Where are you, Johnny?'

He did not answer. Were now strange feelings in him. Heart was not there. Was an engine in its place. Ship's engine. Huge pistons rose and fell. He was beneath these pistons. His body was being hammered by them. All his inside was gone now and was only wind there. Wind seemed to blow round and round all through his frame. Gusts of wind. Were smothering him. Many figures were tramping in him. Voices. All shouting. All talking together. He could hear them. They were walking through him. Third engineer was one.

'You soft old bastard. Didn't I tell you to watch the gauge?'

Chief engineer was another.

'Watch yourself, Reilly. You're getting old now. Be careful. We'll do what we can for you. We won't forget you.'

Was another. And him a greaser. His name was Farrell.

'You sucker. Working longer than anybody else in port. Go and get me some cotton waste. And shift your bloody old legs.'

'I have to keep my job.'

All voices spoke as one now. He could not understand their words. And always this engine was moving, these pistons crushing him. Three o'clock in the morning and no sleep yet.

Mrs Reilly was out of bed. She was downstairs. She looked in the back-kitchen, in the yard and closet. Her husband was not there.

'What a worry he is,' she said, and came upstairs again. And there he was in the bed. He looked up at her. She smiled. He did not smile, but closed his eyes. She spoke to him.

'Where were you, Johnny. I thought you had gone down to the yard. Didn't you hear me calling you?'

'No. Was with children,' he said.

'Are you hungry? Would you like that glass of bitter? You had no supper,' she said, and there was a kindness in her voice, and in the tired eyes.

'Not now. Am tired,' he replied.

'Oh, Johnny. If only you'd stuck out for the £100. It would have been lovely. I was only thinking just now. We could have opened that greengrocer's shop. An' Eileen could have served in it. It would have been grand. We could have got her an artificial arm. They're so wonderful now, these doctors. Artificial arms are just like ordinary ones. You can use a knife and fork with them. If only you'd stuck out, Johnny. And Anthony could have taken out the orders.'

'Shut your mouth, for Christ's sake!' he growled.

Was a silence. Reilly breathed heavily. Light of candle fell upon his face. Was thin and worn. Yellow like colour of fly-paper. Hands were hard. White like coral.

'Johnny, what's the matter, darlin'? Aren't you well?'

'I'm all right,' he said. 'It's this rheumatism, and then I'm thinking of Andy. Lord have mercy on him.'

'Poor Andy,' she said, 'was a lovely lad, wasn't he?'

'It's awful about Eileen,' said Reilly. 'Does she get no compo?'

'Not yet. Company said it was her own fault. If comb fell out of her hair and on to machine she had no right to put out her hand for it. Was an accident, they said. Would give her light job just now brushing rooms.'

'And her with her arm off. The soft sons of bitches,' he growled.

'I had an idea,' she said to him, and stroked his forehead.

'Idea,' he said, and sighed.

'Yes. Couldn't you get Anthony away with you as a trimmer?'

'What for?' he asked. And was a strange look in his eyes.

'To help us, of course,' she said; 'we have to get money somehow or other. We have to live.'

'Don't you get mine!'

'Yes. But it's not enough, Johnny,' she pleaded. 'You know Anthony is a strong lad. He would be all right as a trimmer.'

'I don't want any of my children to go to sea,' he said.

'You're very particular in your old age,' she said, with sarcasm.

'In my old age! Particular! Christ! Shut it.'

'Anyhow he wants to go,' she said. 'Is tired being at home. No work for him. Poor lad. Other lads working and money for cigarettes and pictures. None for him.'

'We're a lucky bloody family,' said Reilly angrily.

'Won't you try?' she asked. 'Will help us all this getting him away as trimmer. Will make a man of him. He wants to go.'

'Make a man of him,' said Reilly, and he laughed.

'Yes. Will make a man of him,' she said, and was angry, for colour had come into her cheeks that looked like taut drum-skins. 'How bloody funny you are.'

'Me funny. Don't kid yourself, woman. I have to see the doctor in the morning. Nothing funny in that. For the love of Jesus shut up about Anthony and everybody else. Why don't you go to sleep?'

He was angry too, for eyes were burning with strange fire. He turned over on his side. Mrs Reilly mumbled to herself. They both lay on their sides with their backs to each other. He thought:

Bring Anthony with him? No. How funny. What made her suggest that? Especially this next trip. No. He would not.

'Are you awake, Johnny?' she asked him.

'I am,' he replied.

'Are you all right? I'm worried about you. Won't you have that glass of bitter that's downstairs?'

'No.'

Of a sudden were strange sounds in that house. And silence was like a fast revolving wheel that has just stopped.

'What's that?' asked her husband.

'It's Eileen. Poor child. In the night her arm pains awful.'

'Go to her.'

His wife got up and went in to Eileen. The girl was sitting up in bed. All dark there for though moon shone light could not get in through high wall that faced window. It had a crack in it.

'What's the matter, child?'

'Oh, mother!' she said. 'Oh, mother!' Mrs Reilly held her child to her. And in her heart a great fear arose. Could feel now tiny heart of child pulsating against her own, whose tick was slow, like little hammer taps, or like dying tick of clock that is worn out.

'Oh my arm!' sighed Eileen.

'There, there,' said the mother. 'Don't cry, darlin'. God's good.'

Was nothing but heavy breathing of mother and little sobs of Eileen in that darkness.

Mrs Reilly shuddered. Eileen clung to her. In the other bed Anthony snored. His curly hair was a dark mass on the pillow.

Mr Reilly turned and lay on his back. He was muttering to himself.

'To-morrow. Pay off. Go away. Pay off. Finish.'

Was not much in life, and we are only like dirt, he felt in his heart. He fell asleep. Was morning when he woke. Nine o'clock.

'I've fried you an egg,' said Mrs Reilly.

'Can't eat anything now,' said Mr Reilly. 'Just make a cup of tea. Have to pass doctor and sign on half-past ten. Where's Eileen?'

'Gone over to the chemist's.'

'What for?'

'Well, I thought you'd want those pills again. For next trip.'

'Pills. Oh yes,' he said, and his voice seemed to be far away. He sat down and drank the tea hurriedly. Then he went into the back-kitchen. As he was closing the door he said: 'Don't let anybody come in here. I'm washing all over.'

He stripped. Was very thin. And he looked at himself in the glass. Ran hands over his body. He said to himself: 'Forty years at the one job. By God! And now finish. Well, many's the stoke-hole and engine-room as has drawn sweat out of you, and you're alive yet. Many a time was ill with eyes bulgin' out of bloody head, and yet I took my rake and slice like a man and fired up. Many places I've been to. Saw many things. Not much in life.' He began to scrub himself.

'Don't splash all over the place,' shouted Mrs Reilly. 'I only scrubbed that place out last night.'

'All right,' he replied.

Was washed now. He dried himself with table cloth that had been on table once and Anthony had spilt tea on it. Was not much of a towel, he said. Again he looked at himself in the glass.

'These varicose veins,' he murmured. 'That's what it is.' And putting on the truss, he added: 'And this. This bloody rupture.'

Remembered fifteen years ago. Was young and strong and worked hard on *Lucania* when her engines broke down in the Western ocean. Heavy shafting to be lifted and he was strong. Was no thought for himself then, only for ship that had to be in New York by Wednesday ten-fifteen p.m. Company were anxious to get passengers for Advertisers' Convention in England, before Red Star liner got them. Remembered that. And Chief Engineer said to second: 'Call the men for'ard, and tell the steward to give each man a tot of rum.' Good job that.

Remembered that. Had the rum. Forgot all about strain on body. Six years later the rupture came. It was bad too. He dressed and went into the kitchen.

'You look all right now,' said Mrs Reilly, and helped him to tie his boots, and fasten his collar on. He put his coat and blue serge cap on. Then he crossed to the door.

'Kiss me,' she said.

He kissed her on cheek. The door banged. Mrs Reilly was thinking.

'God help him! He does look bad this trip.'

Reilly walked down the street. There were some people standing on their doorsteps, and children in gutters. Some women were speaking.

'There's owld Reilly home again.'

'He looks bad, doesn't he?'

'Sure that owld devil's as hard as leather.'

Reilly passed a pub where men were standing outside. Were old seamen out of work and they were talking.

'Hello, Johnny! How are you keepin', old timer?'

'Not bad,' Reilly said.

'He's a tough old devil, all right,' said this man.

Reilly had turned the corner. He had nearly been knocked down by a car. He had jumped smartly out of the way. A man who was young and very tall laughed. He said to the girl who was with him: 'Can't beat that, can you? An old sod like that trying to appear like a schoolboy.'

Reilly walked on. He was near the docks now. He walked down the shed. Were many men in this shed who knew him. They hallooed him. Waved hands.

'Hello there?'

'Hello?'

'How goes it, Jack?'

'How do?'

Reilly smiled and shouted: 'Fine.' 'Middlin'.' 'Not so bad.' 'In the pink.' He was walking up the gangway now. A large number of men were standing about in the alloway, waiting to pass the doctor.

'Hello there?'

'How do?'

'Christ, he's back again!'

'Bloody old sucker.'

'How do, Reilly, old lad?'

All the men shouting and joking with him. He stood by the wall. He had his book in his hand.

'Whose — will you kiss this time?'

' How's your arm?'

'Did you have a bite this time home?'

All men taunting him. Were young men. Could not protest. Must hang on to his job.

'Leave the old fellow alone.'

'He's all right.'

'A wet dream is more correct.'

Reilly's heart was almost bursting. Could do nothing. Was tragic for him. 'I feel like a piece of dirt,' he said to himself. He was nearly in tears through anger, humiliation, threats, taunts.

'Doctor.'

All the men commenced to move down the alloway. Reilly was last. He shivered. Was afraid. He drove his nails into the palms of his hands but hands were hard and horny through much gripping of steel slice. He bit his lip until some blood came.

'Jesus, help me!' he said in his heart. 'Don't shiver. Don't be afraid. Be like the others. Remember now. All at home waiting for you. Waiting. Waiting for money. Little children expecting something. Wife expecting to go to the pictures. Keep cool.' The thoughts careered round and round his brain. He felt he was in a kind of whirlpool. 'Keep calm.'

The file moved along and it came Reilly's turn. He was in the doctor's room now. The doctor was young, and whilst Reilly dropped his trousers down, he cast look of appeal at doctor, whose cheeks were rosy, and his teeth beautifully white. Very clean he was. 'Like those men from University with white soft hands,' thought Reilly as he looked him in the face. Terribly clean. And strong too. The doctor spoke to him.

Reilly looked up at him with the eyes of a dying dog. 'Tell the truth now,' he said to himself. 'Anyhow it's your last trip.'

'How old are you?'

'Sixty-four, sir,' replied Reilly. 'I've been in this ship since she was built.'

'That doesn't mean that you can stay in her for ever,' said the doctor. Was cruel. Was like a stab in the heart. Was bitter, Reilly thought.

'Step over,' he said to Reilly.

The man stepped across and stood before the doctor. He was a head above Reilly. He examined his chest.

Then he looked lower down. He stroked his hair with his hand. He placed his hand on Reilly, and he felt how soft it was. Like silk. Beautiful hands. And his own were like steel. 'How long have you had this rupture, Reilly?'

'About six years, sir. I think I got it in the *Lucania*.'

'You didn't happen to get it anywhere else,' said the doctor.

'Again he is sarcastic,' thought Reilly.

'Oh,' exclaimed the doctor. 'Who's been passing you with these varicose veins?'

There was a bitter taste in Reilly's mouth. Like gall.

'On and off, sir,' he said: 'Dr Hunter always passed me. I can do my work well. Second engineer will tell you that, sir.'

The doctor smiled. ' I don't want to know anything about that,' he said. 'I am quite capable of handling you, thank you.'

'Christ!' muttered Reilly. 'How bitter he can be. Bitter as hell.'

'Bend down,' said the doctor.

Reilly bent down. Doctor looked hard at him. Felt him. All over. Legs, thighs, heels.

'All right,' said the doctor. 'But I won't pass you again after this. Next.'

The blood stirred in Reilly's heart. He was angry. He did not, he could not, make any reply to the doctor. He seemed to fly from that room.

'Did you get tickled?'

'Did you cough?'

'Did you do it?'

Again were voices in his ears as he walked down the alloway. Again were many men waiting to pass through to the pay table. Suddenly a voice of a master-at-arms shouted: 'Pass through as your names are called.'

Pay table was in grand saloon where rich carpets are deep and feet sink into them. Was beautiful and rich. Very quiet. Warm. Beautiful pictures on walls. Great marble pillars stretching up to ceiling. Was a place where first-class passengers dined on trips to America, but crew were not allowed to go there, for crew must stay for'ard in foc'sle. Crew must eat off wooden table through which iron poles were pushed up to deck-head, to hold table and prevent food from upsetting when weather was rough. Was well for'ard, the men's foc'sle. Where, when ship was up against heavy head swell, foc'sle seemed to pitch and toss, and often when she pitched badly food would be flung from table into men's bunks. And was dark too, for port-holes were down near water-line, and must have dead-lights screwed over them, for fear waters poured in, drowning men in their bunks. Men filed past the pay-table.

'Reilly.'

His name now. And he stood whilst another man said: 'Five pounds, eighteen and threepence.' Was handed the notes, and they were new and crackled in his horny hand.

'Your book.' And another man handed him his book.

'John Reilly, ship's fireman.' He passed through another room, where he signed on. He handed his book to the officer. He passed out to the other side, and walked along saloon deck, which crew were not allowed to stand on during voyage, descended the companion ladder, walked along well-deck, and then down gangway. Again many men in the dockshed. 'Union,' one said, and that was seventeen shillings.

'Help the blind!' said a voice, and that was one shilling.

'Here y'are,' and it was a bill for carrying the bag to and fro from ship to house for four trips, and that was eleven shillings.

Near gates were Salvation Army women with boxes, and these rattled, for were full of poor men's pennies, that kept hostels open for poor men. Was also a man holding a large box for collection. A card read: 'For widow of Bernard Dollin. Scalded to death on the *Europesa*. No compensation. Please help.' More shillings. Reilly hung desperately on to his money now. He put two shillings in the box for Dollin's widow. On dock road was a woman selling flags that were made of yellow rag. Was for homes for tired horses at Broadgreen.

'Jesus Christ! For tired horses!' exclaimed Reilly, and laughed aloud. He turned up Juniper Street. At Hangmans he stopped and went in with men who had been waiting for him.

'Have a drink on me, mates,' he said.

The bar-lady served seven pints of bitter. 'Good health, Johnny. Best of luck next trip.'

All wished him good health and good luck. He said 'same to you,' and drank his pint quickly, like a thirsty horse drinking at a trough.

'Same again,' he said to the bar-lady. 'I must go now, lads,' he said. 'See you again. Good luck.'

'Good luck, Johnny,' all said in chorus, and he went out.

He came up the street and again were women talking on steps as he passed. Also children like pigeons in gutters.

'Good-day, Mr Reilly.'

'Good-day,' he said.

'Hello, Johnny, how are you?'

'Not so bad,' he said.

People were nice in one's face, and some people had cursed him when he had gone up the street. Was at his home now. Mother had clean table-cloth on the table and children were waiting for him.

'Hello, dad,' said Clara, and then Anthony said, 'Hello, dad,' and Eileen too. 'Hello, dad,' she said. He kissed them all. He sat down in the chair by the fire. Looked in the flames for a long time. Children looked up into eyes of father who had come to them out of great ocean and dark night and was wonder in their eyes. Mother came in from back-kitchen and said: 'Dinner is ready, Johnny.'

He said he was ready too and sat down. Children were seated now. Wild freshness of youth on their faces was a feast for his eyes, and his dinner was going cold through watching them. He looked at them longingly and blood stirred in him when he remembered humiliations of last trip.

'Lovely children. God help them,' he said in his heart.

The children were finished dinner so they got up and went out.

'Here,' he said, and gave each of them sixpence, and they smiled. He kissed them all. 'How happy they are,' he thought. They went out then.

Mrs Reilly said: 'Did you sign, Johnny,' and he said: 'Yes.'

He pushed back his plate and put his hand in his pocket. Gave her £4.

'Is that all?' she asked, and was a sadness in her voice.

'That's all,' he said. 'Had to give seventeen shillings to union, and coppers here and there. Was going to buy a pair of drawers this trip, but can't afford it.'

'Good God!' she said. 'That's terrible, Johnny.'

'Good Jesus!' he said. 'Can't do any more, can I? You get my allotment money. You can't have it both ways, woman. If you hadn't drawn thirty shillings a week from my wages I could have given you about £8.'

'God! I don't know,' she said, and sighed deeply.

'Can't do any more,' he said. 'Will you go to the pictures to-night?' He stood up and put his hands on her shoulders.

'I don't know,' she said.

'Heavens above,' he said. 'Always something wrong. What would you do if I hadn't signed?' He became suddenly silent. No use to talk like that. Forget all that. Try and be happy.

'Come on, old girl,' he said, 'get cleaned up. We'll go to the theatre or somewhere.'

'All right,' she said. 'You go and have a lie down.'

Reilly went upstairs to bed. He was not long with his head on the pillow before he snored. Below Mrs Reilly cleaned up. When she was finished she washed herself. Changed. Was all ready now and sitting by the fire. Kettle was boiling on the hob. At five Johnny came down. Was feeling a little better after his sleep. He said: 'Good. I see you're ready. Where'll we go, old girl?'

'Anywhere you like,' she replied.

'Righto,' he said, and went to get a wash in the back-kitchen.

When the children came in she said to them: 'Your father and me are going out to the pictures. Now please be good and look after the place.' And to Eileen she said: 'Look after them, Eileen. To-morrow me and you will go somewhere.'

Were gone now and children all alone in house. Mrs Reilly and her husband got on a tram and it took them to the picture-house. Was dark in there but band played nice music and Mrs Reilly said she liked it. He said nothing at all. When picture came it was a story of a man and two women. Mrs Reilly said last time she was at the pictures story was about two men and one woman. Johnny laughed. 'Story was very nice,' he said. Always the people in the pictures were nice looking, and always plenty of stuff on tables and no trouble for them to get whisky. She said women wore lovely dresses. Interval then and lights went up. Band played music again.

'Come on,' he said, and they got up and went outside. They went to a pub, and he said: 'What'll you have, old woman?'

She said: 'A bottle of stout.'

'All right,' he said.

He drank a lemon dash himself. Was all smoke and spit and sawdust in the pub. Many men and women were drinking there. He said: 'It's cosy here.'

'Have another?' said Reilly, and she said: 'No. Not now.'

'I'm having another dash,' he said. When it came he drank it quickly. Back to pictures. All was dark again. In the next seat to them they could hear the giggling of a girl.

'Gettin' her bloody leg felt,' he said and lighted his pipe.

'Ought to be ashamed of herself,' she said, and was looking at a picture of a comic man throwing pies when she said this. He laughed, and she thought he was laughing at the picture and she said: 'He's a corker, isn't he?'

He said: 'I should think so,' and was thinking of the man who was with the girl who his wife said should be ashamed of herself.

'I'm tired,' he said. 'Shall we go?'

'Near the end now,' she said. 'Wait, Johnny.'

Comic man had just been chased by a policeman. He knew it was near the end of the picture. Did not want to stand when 'God save the King' was played by band.

He said: 'Come on,' and pulled her arm. They went out. They hurried home in the tram through dark roads where pale light of gas lamps made all people's faces look yellow as if everybody had yellow jaundice.

'I feel so tired,' he said.

'Will you have a glass of bitter?' she asked him as they were walking up the street.

'No,' he said. 'I'm going to bed now. Too tired for anything.' When they got in he went upstairs. As he was closing the kitchen door, he said: 'Don't be long now.'

Mrs Reilly made herself a drink of tea before she went up herself. She ate some bread that the children had left. 'Poor Johnny,' she said. 'Gets tired quickly these days. Is not the man he used to be: God help him.'

She put out the light and went upstairs. Undressed and got into bed. Candle was burning on table at his side of the bed and light fell on her husband's face. His eyes were closed.

'He is asleep,' she said. Looked at his face. Was very thin, she thought. 'Good God!' she whispered. 'I hope he doesn't catch consumption.' She kissed him on the forehead where many furrows were. She fell asleep watching him.

Morning for going away had come and he was up early. Mrs Reilly and the children were up. Bag was packed and was standing in the corner by the door. Was beautiful and clean for his wife had scrubbed it well. Was hard work for it was made of canvas. All were at the table having their breakfast. Egg each and some bacon. It was the same each sailing day. An egg each and a slice of bacon for the children. Mr Reilly was shaving in the back. Was sadness in his eyes and he did not like looking at himself in the glass whilst he was shaving. He tried to look downward just where razor was scraping. He finished and washed himself. Came into the kitchen. Were two eggs and a piece of bacon for him. He could not eat all that, he said. Wasn't hungry, he told his wife. But she said, 'Try, because you haven't ate much this trip,' and the children were looking from father to mother and to his plate, and each was thinking: 'He will give me the egg that's over.' Mr Reilly started to have his breakfast. His wife said: 'Won't you eat any more?' and he said: 'No.' Children looked only at the mother now, but were disappointed for she said: 'I'll have the odd egg myself.'

Children had gone out into yard. Was quiet now and clock could be heard ticking. Was five past seven by it.

'Must go now,' he said, and voice was soft.

'Now, Johnny,' she said, and got up from the table. Whilst she crossed to the back door to call in the children to say good-bye to their father, she wiped pieces of egg from her mouth, for her husband always kissed her on the lips on sailing day. Children came in. He embraced each one, saying: 'Good-bye. God bless you.' Now his wife. She clung to him.

Nearly in tears he was, for was much in his mind, and 'the heart is a terrible prison,' he said to himself.

'Good-bye, Johnny,' she said. She hung tightly to him. 'God bless you. Take care of yourself now. Don't forget to take the Blaud's pills. Good-bye. God bless you.'

'Good-bye,' he said, and bag was on his back and he was through the door. She closed it and went up to the window, where children were trying to look out in to the dark street and with their noses pressed flat against the window pane.

'Poor Johnny,' she said in her heart. 'Didn't eat much this trip, was looking very bad, poor fellow. Ah, well!'

'Draw the blind down again,' she said to Eileen, for it was still dark and gas was lighted yet. Dark until eight o'clock. The children came away from the window. Mother's eyes were misty and they were looking at her. Reilly walked down the street in the direction of the dock where his ship lay. Was dark, and all silent. Streets were terribly quiet. Everything seemed gloomy and sad. Raining too. Turned the corner now. Argus Street, Welland Street, Darby Street. Good-bye. Good-bye. Juniper Street, Derby Road. Good-bye. Good-bye. Was near the docks now. Some men were coming out of the gate. They knew him for he was just walking under the lamp when they came out.

'Good-bye Johnny. Good luck,' they said.

'Good-bye. Good-bye,' and his voice was a murmur low in their ears. Ship was there. Like a huge beast, sleeping. Was a light from an electric cluster hanging over number 2 hatch. Was like huge beast's eye. Some steam was coming out of the pipe near the funnel. Was like hot breath coming out of huge beast's nostrils. Was slowly waking. And from funnel itself was much smoke coming. It came out in clouds, then in the air became scarf-shaped. All was very silent except for low moaning. Steady whirr, whirr within ship. It came from for'ard where beef-engine was running. Was never stopped for place where food is kept for passengers must always be cool. The morning was very cold. At the gangway the watchman shivered. As Reilly ascended the gangway, the watchman took his nose between his fingers and blew hard into dock.

'Mornin',' he said dryly as Reilly passed him. Reilly made no reply. Was on his ship now. Going for'ard. In some hours to come he would be right down inside this beast. Down inside huge belly. Sweating. Half-past seven. Suddenly many noises filled the air. Ship was full of action. Ship was like great hippopotamus where all ticks were feeding on body. Decks were alive with men. Derricks were moving like long arms, and men seemed like pygmies on the great decks. Crew were now coming on board. All were hurrying towards foc'sle and glory-holes, for first there was best served. Last trip Reilly had to take bottom bunk in firemen's room where rats as big as bricks stood up defiant against the men when they tried to get them in the corner and kill them with big holy-stones. Reilly had a top bunk now. Was first man in. Another man came in. His name was Campbell.

'Hello cocky. You took my bloody bunk,' he said.

Reilly did not reply. Thoughts in him were calm. He said in his heart: 'Your last trip. Keep calm. Remain silent. Stand things for sake of wife and children. When you go home you can get the old age pension.'

'Well, Holy Jesus!' said Farrell, coming in. 'The dozy swine's back again.'

Reilly remained silent. Calmly he unpacked his bag. Was something hard in it. Like a little box. 'Good God!' he murmured. 'Fancy that. Poor Eileen. Bought me a box of soap. God bless the darling child.' He fondled the box as if it were made of solid gold. Were many noises now for foc'sle was full. Again voices in his ears. He wished they were full of cotton wool.

'Old Reilly's back.'

'Oh Christ! Is he?'

'Can't you see him?'

'Hello there. You old sucker.'

Was a message flashing through Reilly's brain. 'Keep calm.' Nine o'clock now. Second engineer came down the crew's alloway. He crushed past a small trimmer. Said to him: 'Tell Farrell to pick his watch.' Trimmer went into foc'sle. Spoke to Farrell. Farrell shouted: 'Outside men.' All the men went out on deck. Some were aleady wearing their dungarees. Some wore their best clothes. Many were drunk. Farrell looked at the men. His right forefinger was pointing. As if he were pointing a gun at them all. They watched him..

'Ryan. Duffy. Connelly. Hughes. Hurst. Thompson. Reilly. Simpson.'

Eight men stepped forward.

'Eight to twelve watch,' he said. 'Stand by till twelve o'clock. Have your dinner. Then turn in.' He walked off amidships.

On the deck also were boatswain and his mate. They picked their port and starboard watches. Look-out men. Day men. Lamp trimmer. Storekeeper. Came a little man, bald, with a sandy moustache. He called eight firemen and they were for Black Pan watch. Then a man named Scully; he picked the 'gentleman's' watch.

Hatches were being put on. The chief engineer was coming along the deck. He was shouting and his face was as red as a turkey-cock. 'God damn you. Can't you hear five blasts on the whistle! Get these men up on the boat-deck.'

Was a terrible fuss now, for no watches should have been picked before boat muster. Was very important because men must be good sailors in case of ship striking iceberg, and helpless passengers to be saved. Was not right to pick watches before this had been done as it gave men a chance to pick mates and make other arrangements. Confusion. All the men diving into bags for jerseys and sailors caps that made some look like monkeys. Was necessary company said even if they looked like monkeys to have ordered ones.

'Like the bloody navy,' said Duffy, whose hat would not fit him and he had just paid five and sixpence for it at the slop chest. 'Robbers,' he growled. 'Dirty robbers.'

The crew ran along all decks and on flush deck some tripped over hatch combings and falls from the drum-ends. Cargo men cursed them. Crew swore too. Reilly was one. Fell right over hatch cover.

'You dopy old bastard. Where were you last night?' growled a ganger. He did not hear the remainder of the sentence. He did not run up companion ladder to the saloon deck, rather he hopped up like a bird. 'I feel like a poor bloody sparrow,' he said in his mind.

All excitement.

'Lower away.'

'Slack your falls.'

'Hey! What the hell are you doin'?'

'Easy there.'

'Heave away.'

'God blast you! How can you lower away with your rollocks like that?'

'Get clear of chocks.'

The boats were ascending and descending. Then a whistle blew. The men dispersed. Reilly went along the deck with Duffy.

'How are you, old timer?' asked Duffy.

Reilly said: 'Not so bad.' They pressed up the alloway. Reilly undressed and turned in. All the men looked at him.

'Oh hell. He's started again.'

'Who? Oh, him. How are you, my pigeon?'

'Leave the old sucker alone.'

'He's all right.'

'Tickle his ribs.'

'To hell with him!'

Duffy's face went red for was fifty himself and remembered sailing with Reilly years ago when he was young and strong and a good worker. Would not let him be put on, he said.

'You're as bad as him.'

'Who said that?'

'I said it.' Farrell was speaking. Was a glint in his eye.

'Come out on deck,' said Duffy.

Reilly was shivering in his bunk. Was cold. For ship's blankets were thin and iron laths of bed pierced through straw palliasse. Was in singlet but no drawers. 'Good Christ!' he said to himself. 'All this over me. All this fuss. All will hate me now.' Some men playing cards at the table were growling.

'Throw the old bastard over the side. Bunk and all.'

'There's always something wrong when he's here.'

'Awful,' said Reilly in his heart, 'and I wanted to keep calm. Say nothing.'

'Come on. Come on the bloody deck!'

'Put a sock in it.'

'Pipe down.'

Silence then for a moment.

'What time is it?'

'Nearly four o'clock.'

The cook, who was half drunk, came up the alloway from galley and said did any of those b—'s want dinner. Was not going to wait there all day for them. Was going to kip.

Seven bells. Four to eight watch were dressing. All had clean sweat-rags round their necks. Some smoked cigarettes, others black shag. They passed out of the foc'sle in silence. Down alloway and along well-deck No. 2. Was a great stink now. Very warm. They could hear the thunder of the pistons pounding. Walked slowly. Some dragged their legs after them.

'Bloody steam up all day. Just to keep you workin'. Lousy bastards.' From the alloway could see the entrance to the engine-room. The steel ladders glistened. All disappeared through the steel door between two high walls of steel, that were black. One wall was scaly with salt. In the foc'sle Reilly fell asleep. He dreamed. Was with the children in a park. Were playing with a rubber ball. All were jolly. Laughing. He bought them ice-cream sandwiches. He stroked their heads. They disappeared. He called after them. Could not find them. 'Hey! Hey!' he called aloud. 'Hey! Where are you all?'

'Where the hell are you? Shut your confounded trap. People here have to do their four hours below as well as you.'

Blood rushed to his head. He had been dreaming all right. Raised his head a little. Very quiet in the foc'sle now. Eight to twelve watch fast asleep. Suddenly he felt cold. Felt in the bed. Was nothing. Felt on top of blanket and his hand was wet. Greasy. Someone had thrown slops on top of him whilst he was sleeping. Was angry.

'Show a leg there! Show a leg there! Seven bells! Seven bells!'

Reilly sat up quickly.

'How soon the time passes,' he said.

Somebody laughed. 'Were you dreaming about her?'

Some were now climbing out of their bunks. Were sullen and silent. They had been drinking heavily and their heads were large and painful. All were ready now.

Five to eight.

'Righto.'

Eight to twelve watch left the foc'sle and towards amidships. Reilly stopped to tie his boot with a piece of string.

'Come on, dozy,' shouted Farrell, and to himself: 'I'll sweat that sucker this trip.'

Descended ladder now one at a time. Reilly was shaking. Each time he was on a ladder his whole body shook. Remembered that trip falling twenty-five feet on his head. They reached the engine-room. Passed through into stoke-hole. Was all heat and smell of water on ashes for men they were relieving had been emptying their bladders. Was much sweat on these men.

'Number 3, you,' said Farrell, and Reilly went on number 3.

A man said to him: 'What time did she pull out?'

'Half-past four.'

'Oh! Must be in the channel now.'

'Yes.'

'Farrell! Are you there?'

Farrell turned round. Reilly was standing there with singlet off and bare to waist. Ribs shone in red glare of furnace.

'What the hell do you want now?' asked Farrell.

Reilly was afraid. Was a sickness at the pit of his stomach. His blood was stirring. It was anxious for rest.

'No. 3. Who is he?' asked Reilly.

'What's that got to do with you?'

'A lot,' said Reilly. 'Isn't he the man I relieve this trip?'

'Well?'

'He wasn't here when I came down.'

'What about it?'

'He should be here. The lousy sod. Look at that.'

'Look at what?' said Farrell, and he smiled.

'You bastard,' said Reilly, but only in his heart.

'The mess he left,' said Reilly. 'The mess he left. What a worker. A pile of bloody ashes here and half the furnace raked out.'

'D'you know who you're relievin'?' asked Farrell.

He bent low towards Reilly, who shivered now.

'Who?'

'My wife's brother,' said Farrell. 'You get on your job, old cock. By Jesus! I'll watch you.'

Was a man stoking up hard at number 4 furnace. Also a little trimmer running to him from between boilers. Had come from bunkers with heavy steel barrow full of coal. Ship lurched and trimmer was pitched forward on to his face.

'You awkward bloody worm,' said Duffy.

'Come on. Christ! Look at him. Standing there,' said Farrell. 'D'you want me to use your slice for you? Hell. Sit down. I'll hold your hand for you.'

'O Jesus!' said the old man to himself. 'Be calm.'

Farrell walked away. Reilly looked towards number 4 furnace. Was a cloud of steam. Duffy had done it on ashes. He could not see him. He looked at his own furnace. Suddenly bent down. Looked right into it. A trimmer had shouted: 'Righto.' Had tipped his barrow for Reilly. Heat was terrible. Reilly took his shovel. Dug into coal and heaved a shovelful into the furnace. Flames roared. Flame licked out at him, scorching his face and thin chest. Reilly said: 'The mean bastard! Knew it would happen. Told trimmer to heave me a load of slack. God strike him dead!'

He shovelled again. Must get her going. Must watch gauge. Gauge going down. Must watch bloody boiler. Might burst. He heaved in again. Flames licked out at him like many little tongues. Suddenly he flung down his shovel. Folded his arms and stared into the roaring furnace. 'How tired I am. How sick and tired of it all. After forty years. O Jesus! How can I go to them? To see her face when I say: "I'm sacked. Too old." How can I? Poor children. Nothing for them. Nothing for them.' Was silent. Tears were running down his cheeks and drying on his chest. Saw in flames all his past life. Every thought. Every word. Every deed. All endeavours, trials, braveries of the flesh and spirit. Was now — nothing. All ended. Nothing more now. Nothing more now. 'What is it all for?' he said in his heart. 'Who cares? Nobody. Who feels? Nobody.' Saw all his life illuminated in those flames. 'Not much for us. Sweat, sweat. Pay off. Sign on. Sweat, sweat. Pay off. Finish. Ah, well!' Were voices in those flames now. Were speaking to him. He understood their language which was in sounds of hot air. And suddenly he said, half aloud: 'All to her. All to the sea.' He gripped his shovel. Then suddenly dropped it. He picked up the steel slice. And suddenly dropped that too. All to her. All his life, hopes, energies. Everything. The flames licked out at him.

'ALL,' he shouted, and leaped.

'Hey! Jesus Christ! HELP! HELP! Reilly's jumped in the furnace.'

Walter Greenwood   Joe Goes Home

The appearance of the ambulance in North Street was a summons to the neighbours. They came to their front doors attracted by the bell and they stood watching until the vehicle pulled up outside the Riley home. They said in hushed tones: 'So they're taking poor old Joe away at last.'

Sympathetic murmurs.

'I guess it's the finish of the old lad.'

'But seventy-five's a good age. And he's been a worker, if ever there was one, by gum, he has.'

They shook their heads, sadly recalling the innumerable years in which Blind Joe Riley, with his long pole tipped with a bunch of wires, clattered round Hanky Park of an early morning knocking on bedroom windows to rouse people for work.

'Ay, all those years and years. It won't seem the same whoever gets the job.'

'It makes you think, doesn't it?'

Inside the house, stout Mrs Bull, the neighbourhood's uncertificated midwife and often unpaid nurse, was washing Joe's hands and face. 'There you are, old lad,' she said, when she had finished. 'Clean as a new pin and fresh as a daisy. How do you feel, Joe?'

He nodded feebly: 'I'm all right, lass.' His withered, toil-worn hands rummaged in the gaping pockets of his ancient coat where he had put all his possessions.

'What are you looking for?' Mrs Bull asked.

'It's all right, Mrs Bull. I was feeling if I'd got all my things.'

'You'd better make sure, then.' She watched him bring forth a small tobacco-tin whose advertisement was worn away; a yellow, bone-handled pen-knife, a pipe and a box of matches. 'I've got 'em all,' he said. 'I'll not be needing anything else.'

His eldest married daughter, with whom he lived, lifted her soiled apron to her nose and sniffed.

The ambulance men came in. 'We're ready, dad, if you are,' the driver said. 'Give us your arm.'

'Nay,' replied Joe, frowning. 'I can walk myself. Where's my stick, lass?'

His daughter passed it to him.

Joe stroked his stained beard and blinked his sightless eyes in the direction where he fancied his daughter to be standing. He said: 'I suppose you didn't know I'd saved up a bit, did you, eh?'

'Don't talk like that, our father.'

'I'll not come back from where I'm going, lass. When they send you to the infirmary, it's dickey-up with you.'

'Yah? What talk, what talk,' said Mrs Bull. 'Be ashamed of yourself, Joe. You'll be out again in a month, fit as a fiddle.'

Joe shook his head. 'No use o' lying about it, Mrs Bull. I've seen too many of 'em go in there. And I've never heard of any of 'em coming out agen – not at my time o' life.' To his daughter: 'There's twenty-two shillings and sixpence in the ornament on my bedroom mantelpiece, lass … It's yours. And my best pair o' clogs and my knocking-up stick – our Albert can have 'em. That stick's been in the family since my grandfather's day. It's a good regular business for our Albert if he looks after himself.'

His daughter began to weep softly.

'I'm ready,' said Joe.

The ambulance driver said: 'We've to take your old age pension book back with us, dad.'

'It's in my pocket,' said Joe. 'I've not been well enough to go for it this week.'

He gripped the table edge and strained to his feet. He would not let them help him. In a moment he was feeling his way to the door like a child just learning to walk. The ambulance attendants kept a pace behind him, followed by Joe's daughter and Mrs Bull.

The men had to assist him up the vehicle's high step.

He sat in the corner of the van, hands clasped on top of his stick, head bent a little, his shabbiness lending a heightened dignity to his unaffected, acquiescent demeanour.

The neighbours stood motionless. Even when Joe's daughter got into the ambulance and the door was closed they did not speak or stir, only stared, eyes shining.

The engine started, accelerated; the van jerked forward. In a minute it had turned the corner and was gone.

Sighs.

'Ay, well,' said Mrs Bull, 'seventy-five's not a bad age. And that's how we'll all go, one of these days.'

Five o'clock struck.

The groups split up. Husbands' teas had to be prepared.

Ethel Carnie Holdsworth   The Sheep

The house looked down on the slaughter yard. It was a grey house, and the yard was grey, saving when the dripping carcases were brought out. Inside the washing machine was always going. Outside was the iron groaning of trains, and their shrill screams from the tunnel.

Peter lived amongst these sounds. He was a small child, with a large head, whose eyes always looked as though he were trying to find answers to muddled questions, which beat forever in his frustrated brain.

Always, he saw the sheep lying there, waiting their turns, by the grey gutter of running water.

Stupidly, stubbornly, he began to hate the slaughterer.

His mother said there had always been sheep, always been slaughterers. That made him worse. Was a thing right because it had always been there?

Once he shook his puny fist at the slaughterer.

His mother took him in, explaining to the slaughterer that he was silly, and that his father was killed in the quarry the day he came to town.

He took it into his head that his father had been one of the sheep.

One day something flew out of Peter's hand.

The slaughterer gave a cry, not unlike a bleat.

Peter's mother ran out.

The slaughterer was shaking his fist, almost as Peter had done. There was blood on the grey yard; but not the blood of sheep.

Peter's mother bleated suddenly, 'He's silly. His father was killed in the quarry ... day he came.'

The slaughterer yelled, pale with pain, 'You shall pay for this. You are responsible for him.'

As for Peter ... he was not listening. He was saying over and over, 'My father was killed. My father was a sheep. My father was killed. He must have been a sheep.'

Katherine Mansfield   Life of Ma Parker

When the literary gentleman, whose flat old Ma Parker cleaned every Tuesday, opened the door to her that morning, he asked after her grandson. Ma Parker stood on the doormat inside the dark little hall, and she stretched out her hand to help her gentleman shut the door before she replied. 'We buried 'im yesterday, sir,' she said quietly.

'Oh, dear me! I'm sorry to hear that,' said the literary gentleman in a shocked tone. He was in the middle of his breakfast. He wore a very shabby dressing-gown and carried a crumpled newspaper in one hand. But he felt awkward. He could hardly go back to the warm sitting-room without saying something – something more. Then because these people set such store by funerals he said kindly, 'I hope the funeral went off all right.'

'Beg parding, sir?' said old Ma Parker huskily.

Poor old bird! She did look dashed. 'I hope the funeral was a-a-success,' said he. Ma Parker gave no answer. She bent her head and hobbled off to the kitchen, clasping the old fish bag that held her cleaning things and an apron and a pair of felt shoes. The literary gentleman raised his eyebrows and went back to his breakfast.

'Overcome, I suppose,' he said aloud, helping himself to the marmalade.

Ma Parker drew the two jetty spears out of her toque and hung it behind the door. She unhooked her worn jacket and hung that up too. Then she tied her apron and sat down to take off her boots. To take off her boots or to put them on was an agony to her, but it had been an agony for years. In fact, she was so accustomed to the pain that her face was drawn and screwed up ready for the twinge before she'd so much as untied the laces. That over, she sat back with a sigh and softly rubbed her knees ...

'Gran! Gran!' Her little grandson stood on her lap in his button boots. He'd just come in from playing in the street.

'Look what a state you've made your gran's skirt into – you wicked boy!'

But he put his arms round her neck and rubbed his cheek against hers.

'Gran, gi' us a penny!' he coaxed.

'Be off with you; Gran ain't got no pennies.'

'Yes, you 'ave.'

'No, I ain't.'

'Yes, you 'ave. Gi' us one!'

Already she was feeling for the old, squashed, black leather purse.

'Well, what'll you give your gran?'

He gave a shy little laugh and pressed closer. She felt his eyelid quivering against her cheek. 'I ain't got nothing,' he murmured ...

The old woman sprang up, seized the iron kettle off the gas stove and took it over to the sink. The noise of the water drumming in the kettle deadened her pain, it seemed. She filled the pail, too, and the washing-up bowl.

It would take a whole book to describe the state of that kitchen. During the week the literary gentleman 'did' for himself. That is to say, he emptied the tea leaves now and again into a jam jar set aside for that purpose, and if he ran out of clean forks he wiped over one or two on the roller towel. Otherwise, as he explained to his friends, his 'system' was quite simple, and he couldn't understand why people made all this fuss about housekeeping.

'You simply dirty everything you've got, get a hag in once a week to clean up, and the thing's done.'

The result looked like a gigantic dustbin. Even the floor was littered with toast crusts, envelopes, cigarette ends. But Ma Parker bore him no grudge. She pitied the poor young gentleman for having no one to look after him. Out of the smudgy little window you could see an immense expanse of sad-looking sky, and whenever there were clouds they looked very worn, old clouds, frayed at the edges, with holes in them, or dark stains like tea.

While the water was heating, Ma Parker began sweeping the floor. 'Yes,' she thought, as the broom knocked, 'what with one thing and another I've had my share. I've had a hard life.'

Even the neighbours said that of her. Many a time, hobbling home with her fish bag, she heard them, waiting at the corner, or leaning over the area railings, say among themselves, 'She's had a hard life, has Ma Parker.' And it was so true she wasn't in the least proud of it. It was just as if you were to say she lived in the basement-back at Number 27. A hard life! ...

At sixteen she'd left Stratford and come up to London as kitching-maid. Yes, she was born in Stratford-on-Avon. Shakespeare, sir? No, people were always arsking her about him. But she'd never heard his name until she saw it on the theatres.

Nothing remained of Stratford except that 'sitting in the fire-place of a evening you could see the stars through the chimley,' and 'Mother always 'ad 'er side of bacon 'anging from the ceiling.' And there was something – a bush, there was – at the front door, that smelt ever so nice. But the bush was very vague. She'd only remembered it once or twice in the hospital, when she'd been taken bad.

That was a dreadful place – her first place. She was never allowed out. She never went upstairs except for prayers morning and evening. It was a fair cellar. And the cook was a cruel woman. She used to snatch away her letters from home before she'd read them, and throw them in the range because they made her dreamy ... And the beedles! Would you believe it? – until she came to London she'd never seen a black beedle. Here Ma always gave a little laugh, as though – not to have seen a black beedle! Well! It was as if to say you'd never seen your own feet.

When that family was sold up she went as 'help' to a doctor's house, and after two years there, on the run from morning till night, she married her husband. He was a baker.

'A baker, Mrs Parker!' the literary gentleman would say. For occasionally he laid aside his tomes and lent an ear, at least, to this product called Life. 'It must be rather nice to be married to a baker!'

Mrs Parker didn't look so sure.

'Such a clean trade,' said the gentleman.

Mrs Parker didn't look convinced.

'And didn't you like handing the new loaves to the customers?'

'Well, sir,' said Mrs Parker, 'I wasn't in the shop above a great deal. We had thirteen little ones and buried seven of them. If it wasn't the 'ospital it was the infirmary, you might say!'

'You might, *indeed*, Mrs Parker!' said the gentleman, shuddering, and taking up his pen again.

Yes, seven had gone, and while the six were still small her husband was taken ill with consumption. It was flour on the lungs, the doctor told her at the time... Her husband sat up in bed with his shirt pulled over his head, and the doctor's finger drew a circle on his back.

'Now, if we were to cut him open *here*, Mrs Parker,' said the doctor, 'you'd find his lungs chock-a-block with white powder. Breathe, my good fellow!' And Mrs Parker never knew for certain whether she saw or whether she fancied she saw a great fan of white dust come out of her poor dear husband's lips ...

But the struggle she'd had to bring up those six little children and keep herself to herself. Terrible it had been! Then, just when they were old enough to go to school her husband's sister came to stop with them to help things along, and she hadn't been there more than two months when she fell down a flight of steps and hurt her spine. And for five years Ma Parker had another baby – and such a one for crying! – to look after. Then young Maudie went wrong and took her sister Alice with her; the two boys emigrimated, and young Jim went to India with the army, and Ethel, the youngest, married a good-for-nothing little waiter who died of ulcers the year little Lennie was born. And now little Lennie – my grandson ...

The piles of dirty cups, dirty dishes, were washed and dried. The ink-black knives were cleaned with a piece of potato and finished off with a piece of cork. The table was scrubbed, and the dresser and the sink that had sardine tails swimming in it ...

He'd never been a strong child – never from the first. He'd been one of those fair babies that everybody took for a girl. Silvery fair curls he had, blue eyes, and a little freckle like a diamond on one side of his nose. The trouble she and Ethel had had to rear that child! The things out of the newspapers they tried him with! Every Sunday morning Ethel would read aloud while Ma Parker did her washing.

'Dear Sir, – Just a line to let you know my little Myrtil was laid out for dead... After four bottils ... gained 8 lbs. in 9 weeks, *and is still putting it on.*'

And then the egg-cup of ink would come off the dresser and the letter would be written, and Ma would buy a postal order on her way to work next morning. But it was no use. Nothing made little Lennie put it on. Taking him to the cemetery, even, never gave him a colour; a nice shake-up in the bus never improved his appetite.

But he was gran's boy from the first ...

'Whose boy are you?' said old Ma Parker, straightening up from the stove and going over to the smudgy window. And a little voice, so warm, so close, it half stifled her – it seemed to be in her breast under her heart – laughed out, and said, 'I'm gran's boy!'

At that moment there was a sound of steps, and the literary gentleman appeared, dressed for walking.

'Oh, Mrs Parker, I'm going out.'

'Very good, sir.'

'And you'll find your half crown in the tray of the inkstand.'

'Thank you, sir.'

'Oh, by the way, Mrs Parker,' said the literary gentleman quickly, 'you didn't throw away any cocoa last time you were here – did you?'

'No, sir.'

'*Very* strange. I could have sworn I left a teaspoonful of cocoa in the tin.' He broke off. He said softly and firmly, 'You'll always tell me when you throw things away – won't you, Mrs Parker?' And he walked off very well pleased with himself, convinced, in fact, he'd shown Mrs Parker that under his apparent carelessness he was as vigilant as a woman.

The door banged. She took her brushes and cloths into the bedroom. But when she began to make the bed, smoothing, tucking, patting, the thought of little Lennie was unbearable. Why did he have to suffer so? That's what she couldn't understand. Why should a little angel child have to arsk for his breath and fight for it? There was no sense in making a child suffer like that.

… From Lennie's little box of a chest there came a sound as though something was boiling. There was a great lump of something bubbling in his chest that he couldn't get rid of. When he coughed the sweat sprang out on his head; his eyes bulged, his hands waved, and the great lump bubbled as a potato knocks in a saucepan. But what was more awful than all was when he didn't cough he sat against the pillow and never spoke or answered, or even made as if he heard. Only he looked offended.

'It's not your poor old gran's doing it, my lovey,' said old Ma Parker, patting back the damp hair from his little scarlet ears. But Lennie moved his head and edged away. Dreadfully offended with her he looked – and solemn. He bent his head and looked at her sideways as though he couldn't have believed it of his gran.

But at the last … Ma Parker threw the counterpane over the bed. No, she simply couldn't think about it. It was too much – she'd had too much in her life to bear. She'd borne it up till now, she'd kept herself to herself, and never once had she been seen to cry. Never by a living soul. Not even her own children had seen Ma break down. She'd kept a proud face always. But now! Lennie gone – what had she? She had nothing. He was all she'd got from life, and now he was took too. Why must it all have happened to me? she wondered. 'What have I done?' said old Ma Parker. 'What have I done?'

As she said those words she suddenly let fall her brush. She found herself in the kitchen. Her misery was so terrible that she pinned on her hat, put on her jacket and walked out of the flat like a person in a dream.

She did not know what she was doing. She was like a person so dazed by the horror of what has happened that he walks away — anywhere, as though by walking away he could escape ...

It was cold in the street. There was a wind like ice. People went flitting by, very fast; the men walked like scissors; the women trod like cats. And nobody knew — nobody cared. Even if she broke down, if at last, after all these years, she were to cry, she'd find herself in the lock-up as like as not.

But at the thought of crying it was as though little Lennie leapt in his gran's arms. Ah, that's what she wants to do, my dove. Gran wants to cry. If she could only cry now, cry for a long time, over everything, beginning with her first place and the cruel cook, going on to the doctor's, and then the seven little ones, death of her husband, the children's leaving her, and all the years of misery that led up to Lennie. But to have a proper cry over all these things would take a long time. All the same, the time for it had come. She must do it. She couldn't put it off any longer; she couldn't wait any more ... Where could she go?

'She's had a hard life, has Ma Parker.' Yes, a hard life, indeed! Her chin began to tremble; there was no time to lose. But where? Where?

She couldn't go home; Ethel was there. It would frighten Ethel out of her life. She couldn't sit on a bench anywhere; people would come arsking her questions. She couldn't possibly go back to the gentleman's flat; she had no right to cry in strangers' houses. If she sat on some steps a policeman would speak to her.

Oh, wasn't there anywhere where she could hide and keep herself to herself and stay as long as she liked, not disturbing anybody, and nobody worrying her? Wasn't there anywhere in the world where she could have her cry out — at last?

Ma Parker stood, looking up and down. The icy wind blew out her apron into a balloon. And now it began to rain. There was nowhere.

D.H. *Lawrence*   Fanny and Annie

Flame-lurid his face as he turned among the throng of flame-lit and dark faces upon the platform. In the light of the furnace she caught sight of his drifting countenance, like a piece of floating fire. And the nostalgia, the doom of home-coming went through her veins like a drug. His eternal face, flame-lit now! The pulse and darkness of red fire from the furnace towers in the sky, lighting the desultory, industrial crowd on the wayside station, lit him and went out.

Of course he did not see her. Flame-lit and unseeing! Always the same, with his meeting eyebrows, his common cap, and his red-and-black scarf knotted round his throat. Not even a collar to meet her! The flames had sunk, there was shadow.

She opened the door of her grimy, branch-line carriage, and began to get down her bags. The porter was nowhere, of course, but there was Harry, obscure, on the outer edge of the little crowd, missing her, of course.

'Here! Harry!' she called, waving her umbrella in the twilight. He hurried forward.

'Tha's come, has ter?' he said, in a sort of cheerful welcome. She got down, rather flustered, and gave him a peck of a kiss.

'Two suit-cases!' she said.

Her soul groaned within her, as he clambered into the carriage after her bags. Up shot the fire in the twilight sky, from the great furnace behind the station. She felt the red flame go across her face. She had come back, she had come back for good. And her spirit groaned dismally. She doubted if she could bear it.

There, on the sordid little station under the furnaces, she stood, tall and distinguished, in her well-made coat and skirt and her broad grey velour hat. She held her umbrella, her bead chatelaine, and a little leather case in her grey-gloved hands, while Harry staggered out of the ugly little train with her bags.

'There's a trunk at the back,' she said in her bright voice. But she was not feeling bright. The twin black cones of the iron foundry blasted their sky-high fires into the night. The whole scene was lurid. The train waited cheerfully. It would wait another ten minutes. She knew it. It was all so deadly familiar.

Let us confess it at once. She was a lady's maid, thirty years old, come back to marry her first-love, a foundry worker: after having kept him dangling, off and on, for a dozen years. Why had she come back? Did she love him? No. She didn't pretend to. She had loved her brilliant and ambitious cousin, who had jilted her, and who had died. She had had other affairs which had come to nothing. So here she was, come back suddenly to marry her first-love, who had waited – or remained single – all these years.

'Won't a porter carry those?' she said, as Harry strode with his workman's stride down the platform towards the guard's van.

'I can manage,' he said.

And with her umbrella, her chatelaine, and her little leather case, she followed him.

The trunk was there.

'We'll get Heather's greengrocer's cart to fetch it up,' he said.

'Isn't there a cab?' said Fanny, knowing dismally enough that there wasn't.

'I'll just put it aside o' the penny-in-the-slot, and Heather's green-grocers'll fetch it about half-past eight,' he said.

He seized the box by its two handles and staggered with it across the level-crossing, bumping his legs against it as he waddled. Then he dropped it by the red sweetmeats machine.

'Will it be safe there?' she said.

'Ay – safe as houses,' he answered. He returned for the two bags. Thus laden, they started to plod up the hill, under the great long black building of the foundry. She walked beside him – workman of workmen he was, trudging with that luggage. The red lights flared over the deepening darkness. From the foundry came the horrible, slow clang clang, clang of iron, a great noise, with an interval just long enough to make it unendurable.

Compare this with the arrival of Gloucester: the carriage for her mistress, the dog-cart for herself with the luggage; the drive out past the river, the pleasant trees of the carriage-approach; and herself sitting beside Arthur, everybody so polite to her.

She had come home – for good! Her heart nearly stopped beating as she trudged up that hideous and interminable hill, beside the laden figure. What a come-down! What a come-down! She could not take it with her usual bright cheerfulness. She knew it all too well. It is easy to bear up against the unusual, but the deadly familiarity of an old stale past!

He dumped the bags down under a lamp-light. Passers by stared at her, and gave good night to Harry. Her they hardly knew, she had become a stranger.

'They're too heavy for you, let me carry one,' she said.

'They begin to weigh a bit by the time you've gone a mile,' he answered.

'Let me carry the little one,' she insisted.

'Tha can ha'e it for a minute, if ter's a mind,' he said, handing over the valise.

And thus they arrived in the streets of shops of the little ugly town on top of the hill. How everybody stared at her; my word, how they stared! And the cinema was just going in, and the queues were tailing down the road to the corner. And everybody took full stock of her. 'Night, Harry!' shouted the fellows, in an interested voice.

However, they arrived at her aunt's – a little sweet-shop in a side street. They 'pinged' the door-bell, and her aunt came running forward out of the kitchen.

'There you are, child! Dying for a cup of tea, I'm sure. How are you?'

Fanny's aunt kissed her, and it was all Fanny could do to refrain from bursting into tears, she felt so low. Perhaps it was her tea she wanted.

'You've had a drag with that luggage,' said Fanny's aunt to Harry.

'Ay – I'm not sorry to put it down,' he said, looking at his hand which was crushed and cramped by the bag handle.

Then he departed to see about Heather's greengrocery cart.

When Fanny sat at tea, her aunt, a grey-haired, fair-faced little woman, looked at her with an admiring heart, feeling bitterly sore for her. For Fanny was beautiful: tall, erect, finely coloured, with her delicately arched nose, her rich brown hair, her large lustrous-grey eyes. A passionate woman – a woman to be afraid of. So proud, so inwardly violent! She came of a violent race.

It needed a woman to sympathise with her. Men had not the courage. Poor Fanny! She was such a lady, and so straight and magnificent. And yet everything seemed to do her down. Every time she seemed to be doomed to humiliation and disappointment, this handsome, brilliantly sensitive woman, with her nervous, over-wrought laugh.

'So you've really come back, child?' said her aunt.

'I really have, Aunt,' said Fanny.

'Poor Harry! I'm not sure, you know, Fanny, that you're not taking a bit of an advantage of him.'

'Oh, Aunt, he's waited so long, he may as well have what he's waited for.' Fanny laughed grimly.

'Yes, child, he's waited so long, that I'm not sure it isn't a bit hard on him. You know, I *like* him, Fanny – though as you know quite well, I don't think he's good enough for you. And I think he thinks so himself, poor fellow.'

'Don't you be so sure of that, Aunt. Harry is common, but he's not humble. He wouldn't think the Queen was any too good for him, if he's a mind to her.'

'Well – it's as well if he has a proper opinion of himself.'

'It depends what you call proper,' said Fanny. 'But he's got his good points -'

'Oh, he's a nice fellow, and I like him, I do like him. Only, as I tell you, he's not good enough for you.'

'I've made up my mind, Aunt,' said Fanny, grimly.

'Yes,' mused the aunt. 'They say all things come to him who waits -'

'More than he's bargained for, eh, Aunt?' laughed Fanny rather bitterly.

The poor aunt, this bitterness grieved her for her niece.

They were interrupted by the ping of the shop-bell, and Harry's call of 'Right!' But as he did not come in at once, Fanny, feeling solicitous for him presumably at the moment, rose and went into the shop. She saw a cart outside, and went to the door.

And the moment she stood in the doorway, she heard a woman's common vituperative voice crying from the darkness of the opposite side of the road:

'Tha'rt theer, are ter? I'll shame thee, Mester. I'll shame thee, see if I dunna.'

Startled, Fanny started across the darkness, and saw a woman in a black bonnet go under one of the lamps up the side street.

Harry and Bill Heather had dragged the trunk off the little dray, and she retreated before them as they came up the shop step with it.

'Wheer shal ha'e it?' asked Harry.

'Best take it upstairs,' said Fanny.

She went up first to light the gas.

When Heather had gone, and Harry was sitting down having tea and pork-pie, Fanny asked:

'Who was that woman shouting?'

'Nay, I canna tell thee. To somebody, I s'd think,' replied Harry. Fanny looked at him, but asked no more.

He was a fair-haired fellow of thirty-two, with a fair moustache. He was broad in his speech, and looked like a foundry-hand, which he was. But women always liked him. There was something of a mother's lad about him – something warm and playful and really sensitive.

He had his attractions even for Fanny. What she rebelled against so bitterly was that he had no sort of ambition. He was a moulder, but of very commonplace skill. He was thirty-two years old, and hadn't saved twenty pounds. She would have to provide the money for the home. He didn't care. He just didn't care. He had no initiative at all. He had no vices – no obvious ones. But he was just indifferent, spending as he went, and not caring. Yet he did not look happy. She remembered his face in the fire-glow: something haunted, abstracted about it. As he sat there eating his pork-pie, bulging his cheek out, she felt he was like a doom to her. And she raged against the doom of him. It wasn't that he was gross. His *way* was common, almost on purpose. But he himself wasn't really common. For instance, his food was not particularly important to him, he was not greedy. He had a charm, too, particularly for women, with his blondness and his sensitiveness and his way of making a woman feel that she was a higher being. But Fanny knew him, knew the peculiar obstinate limitedness of him, that would nearly send her mad.

He stayed till about half-past nine. She went to the door with him.

'When are you coming up?' he said, jerking his head in the direction, presumably, of his own home.

'I'll come to-morrow afternoon,' she said brightly. Between Fanny and Mrs Goodall, his mother, there was naturally no love lost.

Again she gave him an awkward little kiss, and said good night.

'You can't wonder, you know, child, if he doesn't seem so very keen,' said her aunt. 'It's your own fault.'

'Oh, Aunt, I couldn't stand him when he was keen. I can do with him a lot better as he is.'

The two women sat and talked far into the night. They understood each other. The aunt, too, had married as Fanny was marrying: a man who was no companion to her, a violent man, brother of Fanny's father. He was dead, Fanny's father was dead.

Poor Aunt Lizzie, she cried woefully over her bright niece, when she had gone to bed.

Fanny paid the promised visit to his people the next afternoon. Mrs Goodall was a large woman with smooth-parted hair, a common, obstinate woman, who had spoiled her four lads and her one vixen of a married daughter. She was one of those old-fashioned powerful natures that couldn't do with looks or education or any form of showing off. She fairly hated the sound of correct English. She thee'd and tha'd her prospective daughter-in-law, and said:

'I'm none as ormin' as I look, seest tha.'

Fanny did not think her prospective mother-in-law looked at all orming, so the speech was unnecessary.

'I towd him mysen,' said Mrs Goodall, 'Er's held back all this long, let 'er stop as 'er is. 'E'd none ha' had thee for my tellin' – tha hears. No, 'e's a fool, an' I know it. I says to him: "Tha looks a man, doesn't ter, at thy age, goin' an' openin' to her when ter hears her scrat' at th' gate, after she's done gallivantin' round wherever she's a mind. That looks rare an' soft." But it's no use o' any talking: he answered that letter o' thine and made his own bad bargain.'

But in spite of the old woman's anger, she was also flattered at Fanny's coming back to Harry. For Mrs Goodall was impressed by Fanny – a woman of her own match. And more than this, everybody knew that Fanny's Aunt Kate had left her two hundred pounds: this apart from the girl's savings.

So there was high tea in Princes Street when Harry came home black from work, and a rather acrid odour of cordiality, the vixen Jinny darted in to say vulgar things. Of course Jinny lived in a house whose garden end joined the paternal garden. They were a clan who stuck together, these Goodalls.

It was arranged that Fanny should come to tea again on the Sunday, and the wedding was discussed. It should take place in a fortnight's time at Morley Chapel. Morley was a hamlet on the edge of the real country, and in its little Congregational Chapel Fanny and Harry had first met.

What a creature of habit he was! He was still in the choir of Morley Chapel – not very regular. He belonged just because he had a tenor voice, and enjoyed singing. Indeed, his solos were only spoilt to local fame because when he sang he handled his aitches so hopelessly.

'And I saw 'eaven hopened
And be'old, a wite 'orse –'

This was one of Harry's classics, only surpassed by the fine outburst of his heaving: 'Hangels – hever bright an' fair –'

It was a pity, but it was unalterable. He had a good voice, and he sang with a certain lacerating fire, but his pronunciation made it all funny. And *nothing* could alter him.

So he was never heard save at cheap concerts and in the little, poorer chapels. The others scoffed.

Now the month was September, and Sunday was Harvest Festival at Morley Chapel, and Harry was singing solos. So that Fanny was to go to service, and come home to a grand spread of Sunday tea with him. Poor Fanny! One of the most wonderful afternoons had been a Sunday afternoon service, with her cousin Luther at her side, Harvest Festival in Morley Chapel. Harry had sung solos then – ten years ago. She remembered his pale-blue tie, and the purple asters and the great vegetable marrows in which he was famed, and her cousin Luther at her side, where he was getting on well, learning his Latin and his French and German so brilliantly.

However, once again it was Harvest Festival at Morley Chapel, and once again, as ten years before, a soft, exquisite September day, with the last roses pink in the cottage gardens, the last dahlias crimson, the last sunflowers yellow. And again the little old chapel was a bower, with its famous sheaves of corn and corn-plaited pillars, its great bunches of grapes, dangling like tassels from the pulpit corners, its marrows and potatoes and pears and apples and damsons, its purple asters and yellow Japanese sunflowers. Just as before, the red dahlias round the pillars were dropping, weak-headed among the oats. The place was crowded and hot, the plates of tomatoes seemed balanced perilous on the gallery front, the Rev. Enderby was weirder than ever to look at, so long and emaciated and hairless.

The Rev. Enderby, probably forewarned, came and shook hands with her and welcomed her, in his broad northern, melancholy sing-song before he mounted the pulpit. Fanny was handsome in a gauzy dress and a beautiful lace hat. Being a little late, she sat in a chair in the side-aisle wedged in, right in front of the chapel. Harry was in the gallery above, and she could only see him from the eyes upwards. She noticed again how his eyebrows met, blond and not very marked, over his nose. He was attractive, too: physically lovable, very. If only – if only her *pride* had not suffered! She felt he dragged her down.

'Come, ye thankful people, come,
Raise the song of harvest-home.
All is safely gathered in
Ere the winter storms begin –'

Even the hymn was a falsehood, as the season had been wet, and half the crops were still out, and in a poor way.

Poor Fanny! She sang little, and looked beautiful through that inappropriate hymn. Above her stood Harry – mercifully in a dark suit and a dark tie, looking almost handsome. And his lacerating, pure tenor

sounded well, when the words were drowned in the general commotion.
Brilliant she looked, and brilliant she felt, for she was hot and angrily
miserable and inflamed with a sort of fatal despair. Because there was
about him a physical attraction which she really hated, but which she
could not escape from. He was the first man who had ever kissed her.
And his kisses, even while she rebelled from them, had lived in her blood
and sent roots down into her soul. After all this time she had come back
to them. And her soul groaned, for she felt dragged down, dragged down
to earth, as a bird which some dog has got down in the dust. She knew
her life would be unhappy. She knew that what she was doing was fatal.
Yet it was her doom. She had to come back to him.

He had to sing two solos this afternoon: one before the 'address' from
the pulpit and one after. Fanny looked at him, and wondered he was
not too shy to stand up there in front of all the people. But no, he was
not shy. He had even a kind of assurance on his face as he looked down
from the choir gallery at her: the assurance of a common man deliberately entrenched in his commonness. Oh, such a rage went through her
veins as she saw the air of triumph, laconic, indifferent triumph which
sat so obstinately and recklessly on his eyelids as he looked down at her.
Ah, she despised him! But there he stood up in that choir gallery like
Balaam's ass in front of her, and she could not get beyond him. A certain
winsomeness also about him. A certain physical winsomeness, and as if
his flesh were new and lovely to touch. The thorn of desire rankled
bitterly in her heart.

He, it goes without saying, sang like a canary, this particular afternoon,
with a certain defiant passion which pleasantly crisped the blood of the
congregation. Fanny felt the crisp flames go through her veins as she
listened. Even the curious loud-mouthed vernacular had a certain fas-
cination. But, oh, also, it was so repugnant. He would triumph over
her, obstinately he would drag her right back into the common people:
a doom, a vulgar doom.

The second performance was an anthem, in which Harry sang the
solo parts. It was clumsy, but beautiful, with lovely words.

They that sow in tears shall reap in joy,
He that goeth forth and weepeth, bearing precious seed
Shall doubtless come again with rejoicing, bringing his sheaves
    with him –

'Shall doubtless come, Shall doubtless come –' softly intoned the altos
– 'Bringing his she-e-eaves with him,' the trebles flourished brightly,
and then again began the half-wistful solo:

'They that sow in tears shall reap in joy –'

Yes, it was effective and moving. But at the moment when Harry's voice sank carelessly down to his close, and the choir, standing behind him, were opening their mouths for the final triumphant outburst, a shouting female voice rose up from the body of the congregation. The organ gave one startled trump, and went silent; the choir stood transfixed.

'You look well standing there, singing in God's holy house,' came the loud, angry female shout. Everybody turned electrified. A stoutish, red-faced woman in black bonnet was standing up denouncing the soloist. Almost fainting with shock, the congregation realised it. 'You look well, don't you, standing there singing solos in God's holy house, you, Goodall. But I said I'd shame on you. You look well, bringing your young woman here with you, don't you? I'll let her know who she's dealing with. A scamp as won't take the consequences of what he's done.' The hard-faced, frenzied woman turned in the direction of Fanny. '*That's* what Harry Goodall is, if you want to know.'

And she sat down again in her seat. Fanny, startled like all the rest, had turned to look. She had gone white, and then a burning red, under the attack. She knew the woman: a Mrs Nixon, a devil of a woman, who beat her pathetic, drunken, red-nosed second husband, Bob, and her two lanky daughters, grown-up as they were. A notorious character. Fanny turned round again, and sat motionless as eternity in her seat.

There was a minute of perfect silence and suspense. The audience was open-mouthed and dumb; the choir stood like Lot's wife; and Harry, with his music sheet, stood there uplifted, looking down with a dumb sort of indifference on Mrs Nixon, his face naïve and faintly mocking. Mrs Nixon sat defiant in her seat, braving them all.

Then a rustle, like a wood when the wind suddenly catches the leaves. And then the tall, weird minister got to his feet, and in his strong, bell-like, beautiful voice – the only beautiful thing about him – he said with infinite mournful pathos:

'Let us unite in singing the last hymn on the hymn-sheet; the last hymn on the hymn-sheet, number eleven.

Fair waved the golden corn
In Canaan's pleasant land.

The organ tuned up promptly. During the hymn the offertory was taken. And after the hymn, the prayer.

Mr Enderby came from Northumberland. Like Harry, he had never been able to conquer his accent, which was very broad. He was a little simple, one of God's fools, perhaps, an odd bachelor soul, emotional, ugly, but very gentle.

'And if, O our dear Lord, beloved Jesus, there should fall a shadow of sin upon our harvest, we leave it to Thee to judge, for Thou art judge. We lift our spirits and our sorrow, Jesus, to Thee, and our mouths are dumb. O Lord, keep us from froward speech, restrain us from foolish words and thoughts, we pray Thee, Lord Jesus, who knowest all and judgest all.'

Thus the minister said in his sad, resonant voice, washed his hands before the Lord. Fanny bent forward open-eyed during the prayer. She could see the rounded head of Harry, also bent forward. His face was inscrutable and expressionless. The shock left her bewildered. Anger perhaps was her dominating emotion.

The audience began to rustle to its feet, to ooze slowly and excitedly out of the chapel, looking with wildly interested eyes at Fanny, at Mrs Nixon, and at Harry. Mrs Nixon, shortish, stood defiant in her pew, facing the aisle, as if announcing that, without rolling her sleeves up, she was ready for anybody. Fanny sat quite still. Luckily the people did not have to pass her. And Harry, with red ears, was making his way sheepishly out of the gallery. The loud noise of the organ covered all the downstairs commotion of exit.

The minister sat silent and inscrutable in his pulpit, rather like a death's-head, while the congregation filed out. When the last lingerers had unwittingly departed, craning their necks to stare at the still seated Fanny, he rose, stalked in his hooked fashion down the little country chapel and fastened the door. Then he returned and sat down by the silent young woman.

'This is most unfortunate, most unfortunate!' he moaned. 'I am so sorry, I am so sorry, indeed, indeed, ah, indeed!' he sighed himself to a close.

'It's a sudden surprise, that's one thing,' said Fanny brightly.

'Yes – yes – indeed. Yes, a surprise, yes. I don't know the woman. I don't know her.'

'I know her,' said Fanny. 'She's a bad one.'

'Well! Well!' said the minister. 'I don't know her. I don't understand. I don't understand at all. But it is to be regretted, it is very much to be regretted. I am very sorry.'

Fanny was watching the vestry door. The gallery stairs communicated with the vestry, not with the body of the chapel. She knew the choir members had been peeping for information.

At last Harry came – rather sheepishly – with his hat in his hand.

'Well!' said Fanny, rising to her feet.

'We've had a bit of an extra,' said Harry.

'I should think so,' said Fanny.

'A most unfortunate circumstance – a most *unfortunate* circumstance. Do you understand it, Harry? I don't understand it at all.'

'Ay, I understand it. The daughter's goin' to have a childt, an' 'er lays it to me.'

'And has she no occasion to?' asked Fanny, rather censorious.

'It's no more mine that it is some other chap's,' said Harry, looking aside.

There was a moment of pause.

'Which girl is it?' asked Fanny.

'Annie – the young one – '

There followed another silence.

'I don't think I know them, do I?' asked the minister.

'I shouldn't think so. Their name's Nixon – mother married old Bob for her second husband. She's a tanger, she's driven the gel to what she is. They live in Manners Road.'

'Why, what's amiss with the girl?' asked Fanny sharply. 'She was all right when I knew her.'

'Ay – she's all right. But she's always in an' out o' th' pubs, wi' th' fellows,' said Harry.

'A nice thing!' said Fanny.

Harry glanced towards the door. He wanted to get out.

'Most distressing, indeed!' the minister slowly shook his head.

'What about to-night, Mr Enderby?' asked Harry, in rather a small voice. 'Shall you want me?'

Mr Enderby looked up painedly, and put his hand to his brow. He studied Harry for some time, vacantly. There was the faintest sort of resemblance between the two men.

'Yes,' he said. 'Yes, I think. I think we must take no notice and cause as little remark as possible.'

Fanny hesitated. Then she said to Harry:

'But *will* you come?'

He looked at her.

'Ay, I s'll come,' he said.

Then he turned to Mr Enderby.

'Well, good afternoon, Mr Enderby,' he said.

'Good afternoon, Harry, good afternoon,' replied the mournful minister. Fanny followed Harry to the door, and for some time they walked in silence through the late afternoon.

'And it's yours as much as anybody else's?' she said.

'Ay,' he answered shortly.

And they went without another word, for the long mile or so, till they came to the corner of the street where Harry lived. Fanny hesitated. Should she go on to her aunt's? Should she? It would mean leaving all this, for ever. Harry stood silent.

Some obstinacy made her turn with him along the road to his own home. When they entered the house-place, the whole family was there, mother and father and Jinny, with Jinny's husband and children and Harry's two brothers.

'You've been having your ears warmed, they tell me,' said Mrs Goodall grimly.

'Who told thee?' asked Harry shortly.

'Maggie and Luke's both been in.'

'You look well, don't you!' said interfering Jinny.

Harry went and hung his hat up, without replying.

'Come upstairs and take your hat off,' said Mrs Goodall to Fanny, almost kindly. It would have annoyed her very much if Fanny had dropped her son at this moment.

'What's 'er say, then?' asked the father secretly of Harry, jerking his head in the direction of the stairs whence Fanny had disappeared.

'Nowt yet,' said Harry.

'Serve you right if she chucks you now,' said Jinny. I'll bet it's right about Annie Nixon an' you.'

'Tha bets so much,' said Harry.

'Yi – but you can't deny it,' said Jinny.

'I can if I've a mind.'

His father looked at him enquiringly.

'It's no more mine than it is Bill Bower's, or Ted Slaney's, or six or seven on 'em,' said Harry to his father.

And the father nodded silently.

'That'll not get you out of it, in court,' said Jinny.

Upstairs Fanny evaded all the thrusts made by his mother, and did not declare her hand. She tidied her hair, washed her hands, and put the tiniest bit of powder on her face, for coolness, there in front of Mrs Goodall's indignant gaze. It was like a declaration of independence. But the old woman said nothing.

They came down to Sunday tea, with sardines and tinned salmon and tinned peaches, besides tarts and cakes. The chatter was general. It concerned the Nixon family and the scandal.

'Oh, she's a foul-mouthed woman,' said Jinny of Mrs Nixon. 'She may well talk about God's holy house, *she* had. It's the first time she's set foot in it, ever since she dropped off from being converted. She's a devil and she always was one. Can't you remember how she treated Bob's children, mother, when we lived down in the Buildings? I can remember when I was a little girl she used to bathe them in the yard, in the cold, so that they shouldn't splash the house. She'd half kill them if they made a mark on the floor, and the language she'd use! And one Saturday I can remember Garry, that was Bob's own girl, she ran off when her stepmother was going to bathe her – ran off without a rag of clothes on – can you remember, mother? And she hid in Smedley's close – it was the time of mowing-grass – and nobody could find her. She hid out there all night, didn't she, mother? Nobody could find her. My word, there was a talk. They found her on Sunday morning – '

'Fred Coutts threatened to break every bone in the woman's body, if she touched the children again,' put in the father.

'Anyhow, they frightened her,' said Jinny. 'But she was nearly as bad with her own two. And anybody can see that she'd driven old Bob till he's gone soft.'

'Ah, soft as mush,' said Jack Goodall. 'E'd never addle a week's wages, nor yet a day's, if th' chaps didn't make it up to him.'

'My word, if he didn't bring her a week's wage, she'd pull his head off,' said Jinny.

'But a clean woman, and respectable, except for her foul mouth,' said Mrs Goodall. 'Keeps to herself like a bulldog. Never lets anybody come near the house, and neighbours with nobody.'

'Wanted it thrashed out of her,' said Mr Goodall, a silent evasive sort of man.

'Where Bob gets the money for his drink from is a mystery,' said Jinny.

'Chaps treats him,' said Harry.

'Well, he's got the pair of frightenedest rabbit-eyes you'd wish to see,' said Jinny.

'Ay, with a drunken man's murder in them, *I* think,' said Mrs Goodall.

So the talk went on after tea, till it was practically time to start off to the chapel again.

'You'll have to be getting ready, Fanny,' said Mrs Goodall.

'I'm not going to-night,' said Fanny abruptly. And there was a sudden halt in the family. 'I'll stop with *you* to-night, mother,' she added. 'Best you had, my gel,' said Mrs Goodall, flattered and assured.

Rhys Davies   A Bed of Feathers

I

One year Jacob Jenkins, having amassed a little fortune by steady labour in the pit, went for a long holiday amid the rich meadows and stony villages of Cardiganshire. And he brought back to the Valley a wife.

To the Valley people the union was scandalous and unnatural. For though Jacob was sixty and become arid in a respectable celibacy, the woman he brought triumphantly to the Valley was a rose-red blooming young creature of twenty-five, with wanton masses of goldish hair and a suggestion of proud abandonment about her: a farm-hand, as everyone knew not long after her arrival. Ach y fi. Why couldn't the man marry one of the many local widows near his own age? Jacob Jenkins, a deacon for fifteen years, taking to himself a jaunty-looking slut like that!

But Jacob brought her proudly into the home, presented her to his gaping sister Ann, who for minutes was shocked into silence, and then to his half-brother Emlyn, who accepted her with amused indifference.

'Come to mother us orphans, have you?' Emlyn said with a grin.

'Indeed now, have I been useless, then?' Ann, forty-five and shrewish, demanded at last. She turned to Jacob's wife. 'An awful business you'll find it, looking after colliers,' she said with an unpleasant grimace.

'With two of you not so hard the work will be,' Jacob said.

But Ann announced, drawing off her shawl and folding it calmly: 'Oh, now that you have married like this, so late and cunning, no need is there for me here. Go as a housekeeper I will, somewhere in the country.' Her lips were bloodless, her big body taut with scorn. She loathed the wife at first sight.

Jacob said indifferently, 'Your own way you must go, Ann fach.' He had eyes only for Rebecca now.

'No disturbance do I want to make in this house,' Rebecca said, tapping her foot nervously.

But Ann ignored her and went out. Emlyn, child of their father's second wife, spat into the fire and sat down in satisfied acceptance of the new menage. And he said to Jacob, when the young wife had gone upstairs to take off her new clothes:

'Jacob, Jacob, a sly taste for women you hid in you. And a juicy taste too!'

Jacob lifted his lizard eyelids.

'Easy capture she was,' he said. 'A lot of silly bumpkins were after her, with nothing in their pockets, and a liking for dear things she has. Think you she is worth a brooch that was fifty shillings and a bracelet that cost the wages of ten days' work?' His grey old collier's face shone exultingly.

Emlyn laughed. 'Worth every penny she is, no doubt!'

Jacob looked at him in senile rhapsody.

'Ah, every penny. A fool I was to stay single for so many years. Take advice from me. Don't you be a frog and remain unmarried for so long. A rare bed of feathers is a woman.'

Emlyn stretched his length in yawning indifference. He was not yet thirty, tall and easy with supple strength, and no stranger to the comforting ways of women.

'Don't hurry me now,' he laughed. 'Satisfied I am as things are.' He looked at Jacob. 'But you want me to go? Ann says she is going, and you want to be alone?'

But Jacob shook his head. 'No, stay you as a lodger, Emlyn bach. An expensive woman Rebecca is going to be I am thinking, and not for ever do I want to work in the dirty old pit. Take some of the expense off you will if you will pay us so and so.' Rebecca came back into the room just then, and he said to her: 'Willing you are that Emlyn shall stay as a lodger? Asking he was if we would rather be alone.'

Rebecca's dark watching eyes suddenly became filled with tears.

'Oh,' she said again, faltering a little, her tearful glance upon the young man, 'no disturbance do I want to make here. Emlyn, stay you will, won't you?'

Her thick hand played with the blood-red stone of her bracelet; and her eyes looked a little weary in the shining fruit-like freshness of her face.

II

Rebecca did not become a collier's wife easily. She would *not* boil enough water for the baths, she neglected to dry the sweat-damp garments that Jacob and Emlyn threw into a corner of the kitchen as they undressed to wash in the tub before the fire, she couldn't patch moleskin trousers, she couldn't make broth as a Welsh collier likes it — thick and heavy with carrots, onions and leeks. This last fault was hard to overlook, though both Emlyn and Jacob were strangely forebearing with the young woman.

'Thin is her broth and heavy her jam pudding,' Emlyn muttered. 'No hand has she for tasty cooking.'

'Give the woman time,' Jacob answered with warmth. 'More used to cows' teats her hands have been, remember.'

At first, too, she seemed to dislike being present in the kitchen when the men bathed, to hand them this and that as they stood naked in the tub, and to wash the coal-black off their backs, as the women do in the miners' cottages. But gradually she got accustomed to it, even to washing Emlyn's back, while Jacob, having taken precedence in the tub, read the paper or dozed before the fire, attired only in his flannel shirt. For such is the bucolic simplicity of the miner's cottage life; and Rebecca did not mind, presently.

Though she dreamed of a better life. True, this Valley was far nicer than the country of Cardiganshire. Here there were shops filled with blue and red silks and satins, fashionable hats, beads, and thin delicate shoes. Here was a cinema too. The chapel was crowded with observant faces, and she had a position there, as the wife of a deacon. Yet she craved for something else, she knew, gazing at her handsome face in the mirror, that some other wonderful thing was escaping her. And as she realised that, a strained and baffled look would come into her searching eyes and she would cross her pressing arms over her body, a half-strangled moan escaping her distended lips.

There were some evenings when she was left alone, Jacob in the chapel attending to deacons' business; and Emlyn was always out. She had not made friends yet, and in those long weary evenings she would sit and brood over a novelette, her face a little paler after the work of the day. Or she would go into the parlour and lie down on the sofa in the darkness, or stand at the window and watch with gleaming eyes the few people pass. And then perhaps she would go out for a short walk, to the main street, where the men were gathered in little groups about the street corners, peaceful in the night, the hills rising up tall and secretive, each side of the hushed vale. But she would return with a greater loneliness in her heart.

Jacob would come in to his supper and sink with established familiarity into his chair, his face fixed in a contented leer.

'Well, Rebecca,' he would say, watching every movement she made, every expression shifting on her face, 'what have you been doing tonight?'

He never touched or caressed her out of bed. But his pale eyes watched her with a possessive satisfaction that crept about her like the tight embrace of a snake. Sometimes she would notice his large oaken hand tremble as it rested on his knee.

Then she would go into the kitchen and wait until the painful throbbing of her heart was stilled.

And he was aware of that, her sheering off from him, like a flame from an icy blast. A strange lipless grin would come to his face then. Still the female was not his. The contented leer passed from his face and in his eyes a fanatical glare shone. As it shone when he prayed aloud in chapel.

III

One Sunday morning she said:

'Staying home from chapel I am this morning.'

Her face was rather yellow, though her cheeks as yet had not quite lost their blooming rose.

'Not well you are?' Jacob enquired gently.

'I will make apple dumplings instead,' she promised, moving away into the kitchen.

'Don't you stay too long over the fire,' he said, looking for his bible and bag of peppermints. And he went out, dressed in his deep Sunday black.

She was alone. Emlyn had gone to the whippet-racing, the Sunday morning amusement of those colliers who have the courage to scorn the chapel respectability; but she wished he was home, so that she would have someone young to talk with. That morning the house had seemed like a dark and silent prison about her soul, and yet she would not have stirred out of it, fearful lest she would cry aloud in the chapel. She worked, going from room to room with a duster, working without method, only conscious that she must move. She prepared the apple dumplings. A little later Emlyn came in. He brought with him a dog, one of the whippets.

'It isn't yours?' she asked, gazing fixedly at the slim animal. It had a beautiful sleek body, long and narrow, its glistening fawn coat like velvet, the most delicate-looking dog she had ever seen. 'Ah,' she cried in sudden excitement, 'lovely he is.'

'Keeping him I am for a while,' Emlyn said, taking the dog's head in his hand with a slow pressure that she watched, bending to stroke the animal. There was a bright glint, almost of passion, in Emlyn's eyes as he held the dog's head tight in his hand.

'Oh, he doesn't like me!' she cried childishly as, her hand touching his sleek coat, the dog winced away. Shaking his head free, the whippet looked at her with a swift regard. Then, sniffing the air delicately, he moved his head towards her, his long narrow head that invited the grasp of a hand. And, fearful but fascinated, her hand moved down over the head until it spanned the jaw in a light and trembling clasp.

'There!' Emlyn said in a satisfied voice, 'he likes you.'

Slowly she released the head. The dog turned to Emlyn with a nervous look, as though he wondered at some atmosphere in the air.

'My little beauty!' Emlyn cried suddenly in delight. 'Just like a funny little child you are.'

Rebecca got up slowly, stood watching them, her eyelids dropped, her face inscrutable. Emlyn was as though unaware of her and was caressing the dog, uttering little noises of satisfaction. He passed his large strong hands over the slender body of the dog, slowly up and down, the thumbs on the back and the fingers over the belly.

'Soft and glossy as the back of a swan,' he whispered ecstatically.

The dog was quivering under his grasp.

'Hurting him you are!' she exclaimed.

'No,' he said, 'he likes it.' And his powerful collier's hands, that spanned the animal's slim body, were certain and intimate in their caressive grasp.

Then when Emlyn released him, the dog immediately lay down on the mat, contendedly burying his head between his paws. Emlyn looked up.

Rebecca was still standing against the table, taut, her eyelids drooping. There seemed a strange tension on her face. Neither spoke for a minute or so and at last her voice, unquiet and unwilling, broke the silence:

'What will Jacob say, bringing one of those dogs in on a Sunday?' Jacob, as was proper in a deacon, sternly condemned whippet-racing.

'Ah! what will he say?' Emlyn repeated, a little grin on his mouth.

And then he stared at her, his full moist lips distended in that jeering grin. For a moment she looked back at him. Her eyes seemed to go naked in that moment, their blue nudity, chastened of weariness and pain, gleaming full on him.

She moved away, went into the kitchen and sank upon a chair. The yellow pallor of her face was again evident. She looked as though she wanted to be sick.

Jacob came in, his face still exalted from the chapel prayers. Immediately he saw the sleeping dog.

'Whose is that?' he asked sternly.

'Keeping it for a while I am,' Emlyn said fondly. 'A little angel he is.'

'Bah!' Jacob uttered, violent wrath beginning to burn in his shrunken cheeks. 'Bring you one of those animals in this house? Come I have from the Big Seat of the chapel, the words of our prayers still full of fire in my heart, and this vessel of wickedness my eyes see as I enter my house!'

'Ach, Jacob, if wickedness there is, blame you the men that use the animal.'

'He is a partner in your Sabbath abominations. Take him away from here.' A storm was gathering in Jacob's eyes.

'He likes the warmth of the fire. Look, Jacob, innocent as a little calf's is his face.'

The dog had lifted its head and was gazing at Jacob with a pleading expression in his glinting eyes. But his gaze made Jacob more infuriated.

'Out of these rooms where I move,' he began to shout. 'Take him back to his owner or tie him to the tree in the garden. Put evil in the house he does.'

Rebecca had come into the room. She said, her voice scarcely above a mutter: 'Comfort let the little dog bach have, Jacob. Delicate he looks and company for me he'll be.'

Jacob turned to her. 'Ignorant of the wicked sports he is partner to you are, Mrs Jenkins,' he replied angrily. 'No, let him go out of this house.'

Emlyn began to grin. He was really indifferent. The grin on his handsome tolerant face was irritating to Jacob, who began to moan:

'Ach, awful it is for me to have a brother who spends the Sabbath mingling with abandoned and dirty-minded men. Take you warning, young man, the Lord is not mocked and derided long.'

'All sorts come to our races,' Emlyn reflected comfortably, 'and happy and healthy they seem. No sour faces such as gather in the chapels.' He called to the dog and lazily took him to the garden.

IV

That night she dreamed of hands.

They were upon her breasts, outspread and clasping; and there was such a pain beneath them that her lips moved in anguish. She did not know whose hands they were, her mind strove to discover. A horror came upon her, she seemed to struggle. But the hands were immovable and finally she submitted, drifting into the gloom and the horror, moaning until she woke in the darkness, hearing the bell of the alarm clock.

'Jacob,' she called, louder than usual, 'Jacob.'

Jacob grunted. He had been deep in slumber. Rebecca got out of bed and lit the candle. Then Jacob, his face grey and corpse-like in the dim light, moving his limbs with the effort of an old man, followed and put on, with grunts and sighs, his thick striped flannel drawers.

She went downstairs, after calling Emlyn. Her mind was still drugged with slumber and in her too was the shadow of that unbearable pain. With mechanical drugged movements she set about the usual tasks – blew the fire into a glow and set the kettle, prepared the breakfast and the men's food-tins for the pit. She was in such an abstraction that when she turned and saw Emlyn, who had silently entered in his stockinged feet, she shrank back with a little cry.

'What's the matter with you?' he exclaimed.

For a moment or two she stared at him. His face! Ah, she had never seen it before, not as she saw it now. Her heart seemed to dart in a flame to her throat, her lips could utter no word. And there he stood, strange and watching, looking at her curiously.

Then she woke with a jolt and bent her head to cut the bread.

'Make a noise coming down you ought to,' she said. 'Not quite awake am I, early in the morning like this.'

Emlyn began to whistle with a shrill male energy that made her shudder and went into the kitchen for his boots.

Jacob came down, coughing. He seemed to creak as he sat in his chair, his face like a wrinkled stone.

They all sat down to breakfast, Rebecca between them. There was cold ham and thick black tea. Jacob began to grunt:

'Wheezy I am again this morning. Glad I'll be when I'll be able to lie in bed longer.'

Rebecca was looking at her husband. As he uttered the last word he glanced at her and a cunning grin came over his face. She felt her stomach rise, her mind reel.

'Jesus, white you've gone, Rebecca,' Emlyn said quickly.

Jacob looked at her calmly. The cunning grin had become an obscene and triumphant leer.

'Well, well, one must expect such things now,' he said.

'What!' exclaimed Emlyn in a sharpened voice. 'True is it, Rebecca?'

She suddenly swept her hand before her, upsetting her cup of tea.

'No,' she said loudly, 'no.'

'Ach, you don't know,' said Jacob. 'And there's a mess you've made, Mrs Jenkins.'

'No, it's not true,' she repeated loudly. Her eyes glittered.

Jacob sniffed as he rose from the table and loosened his belt.

'See we shall,' he continued hatefully, sniffing laughter over the words. 'Think you you are different to other women?'

She sat, her face stretched forward like an animal suddenly aware of some ominous portent. The men gathered their things together.

'Take you heart, Mrs Jenkins,' Jacob said.

She watched them go off – they worked side by side in the pit, on the same seam. Her husband's back suddenly roused a fury of hate in her – she could have clawed in venom the coarse thick neck above the cotton muffler. But Emlyn – going through the door last – turned and smiled at her, a quick brilliant smile that rippled in a delighted shudder over her, until her own moist mouth reflected it.

She removed the breakfast things. How quiet and familiar the house had become! She thought of the day's work in a sudden access of energy; and then she began to sing *Merch y Ydfa*. The rows of polished plates standing on the dresser pleased her – how pretty were the little Chinese bridges and the sleeping trees! She plunged her hands into a bowl of cold water and enjoyed the shudder that ran through her blood.

Then the bark of a dog made her lift her head quickly. She went in haste to the pantry and filled a pan with pieces of bread, pouring milk over. Again came the bark, and she hurried out with the pan to the back garden.

The whippet stood outside its roughly made kennel.

'Well, well now,' she called soothingly, 'is he hungry then?'

She knelt on the earth before it, holding the pan for it to eat; and as the animal ate she admired again the fawn sheen of his coat and the long delicate shape of his body, which quivered in pleasure.

V

Then from that morning Rebecca seemed to awaken as from a long and dull slumber. Her eyes became wider, a blue and virgin fire glowing beneath the thick lids; and as she went about, her body walked with a taut and proud grace, flaunting a fierce health. Her voice became plangent and direct, coming from her heavy lips.

'Ha, agree with you does married life,' Jacob said.

She slowly turned her head to him.

'Ha,' he repeated, 'rich and nice as a little calf you are now.' And he added with lecherous humour, 'Afraid of you I was at first, in Cardigan. More like a Bristol cow you were then.'

She pressed her hands down on her hips, lifting her shoulders and looking at him with drawn brows.

'Not angry with me you are?' he asked with childish complaint. 'A compliment I was paying you.'

She said, a metallic sharpness wavering in her voice: 'Don't you watch me so much. Continually your eyes are watching me.'

Curiously, he dropped his head before her anger. For the first time she realised her power.

'Like a prison keeper you behave,' she added. 'Always you are staring at me as if I wanted to hide something from you. Suspicious of me you are?'

His instinct was aroused by her question.

'Something to hide you have, then?' he asked, jerking his head up.

'What can there be to hide!' she exclaimed with such artless surprise that again his face became expressive of his relentless lust for her.

'Only a thought passing in my head it was,' he muttered.

She roused herself. She seemed to glitter with an ominous vitality, female and righteous.

'A dirty old swine you are,' she said loudly.

He received this with silence. Then his voice became plaintive and ashamed; he said:

'Harsh you are with me, Rebecca. Forgive an old man's errors you must.'

He looked at her with abject pleading in his eyes. She stared back at him. And still she saw behind the flickering childish pleading in his eyes the obsessed leer of the old man, the relentless icy glitter of his lust. She drew back and her voice had something of a threat in it as she said:

'Well, don't you be so suspicious of me at all.'

She went upstairs to their bedroom.

The evening sun invaded the room with a warm and languid light, a shaft falling on the scarlet counterpane of the bed. The soft glow soothed her. She gazed in the mirror and, biting her lower lip, softly murmured his name. 'Emlyn, Emlyn.' Her head dropped, she sank on the bed and covered her face with her hands. But when she lifted her head again she was smiling. She went to the dressing-table and combed her hair. She passed into Emlyn's room and began to look for some odd jobs to do. She looked over his garments to see if any buttons were missing. All were in their places, and then she opened the drawer in which he kept his ties and collars. As usual, the drawer was untidy. She began to fold the things.

Among other oddments she found a scrap of paper upon which was scrawled *May Morgan, 30, Glasfryn Street*, and she stood up to scrutinise it carefully. Then she tossed it back into the drawer with a gesture of disdain.

When she went downstairs Jacob was sleeping in his armchair, his hands clasped over his stomach. His mouth had dropped open and a thin line of saliva was descending from it. Her senses were marvellously tranquil; she moved about with soft intimate movements, her face relaxed as though she were utterly at peace with the world.

Jacob ate his supper with chastened solemnity. She dreamily watched his wad of bread and cheese decrease. He took her long silence as a sign of grieved anger against him, and he anxiously studied her face, eager to see a sign of compassion.

Emlyn came in and joined them. He was slightly tipsy, and his face, handsome and flushed, seemed to give off a ruddy heat of ardour. He sat at the table and gazed round, a critical smile on his lips.

Jacob sniffed with deliberation.

'God, we had a talk to-night!' Emlyn exclaimed.

'About what?' asked Rebecca.

'Socialism,' he said exultingly.

Jacob sniffed again.

'Wisdom was in your talk, no doubt,' he said suavely. 'Godly seems socialism after five or six pots of beer.'

'Jacob, Jacob, a hard-bottomed old Tory you are getting. No wonder you are getting such a grizzler.'

'All your evenings you spend like that?' Rebecca asked.

'I like mixing with men,' Emlyn said, 'to save my mind and joints from getting stiff.' He laughed uproariously at this. Rebecca and Jacob remained grave and unsmiling.

'And your pockets from keeping full,' Jacob added unctiously. 'A poor old mongrel you will become, not worth a penny.'

'Ha,' Rebecca cried swiftly, 'a runner after women he is too I should think.'

Emlyn turned his bright, glazed eyes full upon her.

'The wrong way you put it, Rebecca,' he said softly, 'nowadays the women it is who have the pleasantest tongues.'

She drew back her head. Her bosom seemed to rise in a storm.

'Vain as a silly peacock,' she jeered, 'nothing is there in you for a woman to get excited about.'

He laughed again, loudly. There was a coarse maleness in his laughter, a flood of primitive strength.

She sat there, high and proud, the colour deepened and vivid in her face. Jacob seemed to ignore them, sucking up his tea with solemn contempt. He knew that his half-brother was lost to the Baptists for ever. His former protests and denunciations had all been in vain, and now Emlyn interested him no more.

Supper finished, Jacob sat by the fire to read a chapter of the Scriptures before bed. Emlyn lit a cigarette and restlessly began to study a racing list which he took from his pocket.

Rebecca cleared the supper things into the kitchen. Her heart beat with a hard painful throb that was unbearable, and as she carried the crockery into the kitchen she seemed to sway with a slight drunken movement, her head drooping.

And as she was washing the dishes Emlyn came noisily into the kitchen and kicked off his boots. Then he turned and looked at her. Through the dim candlelight his eyes shone down on her like a cat's. She crouched over the pan of water in sudden fright: she thought he was going to advance on her and take her there, suddenly and silently. She began to pant in fear.

They heard Jacob noisily clearing his throat and spit in the fire, and the spell was broken. But Emlyn, with a sleek, drunken smile, came over to her and pressed his hands over her swelling breasts. She moved in anguish and stared at him with remembering eyes. Ah, his grasp was familiar, this agonising rush of her blood suddenly familiar: she remembered her dream. Only the dark horror that had wrapped that dream was not here.

She lifted her face; mutely they stared at each other. Then with a shy and ashamed look she resumed her work.

He went back into the other room, whistling.

VI

Each day passed in an ecstasy of dreaming. When she rose in the early morning she took greater care of her appearance. But it was a relief to see the two men go off to work – then she was alone to dream as deliriously as she liked. Perhaps she was the only collier's wife in the district who was dressed as though for a jaunt when the men returned from work. She bought a flimsy apron to wear over her frock, and a box of powder to soften the colour of her face: she began to look subtle. Once Jacob exclaimed irritably:

'What's come over you, woman! Extraordinary in your ways you are getting. No respectable woman dresses like that this time in the afternoon. Follow you how the others in the street are – hard-working women they look. A laughing stock you will make yourself.'

Rebecca tossed her head.

'Sluts they look,' she said, 'and sorry I feel for them.'

'Half a dozen children you ought to have, Mrs Jenkins,' Jacob answered warmly, 'and come to your senses you would then.'

Emlyn broke in:

'*Out* of her sense! Like to see women become machines of flesh you do, Jacob. Use them until their wheels are worn out. Yes, use them, that's all you see in women.'

Jacob became angry. 'A worshipper of women I am,' he cried in the manner of a baptist preacher. 'Did not Jesus Christ come through a woman! And when I see one give herself over to frip-fraps and idle her flesh all day, vexed and disgusted I become.'

'I work all day and change at four o'clock,' Rebecca cried hotly, 'because bright I want to be by the time you come home.'

'Bright with a blouse and petticoat!' Jacob jeered. 'Bright enough it is for me to know that my wife you are. Without meaning are the clothes that cover your body.'

Rebecca shrank back. She went about her work without another word. Not until the time came for washing Emlyn's back did her averted and ashamed face lift itself in ardour again.

She usually washed the thick coal dust off his back with movements that were far too delicate, so that it took a long time before his flesh shone white again. But he did not complain, crouching in the big wooden tub, and did not shiver, like Jacob, for whom she was never quick enough – the nightly bath was always unpleasant for him.

This evening she felt vengeful. Jacob had had his bath and was sitting in his shirt before the fire in the other room, warming his naked legs. She scooped water over Emlyn's back and passed the soap over the collier's black skin. And with her two hands, softly and ah, with such subtle passion, she began to rub the soap into his flesh, disregarding the rough flannel used for that task. Into the little hollows of his muscular shoulders, down the length of his flawless back, over the fine curves of his sides, she caressingly passed her spread hands. Beneath them his flesh seemed to harden, draw itself together as though to resist her. But – she could feel another answer to her quivering touch. She became exhausted, her breathing difficult. So she rested for a moment or two, and then, as he moved restlessly in his crouching attitude, she took a bowl of clean warm water and poured it over him. The flesh gleamed out, white-gold, a delicate flush beneath, like a heap of wheat burned hot in the sun.

'There,' she breathed, 'you must use the towel yourself. Tired I am.'

He did not answer, neither did he move up from his crouching. She went into the living-room. Jacob, his hands clasped over his stomach, was dozing before the big fire. In his multi-coloured flannel shirt he looked gaunt and grotesque. She went up to the bedroom. Her eyes were gleaming with a kind of remorseless brilliance; her mien was profligate and mobile. She squatted on the floor like some brooding aboriginal dark in the consciousness of some terrific deed hovering. She squatted there, dark and brooding, and heard his steps approach, behind her. His hands upon her shoulders and entering her bosum. A shock, icy and violent, went through her: she dropped her head. Yet she felt as though she lay amid the softest velvet, folds of soothing dark velvet about her. No word was spoken and presently she was alone.

VII

Then came the time of the Cyfarfod, the Big Meetings in Jacob's chapel – a week of important services. A well-known preacher and other ministers came: every night there would be a long service, with *two* sermons. A week of fiery oratory and prayers like flaming gas. Jacob, his deacon's face pompous and weighty, directed Rebecca to see that his Sunday clothes were spotless, that there were seven clean stiff collars ready, that a new heart-shaped tie was bought.

As these instructions were given Emlyn blew whiffs of cigarette smoke to the ceiling, a secret and ironical smile on his face. Rebecca saw it with a shudder. Jacob added:

'Enjoy the preaching you will, Mrs Jenkins. The sermons of Mr Prys-Davis can make you cry, enjoy them so much you do. Sometimes, so great is his shouting that crack like a wall does his voice.'

She was silent. Emlyn broke in:

'Darro, Jacob, those meetings are only for brainy men and old women who cannot take pleasure in anything else.'

Rebecca thought this incautious and she said quickly:

'Oh, enjoy them I shall, Jacob. Little outings they'll be for me, instead of staying in this house every evening.'

Emlyn drew in his stretched legs and spat in the fire.

'Gluttons for religion you two are,' he jeered.

The Cyfarfod opened on the Sunday; there was no hot dinner that day, as Rebecca went to the three services. She arrived home at ten o'clock that night, her eyes rather wild and obsessed. Jacob had stayed back with the deacons in the vestry.

Emlyn was reading a periodical, waiting for his supper.

'God!' he exclaimed, 'their beds people ought to take to that chapel.'

'The preaching was good,' she said slowly. Her cheeks seemed to sag, her face was rather pitiful. He watched her.

'Enjoy it you did!' he laughed.

'I *did* cry,' she answered in a subdued voice.

He rose from the chair and clasped her shoulders. But she drew away a little, her head dropped.

'Ah, foolish you are like all of them,' he said, 'all those damned hypocrites.'

She shrank further away. She was in that mystical state that by prolonged hymn-singing and prophetic preaching can so easily be induced in Welsh people.

'No, no,' she muttered, 'peace was there to-night.'

But he followed her, slowly and sinisterly, and as she reached the table pressed her back over it in his destroying embrace. He caught her unwilling mouth and warmed her with his lips. She tasted the sweet languorous contact of his dripping tongue. She could have screamed in the violence of her soul. Her hands clasping his shoulders, she could have torn him in her agony of hate and lust.

'Tuesday,' he whispered, 'Tuesday you stay home.' Then he let her go and went back to his chair.

Silent and still, she remained for some moments by the table, her arms across her face. Presently she muttered:

'What am I to say?'

'Oh, tell the old fool that your sickness is coming on again. You know, deceive him with soft soap.' His voice was coarse and brutal.

Jacob came in, fiery banners still burning in his soul. His long, arid face was lit with them. He began immediately, sitting down to supper:

'The children of Israel sit down to their meat with thanksgiving to the Lord who gave it them. With singing voices and loud music we have praised his name, and on our bended knees given up our sins. We have listened to the voice of one whose soul is deep with wisdom. Out of his mouth has come big words and exalted phrases.'

Emlyn listened gravely and said: 'Ach, Jacob, strange it is to me that you are not a local preacher yet.'

But Jacob waved this derision aside:

'The wicked shall mock in their ignorance. How can they see the hands of the Lord in their whippet racing and games of painted cards? But with the people of Sodom and Gomorrah they shall sit in misery.'

He ate his supper with austere dignity, seated patriarchally in his armchair, his jaws working rhythmically. He looked rather fearsome. Rebecca did not say a word, but presently he turned to her:

'Rebecca Jenkins, say you that the meeting moved you?'

'Yes.'

'Did not the wings of angels beat about the singing!'

'Very beautiful was the singing,' she answered.

'Tired you look,' he said sternly.

'Well, after three long services – '

He bent his head to her; there seemed to be iron and fire in his voice as he said:

'Yes, a good wife you have been to-day. When we were singing did I not think, Blessed is our union to-day: my wife Rebecca lifts up her voice with mine in Cyfarfod, her voice is as my voice, her body is with my body here.'

She met his burning stare. Every emotion seemed to flee from her consciousness and she seemed to taste death in her. The fiery purpose of these eyes blasted her.

Emlyn seemed not to hear or see anything; he ate his Sunday night cold beef with head bent at the other end of the table. When he had finished he went back to his periodical, stretched his legs into the hearth, and casually lit a cigarette.

Rebecca's steps dragged with weariness and dread as she cleared away the supper things.

And the following two days she waited in a kind of numbness, her eyes glittering obsessively under her sullen brows. Tuesday, as Jacob hurried over his bath, she told him quietly:

'I am going to stay home to-night and rest.'

'Why, Rebecca fach?' he demanded.

'I – I,' she muttered, her eyes cast down, 'something comes over me lately. I could faint, so crowded does the chapel get.'

His face hung over her, she could hear the roused intake of his breath.

'Better ask Mrs Watkins next door to come in and keep you company,' he said slowly.

'Don't you be silly about me,' she answered hurriedly. 'A little rest is all I want.'

'Broody you will get, alone,' he went on fussily. 'Think you it is –'

'Oh go on, like an old woman you are, making a bother. Wait you for plainer signs.'

'All right. But take care of yourself.'

Later she went into the parlour and pressed her hands on her head in an agony of mingled loathing and fear. She felt as though she bore a sword within her, a glittering blade which might at any moment split her being in two. She crouched behind the door, covering her head, her face contorted and ugly; she heard Emlyn go out and she went to her task of clearing the living-room after the men. Then Jacob came down-stairs in his chapel clothes and after an admonishment that she was not to do too much, went off in dignified haste to that meeting.

Slowly she went upstairs and entered her bedroom. Slowly and carefully, as though she were following some definite and dictated plan, she removed her clothes. Her face was repulsive, contracted in an orgasm of primitive realisation, her eyes fixed like balls of blue marble, her lips thick and distended. Unclothed, her body looked hewn out of pure hard flesh, barren of light and shade, solid flesh of marble, hard and durable. Her breasts sloped forward like cornices of white stone, her thighs were like smooth new pillars. From her head her loosened hair fell upon the polished stone of her shoulders. For moments she stood still in her gleaming nudity, as though she had indeed turned into a hewn white stone. Only when she moved to the bed there was the sudden grace of life.

She heard the click of the front door latch.

He was mounting the stairs; she called out in a voice strange to her own ears:

'He has gone, Emlyn.'

Emlyn went back to the front door and locked it.

VIII

She came downstairs and into the living-room. Emlyn was sitting in the armchair, smoking easily and contentedly.

'Are you going to stay in then?' she asked.

He smiled at her, a fatuous contented smile.

'Don't you be nervous,' he said lazily, 'or suspicious Jacob will get at once. I am going to sit in this chair until he comes in.' He lay back deeper, his legs hanging limp. 'A task it would be for me to go out to-night.'

But Rebecca burned with a vivid heat that showed in her mottled face and lithe powerful movements. She looked flushed with strong life.

Emlyn watched her move through the living-room and said in a sniggering whisper:

'A marvel you are, Rebecca darling.'

'Ach!' she exclaimed, making a gesture of disgust.

'But considerate of you I've been –' he said calmly.

Her cheeks flushed a deeper red.

'But you wait –' he continued.

His lechery was like the stinging of a whip on her quivering flesh. Again, cleaving up through her desire for him, she felt a sword of destruction within her. She looked at his throat with haunted eyes.

'Now Rebecca,' he coaxed. 'take things in a natural way. Be ready for Jacob.'

But she dropped on her knees, bowed down on the floor before him, crouching, her arms shuddering over her breasts.

'What shall we do!' she cried, her distorted face thrust to him. 'Living in this house together. What shall we do!'

He leaned to her rather angrily.

'Rebecca, Rebecca, use control on yourself. Shocking this is. What if he came in now!'

'How can we live together here now!' she moaned.

'Ach, certain we can,' he said sharply.

She drew back.

'But how can it go on. Two men, and you his half-brother,' she cried again. There was horror in her face and her eyes seemed utterly lost.

He stooped before her and pressed her between his thighs, lifted her up with his hand, looked at her long and steadily.

'Go on we will be all right. You leave it to me. Rebecca, enjoy it you should. A little secret between ourselves.'

She laid her head on his thigh and burst out:

'Oh, I love you Emlyn. Only with you I want to be. Horrible it will be for me to go to bed with Jacob again. That it is will kill me. Always I am thinking of your arms and your mouth kissing me.'

'Ah! a few good times we will have.'

She wrenched herself free.

'No,' she cried with anger, 'one or the other!'

'Don't you be a fool now! Go you cautious and everything will be all right.' He became impatient with her, and her dramatic and hysterical mien alarmed him. Jacob might come in any moment. 'Can't you take patience with an old man like Jacob. Only a little soft soap he wants.'

'Ha!' she answered venomously, 'a part of his God I have become. When I am with him in the night sometimes he prays as though he was praying through me. Like God he makes me feel.'

Emlyn laughed.

'Don't you laugh!' she shouted.

'Shut up,' he said quickly.

'Well, don't you joke about this.'

He sat back and was silent. Anything to calm her. She went into the kitchen and put the kettle on. And it was just then that Jacob came in.

'No supper laid!' he exclaimed.

'I was just starting –' Rebecca said, coming into the living-room.

Jacob gazed at her. More colour you have than before I went,' he said. 'In the first prayer I asked God to see to your comfort. For indeed ill you looked.'

She stared at her husband without a word.

'Ignorant that she was unwell I was,' Emlyn said hastily, 'or stayed in I would have, to keep her company.'

Jacob slowly turned his gaze to Emlyn.

'So alone she's been most of the evening!' he said as though pondering over the fact.

In a caught, nervous voice that sent a flame of anger over Emlyn, Rebecca said:

'Go on, don't you worry about me. Accustomed to being alone I am.'

'Not very lonely were you in the evenings in Carmarthen,' Jacob said. 'Seemed to me it did that plenty of louts were hanging about.'

'Louts they were,' she answered, regaining something of her natural demeanour. 'And innocent of any behaviour I was.'

Jacob went to hang his coat up in the passage-way. And Emlyn shot an angry glance at Rebecca, who tossed her head. There was a strange glint in her eyes now.

During supper she was mostly silent, replying in a short vague fashion when the men spoke to her. She seemed occupied with some problem, her brow rather sombre. And in that mood Emlyn was afraid of her.

Then from that night something entered the house. It was in the air like the still presence of death, it was in the drawn tension of Rebecca's paling brow, it was in the forced jocular humour of Emlyn. And, too, in the frozen drop of Jacob's eyelids as he sat in his chair, silent for long periods, there seemed a kind of foreboding, a chill.

Rebecca's conduct sometimes infuriated Emlyn. She would look at him with a long and shameless intensity when the three sat at a meal together: the expression of her whole body seemed to cry their secret. Once when they were alone he said to her:

'Behave yourself, you fool. You make your thoughts plain as A.B.C. Old Jacob might be, but not a blind ape is he.'

She set her jaw sullenly. 'I know,' she said.

'How is it you act so childish then!' he exclaimed savagely.

He was a different Emlyn now. She saw him contemptuously, his fear. Yet she was determined to force the issue. She said coldly: 'A rabbit's mind you've got.'

'Rabbit be damned. Worse it would be for you if Jacob found out.'

She drooped towards him. 'Then always we could be together!' she whispered with a sudden change of mood, her eyes gazing ardently upon him.

He let her caress him: until he fixed his mouth upon her's with a fury that satisfied her. But with that he too had to be content. Rebecca was becoming wily.

'To-morrow night,' he muttered drunkenly, 'he will be at the deacons' meeting.'

'Suspicious he is getting,' she said derisively. 'Not a blind ape is he.'

'Hell and Satan take him,' he went on, 'my female you will be to-morrow night.'

She laughed.

IX

Tramping together to the pit in the early morning, Jacob said to Emlyn:

'What is coming over the woman. Noticed you have, Emlyn, how changed she is?'

'Yes,' Emlyn answered irritably, 'trying she is. Look you, my vest wasn't dry this morning and my trousers was still damp in the corner where she threw them yesterday. And like a peevish owl she is in the mornings now.'

'Ah,' muttered Jacob, 'more to complain of I have.'

Emlyn glanced aside at his half-brother's face. Its sharp grey profile was outlined in the keen air as though cut out of cardboard, and it had a flat, dead expression. Emlyn felt a moment's pity for Rebecca: what joy could *she* have from this arid mechanism of dry flesh walking beside him.

'Happy you seem with her,' he said with a note of surprise.

'She keeps herself cold to me,' Jacob said. 'Yet like a playful little mate she was before we were married.'

'Difficult is the first year or so with a woman like Rebecca,' Emlyn observed wisely.

'Mine she is,' said Jacob with sudden intensity. 'Yet I will have her.'

Emlyn said nothing. They tramped along, up the hill towards the pit in the far reach of the quiet vale. Emlyn became aware of something grim and warning in Jacob's demeanour as he strode silently by his side. His face was still grey and inscrutable, but in his movements there was some dark austerity, like a warning. What was brooding in that shut resentful mind?

They were joined by other colliers, dark-browed under their caps, tramping in a ragged black procession to the pit, under the dawning sky. Across the bridge the sound of their footsteps softened in the thick black coal dust, they tropped into the alley-ways between the black-coated sheds and the lines of small coal trucks, up to the lamp room, where they were given their polished lit lamps.

Jacob and Emlyn kept together: they worked side by side. At the shaft they waited their turn to enter the cage. The two wheels aloft spun against the metal sky and dropped their thick and shining ropes taut into the gaping hole beneath: one cage emerged and clashed loudly into stillness. Jacob and Emlyn, with fourteen others, crowded in, and ahead a bell clamoured. The cage descended like a stone.

Arrived at the bottom, a brick-walled tunnel sloped away in the shrill electric light, slimy and dripping. The colliers tramped on, at the side of the rail track, until the walled tunnel ceased and the workings began, propped up by timber. Now light came only from the tiny flames of their lamps. The narrow rail track twisted its way with them, between the walls of rock and timber, the thin rails like twin nerves going deeper and deeper into the rich silence of the earth.

The two half-brothers trudged on without a word, stooping under the beams that held the earth above, splashing through the pools of black water, until they were alone in their own working.

It was a small clearing thick with props of timber and heaps of stone: at one side the coal face gleamed and sparkled in the lamplight, jutting generously and lively out of the dead earth.

Jacob was looking at the roof examiningly.

'Lewis put it all right afterwards?' Emlyn inquired.

'He's been here,' Jacob said. He put his hand on a prop and tried to move it: there was a faint creaking sound. 'It's all right,' he added, and passed to examine another part of the clearing. Emlyn threw off his upper garments and began to attack the coal face; soon he was absorbed, sweating, in the task of removing the coal from its bed, oblivious of Jacob, who, half-naked also, was working twenty yards away, still fumbling with the timber props and beams.

The hours passed and at ten o'clock the two men paused for a meal. Emlyn's face and body was now black with dust, save where the sweat ran down in streaks; tense from his labour crouching under the coal face, his eyes shone out blood-red and liquid.

'God above, how difficult the seam is getting, Jacob,' he panted, looking round for his food tin. 'Where's my box?'

'Here,' came Jacob's voice. He was standing, a dark crouching shape beyond the lamplight, ten yards away.

'What you doing there?' Emlyn asked. 'Still messing with the timber?' He advanced, ducking his head under the low beams.

Then something moved overhead, as he ducked: there was a sharp creak followed by a tearing as of wood slowly snapping. Emlyn turned sharply, and his face showed taut and vulnerable for an instant. Then the space was choked with stone and dust.

Jacob clambered down from his perch in the darkness, ran shouting through the clearing, out into the other workings. His hoarse shout for help leapt with a peculiar deadened sound through the still, hot tunnels.

Men came running up, ducking like strange other-world creatures in the dark alleys, wild-eyed and tense.

'A fall,' Jacob shouted, 'my brother is under.'

There were cries of dismay when they saw the heap of stone.

'Jesus!'

'Quick! Hell, what a job.'

'Ach, not much hope is there.'

They crowded round, worked with feverish haste, shovelling, pulling away with their hands, the rock and earth. Jacob clawed like a possessed beast at the rubble, his eyes glaring maniacally.

'Right on the head, right on the head,' he kept shouting. 'I saw it falling.'

'Stay you away,' one collier muttered, 'we'll get at him soon enough.'

A large stone had caught him – it lay upon his shoulders. There was a heavy smell of blood. They heaved at the rock. Jacob left them alone to their final task. He stood leaning against a prop, his head sunk in his shoulders. He heard a collier's sharp intaken breath as he muttered:

'Christ! a bloody mess.'

And Jacob's nostrils quivered and paled in the stench of blood.

X

They laid him, a shape covered in some dark coarse cloth, on his bed and, their faces closed and grave, went out softly – the four colliers who had brought him home. They heard the wild shrill weeping of Jacob's wife in the living-room and the comforting voice of her neighbour. Jacob shut the door behind them and upon the little crowd of people gathered on the pavement.

Rebecca's frightened voice was lapsing into sobs now. As Jacob entered the living-room she lifted her head from the woman's arms and he stared at her fixedly. Her wild face was drenched with tears, her mouth moving pitiably in its sobs.

'Hush, Rebecca,' he said sternly.

The neighbour protested. 'Let her work it off. Natural it is for her to be frightened. Low enough she has looked lately.'

But his face was stern and sombre, his eyes fixed in a cold, remorseless stare.

'I will wash and change,' he said, 'and go out. Many things are there to arrange. Stay you with her, Mrs Evans, until I come back this evening.'

Rebecca burst into further tears.

'Don't leave me alone in the house,' she wept.

'Why should you fear death?' said Jacob darkly. 'Life it is that we should fear.' And he strode into the kitchen to wash.

Later he went out of the house without another word.

'Strange he is,' commented Mrs Evans. 'Affected by the accident he must be. Daft in the eyes he looked.'

'Yes,' Rebecca whispered, 'it is of him I am frightened.'

'Tut, tut, harmless enough is old Jacob Jenkins,' said the other. 'Shaken him has his brother's death! Fond of each other they were.'

Rebecca shook her head. And she could not keep her hands from trembling. There was a stern and terrible presence in the house, a horror that was closing round her tenaciously and icily, like a freezing drug gripping into her consciousness. What had she seen in Jacob's face when he looked at her? What dark warning had been there?

Trembling and pale to the lips, she awaited his return. He arrived back about seven o'clock and asked:

'Have you lit the candles for him?'

Mrs Evans said they hadn't, and Jacob took two brass candlesticks from the mantelshelf.

'I will go back now then,' Mrs Evans said. Rebecca made a gesture towards her, then sank into her chair: and the woman went off, after a sharp inquisitive glance at Jacob.

In silence he fixed the candles and lit them. At last Rebecca said tremulously: 'Is it arranging about the funeral you were?'

Without looking at her he answered:

'I have been on the mountain. I fled to the hills for silence and prayer.'

'Awful for you it must have been,' she whispered. 'Killed at once he was?'

Jacob slowly raised his head and looked at his wife.

'No. I had words from him before he died.'

Her eyelids dropped quickly, she moved nervously in her chair. He took the candles and went to the stairs. There he turned and said:

'Come you up when I call, Rebecca Jenkins.'

With a numbed heart she watched him. Ah, what terrible meaning was in his voice and his look. There was something he knew. Her faculties seemed to shrink within her, she felt the horror grip at her will. He knew, he knew. She was seized with panic and yet she could not move. Like a lodestone the will of Jacob held her in its power, she could not move out of the warning of his look. She would have to go to him and tell him all. Emlyn was gone and there was no strength to which she might cling. She would have to tell him all and pray for his forgiveness. She would serve him and give of her body, all she had, to the last shred of her being. She would content herself with buying pretty clothes and going to chapel to display them, she would make a friend of young Mrs Rolands and they would go out together in the evenings. Tearfully she thought this, her head sunk in her shoulders, her hands still trembling, while the minutes passed. Her face began to look wild and obsessed. Suddenly she dropped her face into her hands and moaned aloud. No, no, she could not bear the thought of living alone with Jacob, it would be horrible, horrible now.

'Rebecca!'

Violently she started in the chair.

'Rebecca.' His voice was stern.

She forced herself to answer. 'What do you want?'

'Here I want you.'

She stood up and her body seemed to droop within itself. She heard him go back into Emlyn's bedroom. What did he want of her up there, what could she do! But she knew that some awful revelation was waiting, that the deathly horror was gathered in that room for her. For a moment she looked round wildly, as though to flee. And yet there was something reassuring in this familiar room, her living-room, where she had laboured and lived in so much loneliness the last year. Ach, she would face him. What if he *did* know! She had something to tell him. An old man like him. She would not stand in fear of any man. Yet she felt her heart plunging as she slowly climbed the stairs, into the silent darkness of the upper floor.

The door of Emlyn's bedroom was shut, and for a moment she crouched before it in acute dread. Then again came Jacob's voice, sharp, imperious:

'Rebecca.'

Why should he bully her! The old fool. She opened the door and entered quickly, demanding: 'What do you want?'

The two candles were burning on the little mantleshelf. Jacob was seated beneath them, the Bible open on his knees. He did not answer her question as she came in – only stared at her with his deadened eyes fixed unswervingly upon her. Then he rose, put the Bible on the seat, and took up a candlestick. Sombre and tall in his black clothes, his sere face began to kindle with a dull wrath. The shape on the bed had been covered with a white sheet.

She crouched against the washstand by the further wall, and again her strength ebbed from her, her face paling to the lips. But she forced herself to speak, her voice coming in a dry gulp:

'Afraid you make me, Jacob! How is it you are so strange?'

He advanced to the bedside, holding the candle aloft.

'There,' he said, extending his finger downwards over the corpse, 'there is your dead.'

She stared at him. He went on: 'Come you and look for the last time.'

Her mouth had gone dry, she could not move her tongue to any word. She lifted her hand to her face, and her eyes were livid with fright.

'Come,' he repeated.

She did not stir. His brows drawn, stern and righteous wrath in his countenance, he went to her and took her arm in his stony grasp. She quivered away from him, a curious sound coming from her lips, but, tightening his grasp, he drew her to the bedside. Her face had become sickly and loose, her breasts panted. Stonily Jacob looked down on her.

'Gather yourself together, woman. Make yourself ready to look for the last time on what you have worshipped.'

For a moment she went stiff and taut in his grasp, then, had he not held her, she would have fallen to the floor like a heap of rags. He put the candlestick down on the little table at the side of the bed, and with one gesture swept the white sheet away from the head and shoulders of the corpse.

She saw. Jacob had taken the canvas wrapping from the filthy wax of the head and the horror lay there revealed in its congealed blood. Rebecca's body quaked, her back bent forward, she screamed at last. Then Jacob half carried, half dragged her to a chair and sat her on it, as she moaned, her head dropping pitiably on her breast.

He went back to the bed and covered the corpse. Then he took up the Bible again and sat down. And he began to read aloud:

'And early in the morning he came again into the temple, and all the people came unto him; and he sat down, and taught them. And the scribes and Pharisees brought unto him a woman taken in adultery; and when they had set her in the midst,

'They said unto him, this woman was taken in adultery, in this very act.

'Now Moses in the law commanded us, that such should be stoned: but what sayest thou?

'This they said, tempting him, that they might have to accuse him. But Jesus stooped down, and with his finger wrote on the ground, as though he heard them not.

'So when they continued asking him, he lifted up himself and said unto them, He that is without sin among you, let him first cast a stone at her....'

For a moment he was silent, glancing up at Rebecca. Her head still dropped on her breast, she sat immobile as one dead. He went on:

'When Jesus had lifted up himself, and saw none but the woman, he said unto her, woman, where are those thine accusers? hath no man condemned thee?'

'She said, 'No man, Lord.' And Jesus said unto her, 'Neither do I condemn thee: go and sin no more.'

He closed the book, went on his knees, and, leaning his elbows on the chair, prayed:

'Lord, who am I to condemn my wife Rebecca? Thy son forgave the woman taken in adultery and now I ask thee for strength to do likewise with Rebecca. Gone far in sin she has, dear Lord, looking with desire on the flesh of my brother Emlyn. And thou hast punished him with this visitation of death. The voice of the world would say, Stone her, cast her out, let her go from thee into the highways and bye-ways. But have I not read the words of thy son! And what the great Jesus said has opened my heart in pity. Lord, forgive her her great sin against me. To-night the hills cried out to me to slay her, the rocks mocked at my anguish, her name was written in letters of blood upon the sky. For before he died did not Emlyn confess to their behaviour together? Lord, she has done evil while her husband laboured for thee in thy chapel. Visit her with more punishment if thou wilt. Let her beauty shine no more, let her countenance be marked with grief, let her belly sicken her. But she shall rest quietly in her home with me, for I will not harden my sorrowing heart against her. For little Jesus's sake. Amen.'

He rose. Rebecca had covered her face with her hands. He went to her and touched her hair. She moaned.

'Ah,' he muttered, 'a fool you have been. Think you your sin would not be found out?'

She flung up her head; her face had gone loose and mottled, twitching in tears.

'He told you —' she sobbed.

'But already I knew,' he cried harshly. 'Think you I have no eyes, no sense to see how you flaunted yourself before him, and how his eyes burned with lust for you! Then confess to me he did before he died that given yourself to him you had.'

Jacob, after one of the Big Meetings had gone up to his bedroom and found a certain belonging of Emlyn beside the bed.

She got up, crouched against the wall, swaying and sobbing. She felt all her life falling to pieces, there was no hope or happiness anywhere. Then Jacob's hand was laid upon her arm.

'Come, Rebecca. Young and pretty you are. Like a little wanton mare frisking in a field you have behaved. But look you now, settle down to life you must and there's peaceful we'll be together —'

He drew her to him. He passed his large strong hands over her, his sunken eyes began to kindle. She swayed in his gentle embrace. Then his arms closed like oak about her, and she lifted her face. It was like a shining hot flower. She was his now.

Teddy Ashton The Great Chowbent Football Match

It was talk about the cup ties that started the idea. When Jimmy Jabbers, who was employed as a collier at the Midge Hole pits, was enthusiastically giving opinions and prophecies about the English Cup in the Gamecock Inn at Chowbent (which, though it is not on the map, is in England all the same, and not, as some might suppose, from the Celestial suspicion in the first syllable, 'chow,' in China), Lung Jerry, one of the spinners at Cribbalot's cotton factory, exclaimed: 'Oh, chuck it! Is there nowt to talk about but silly futebaw an' crazy crowds that goes to watch it? It's futebaw, an' nowt but futebaw, fro' th' first sup to turnin'-out time.'

'Allow me to tell thee,' said Jimmy Jabbers, 'that there's more in futebaw than ever theau had in thy head. It requires as much skill to be a good footbawer as to run a Parliament.'

'Get off wi' thee,' replied Lung Jerry, 'any foo' con play at futebaw.'

'I don't know about that,' put in Billy Butterbuck, a little chap who worked in the foundry. 'Th' wife says I'm as big a foo' as ever she came across; but I don't think I should ever make an international if I kicked myself to deeath.'

'Thy wife's a good judge, Billy,' retorted Lung Jerry.

At this point there entered Ike Blitcroft, the landlord, commonly nicknamed 'Owd Neaw-then' (now-then) from his constant use and repetition of that phrase. 'Neaw then,' he would say, 'It's time yo' were bein' quieter,' or 'Neaw then, Billy, it's time theau were settlin' thy shot,' or 'Neaw then, we'll ha' no fallin' out,' and so on.

'Oh, Neaw-then,' shouted Jimmy Jabbers, 'we're talkin' about futebaw. Lung Jerry says it's a mugs game; that it needs no brains to run a baw through eleven men an' shoot it into th' net.'

'Aw I can say to that,' said Owd Neaw-then, 'is let him have a try, neaw then.'

'By gow', that's given it me,' cried Jimmy; 'a gradely champion idea. Let's get a futebaw match up. Us Gamecock Inn lot could play th' Miners' Arms lot across th' road. Jack Snubble, what's theer every neet, has been talkin' about gettin' a team up to challenge anybody in

Chowbent to play for a prato pie (potato pie). Let's have a go at 'em. If we can't lick that crew, an' get a gradely good prato pie for nowt, we're not worth buryin', are we hek as like!'

The suggestion scooped. They were all eager to have a football match with the frequenters of the Miners' Arms – all except Lung Jerry, who sat silent.

'Has theau nowt to say, Jerry?' asked Billy Butterbuck. 'Theau'll ha' to be one o' th' team, theau knows.'

'I'd rayther not,' answered Jerry. 'Th' doctor says I've to keep out of anythin' risky or violent. I've to be very careful o' my liver.'

'Oh, be hanged to that tale!' said Jimmy. 'Theau'll ha' to play. We can't let a tall lung chap like thee, that would do champion for goal, slink out o' th' sport. We'll make thee goaler; that's safe enough. Theau's nowt to do but fist th' baw out whenever it comes at thee.'

'No runnin' about an' puncin'?' inquired Jerry.

'Not a bit,' replied Jimmy. 'All theau'll ha' to do will be to stand between th' posts an' keep th' baw fro' going through,'

'Theau'rt sure there's no danger?' said Jerry. 'It would never do for me t' get a punce i' th' liver.'

'No danger, not a bit,' said Jimmy. 'It's as safe as porridge.'

So Jerry was persuaded, and the match arranged.

Owd Neaw-then was umpire for the Gamecocks, and Owd Chucker – the landlord for the Miners' Arms – for the Miners. Owd Ragface – so nicknamed because his features seemed falling to pieces – who had once been up to see a final at the Crystal Palace, yet never got there, but did 'seven days' instead, because he lost his railway ticket on the way (and he swears that this is the true, tragic version of the tale), was appointed the referee, as being, because of his addled journey to see a final in London, an authority on the game.

'We'll play on th' owd brickfield just behind th' Gamecocks,' suggested Jimmy Jabbers. 'We can borrow some goalposts; there's lots of lads plays there; an' the Miners have got a baw – a good classic baw, too, for th' Bowton Wanderers played wi' it when they licked Manchester City.'

The match was fixed for the Saturday following, and Jimmy Jabbers, who was to captain the Gamecocks, was busy selecting his team.

'There's Lung Jerry for goal,' he said; 'that's all right. See as theau never lets th' baw slip through once, Jerry.'

'I'll do my best, so lung as I don't excite my liver,' muttered Jerry. 'But I mustn't upset my liver at no cost.'

'I'll play centre-forrud,' said Jimmy; 'Billy Butterbuck an' Owd Blackpuddin' can play left wing, while Owd Sneezer and Ruchut Bobswoth can play reet wing.'

'Ruchut' – which is the northern vernacular for Richard – Bobswoth was the son of a farmer, or rather milk merchant, who lived a couple of miles away. He was courting Owd Neaw-then's daughter, Ann.

Ruchut grinned, and expressed his willingness to play 'reet wing.' He thought he would show off, and shine in Ann's eyes. She would certainly be watching the match. He had already told her about it.

'Our team's nearly complete neaw,' said Jimmy Jabbers. 'We'n geet all but full-backs, an' we must have two gradely solid men for that job – two that'll need some shiftin'. I think we'll ax two o' th' Chowbent fat club – Tom Rappit an' Jack Spadger would do.'

'But we want 'em nimble as well as fat,' said Billy Butterbuck. 'Fat of itsel – sheer naked fat, as one might say – is no use. We want fat that con frisk a bit.'

'Well, we'll see what we can do,' said Jimmy; 'leave it to me. Meanwhile, yo' chaps train yoursels as much as yo' can – run up an' down th' backyard every neet for half-an-hour. For we must give this Miners' lot a gradely good bastin' an' cop that prato pie.'

On the Saturday afternoon, at three o'clock, the rival teams – the Gamecocks and the Miners – met on the brickfield, which was damp, soft, and slippery, for though the day was fine (yet grey, and threatening wet) there had been considerable rain during the week.

There were about a hundred spectators, friends and 'pals' of the two teams, and a number of lads; but no ladies – except Ruchut's sweetheart, Ann, who stood at the yard gate at the rear of the Gamecock, which was close to the field.

'Well,' said Knockkneed Dan, a spinner from Cribbalot's factory, as he surveyed the two teams, 'they're a rum-lookin' lot. There'll be some rare comic futebaw on this programme. There's only Ruchut Bobswoth that's geet anythin' like a futebaw costume; t'others have simply pulled their coats an' waistcoats off, an' rowled their breeches up. There will be some slutch stirred up to-day. Why, an' ther's some o' th' Miners' lot wi' clogs on – there's Daff Waggle for one.'

'I'll bet as th' Miners win,' cried Bowlegged Ben, a collier.

'Well,' said Knockkneed Dan, 'there's nowt worth bettin' on here. If it were a thing possible in nature an' futebaw both sides would lose, for that's all they're fit for. However, I'll ha' thee a bob on. It'll be patriotic to back th' Gamecocks, though I'd as soon back a crow at a bird-singin' contest.'

When the two captains, Jimmy Jabbers and Jack Snubble, met to toss up, Jimmy said: 'Before we toss up I have a protest to make. I object to Daff Waggle playin' i' clogs. It's again th' regulations an' th' British Constitution. I appeal to th' referee.'

'Neaw, clogs must not be used,' decided Owd Ragface, the referee. 'That's th' law, an' we must stick to th' law.'

'But I've no shoes,' said Daff Waggle.

'Theau must go an' borrow some, then,' retorted Jimmy.

'We might arrange it this road,' said Ragface, thoughtfully; 'that Daff be permitted to run about in his clogs, but every time he wants to kick at th' bawl he must take 'em off.'

'That's a foo's idea,'said Daff. 'Where will th' baw be while I'm pullin' my clog off to punce?'

Ragface being, despite his renowned journey, only human resented his wisdom being termed folly. 'I'm th' referee,' he said, 'an' I'll be obeyed. Theau can't play i' thy clogs, so theau must either get some shoes or go off th' field.'

The difficulty was got over by one of the Miners' supporters, who had come to be a spectator, and, as it happened, had a pair of shoes on, temporarily exchanging his footwear with Daff.

Then the game began. The Miners won the toss, and decided to play downhill the first half – the ground, which was all bare clay, sloping considerably. On the right boundary was the old clay pit, half full of water.

Ragface, the referee, blew his whistle – a little bicycle whistle someone had lent him – and Jimmy Jabbers kicked off.

'Laws, how they shape!' said Knockkneed Dan, critically whiffing his old pipe. 'Some runs like scawdent cocks, others like owd hens in a fit, an' others as if they'd geet their breeches glued on; while they punce as if they were freetent o' their legs flyin' off. Laws, I never seed such gam! Hello, ther's Jimmy Jabbers tryin' to dribble; owd fat Fuzziker is runnin' at him – he's charged him – they're both down i' th' slutch! Laws, what a sight! Fuzziker went flop on little Jimmy, an' flattened him out. They're gettin' up. Jimmy is scrapin' the slutch out of his mouth and earholes, while Fuzziker's daubed fro' head to foot, an' I believe he's brasted his nose. Well, it's cheap at th' price is this show! Hello, there's a scrimmage on neaw! Owd Ragface is in th' midst on it; he's blowin' his whistle! What's up?'.

'Throw up,' said Ragface to the players, who were wondering what he had stopped the game for.

'Throw up? What for?' demanded Jack Snubble. 'Is it a foul?'

'Not as I knows on,' said Ragface, 'but I'm havin' a throw up.'

'What for?' asked Jimmy Jabbers, indignantly.

'That's my business,' said Ragface, 'an' I'll not be taught by nobody. I can't ha' yo' swarmin' round me an' nearly knockin' me down. There's room enough without that; yo'n all th' field to play in. It's not good enough. So to save myself I blows th' whistle, an' we'll ha' a throw up.'

'Here, this'll not do,' said Billy Butterbuck. 'We must ha' futebaw according to th' rules.'

'If yo' don't shut up I'll ha' yo' all suspended,' said Ragface, with dignity. 'I knows th' rules o' futebaw, an' th' rules as to referees, an' I'll be taught by nobody. Haven't I been to th' Crystal Palace? So I say "throw up",' and he flung the ball high in the air, adding, 'There yo' are; yo' con kick it or leave it as yo' like. If I'm to see this match through I must tak' care o' my skin, an' I'll have a throw up whenever my carcase is in danger. An' if yo' don't like it yo' must rub.'

After half an hour's play, by which time most players were covered from head to foot with mud, and a few of them limping, the Miners scored a goal; and there was jubilation amongst their supporters.

'What th' hek did tha' let that baw go through for?' said Jimmy Jabbers, angrily, to Lung Jerry. 'Any child could ha' stopped it. Theau deliberately jumped out o' th' road, an' leet it go through.'

'An' yo'd have done th' same if yo'd been i' my place,' said Lung Jerry. 'It would ha' struck me slap on th' liver if I hadn't, an' it were comin' like a cannon baw, an' I have to be careful o' my liver.'

'Theau bletherin' yorney!' roared Jimmy. 'To Wigan wi' thee an' thy liver! But I'll tell thee what, so pay heed. If theau lets 'em get another goal I'll pur thy liver out mysel'. Aw as theau needed to ha' done were to ha' gan th' baw a welt wi' thy fist, an' knocked it back. Let another go through if theau dare!'

Up to half-time there were no further scores. During the interval both Gamecocks and Miners refreshed – including the referee, who insisted on having two free pints before he went back to the field.

Soon after play was restarted the Gamecocks got a goal, making the score even – one-one. After this the game became alternately furious and flabby.

The referee was knocked down, a dozen players on top of him. When he got up, battered and bruised, he said: 'I'll stop this wark. Where's my whistle? Has anybody seen it? Laws, I believe I've swallowed it! I can feel somethin' goin' pip-pip in my inside!'

'Theau must whistle wi' thy fingers,' said Jimmy Jabbers. 'Let's get on wi' th' game.'

Both teams were getting tired, and it was amusing to see them crawl and spurt about. The Gamecocks scored again, making the game two-one; and then the Miners desperately tried to equalise.

Ruchut was running up the left side with the ball, his sweetheart, Ann, watching him from the back gate. Suddenly, as he was nearing the edge of the clay pit, Daff Waggle ran at him like a bull, and charged him. The two rolled over and disappeared into the pit. Ann screamed, and came running up the field.

'Oh, my chap, my chap!' she yelled.

'Offside,' cried the referee.

'Oh is he drowned?' she cried.

'Neow, they're both crawlin' out,' said Knockkneed Dan. 'There's no harm done. They're only a bit damp. Tak' him home, Ann, an' hang him up to dry in front o' th' fire. He'll soon be aw reet, I dare say,' and Dan turned to Bowlegged Ben. 'Th' poor lass fears if she loses Ruchut she's jiggered. She's certainly not very ticin', is she?'

As Ruchut and Daff Waggle left the field to change their clothes there were only ten men left on each side to finish the game.

The Miners made a great attempt to get another goal. While one of the forwards shot, three more of the players rushed the goalkeeper – Lung Jerry.

The ball went through, and Lung Jerry lay on the ground calling for help.

'Get up,' said Jimmy Jabbers, 'theau'rt not hurt.'

'I'm done for this time,' said Jerry; 'my liver's brasted, or somethin' else fatal. Yo've wickedly deceived me. Yo' told me that goalin' were a safe job – an' here I am, killed at it. Oh, my! I can't get up! Somebody go and prepare my wife for th' doleful news. Oh dear, I'm done for! My liver's gone, an' aw my ribs is broken! Why did I ever allow myself to be lured into this job? If I'd only had sense enough to ha' kept out of it I should ha' been alive and well this very minute. Oh, my! I'm done for!'

'Shut up, theau softey,' said Jimmy Jabbers; 'there's nowt to do wi' thee! Come on an' have a pint an' a plate o' hot prato pie, an' then theau'll be aw reet. Th' match is finished; th' time's up; it's a draw – honours even. But we'll have another do some day. We'll lick this Miners' lot yet.'

'I'm not havin' any more, never no more,' said Lung Jerry. 'If I survive this fatal wound, which is doubtful, yo'll ha' to get a fresh goaler. No more futebaw for me. Oh, my liver, my liver! that th' doctor said I'd to tak' care of – oh, my liver!'

'Get some pluck, an' theau'll manage without liver,' said Jimmy, helping Jerry to his feet. 'Come on, an' have a wash, an' then theau'll be aw reet for tacklin' th' prato pie.'

Hannah Mitchell   May Day

'Hast had one of these 'ere *Northern Voices*,' asked Dick Kilshaw of his workmate, Tom Bates, one Monday morning.

'Ne'er yerd on it,' he answered, 'an iv it's awt like them voices aw yer awhoam when we'n a short wick aw dum't want to yer on it noather. Is it one o' them Spiritualist dodges?'

'Naw, tha gret gobbin, it's a papper coed th' *Northern Voice*.'

'Oh, is it owt like Teddy Ashton's owd *Northern Weekly*? By gum, that wer' a gradely good papper, wi' sum reight hankey stuff in it.'

'Well, it's noan just t'same as th' owd *Northern Weekly*, but yo med say it wer' upo' summat same tack to mak' th' world a bit breeter fur us aw; it's a Labour papper.'

'Labour, is it? Weel, awst noan beigh one then, fur aw reckon nowt o' these Labour chaps, they're awlus causing sum mak o' bother, ayther a strike or a lockout or boath, same as ween just had at th' co-op., or else makking fooes o' theirsels, same as they did t'other Setday at Belle Vue. Aw seed a whol' ruck on 'em at Ardwick Green afore they seet off wi't procession, an' they favvered th' lost tribes of Israel to my thinking. One felly luked as if he'd come eawt o' Wall's owd ghost show wi' a yaller cloak an red shoan. An' a woman wi' him drest up same as a gipsy wi' a tamborine thing in her hand. They seem as they letn their wives do owt they like. An' ther wur a lot o' childer an' a lurry wi' red and yaller banners, an' it had on one 'Russia Leads the Way,' an' aw thowt that's a rum go, chus heaw, fur they wur reight at th' back o' th' procession. An another banner hed sommut abeaut 'Communionism' on it, an aw sed to eawr Bill as wer' wi' me, 'Tha sees neaw they're nowt but a lot o' atheists or they'd noan bring th' 'Communion' into the streets i' that fashion. Aw co that reet deawn blasphemy, an' if Bishop Welldon yers tell on it ther'll be summut said i'th' Cathedral abeawt it, awl bet a hapenny. They wer' sheawtin summut abeaut *New Leaders*, an' by gum they wanted sum, for them owd chaps i'th' front luked rare an' teight, an' sarve 'em reet, traipsin' off to Belle Vue like a lot of meawntibanks when they cud ha' gone to th' foatbaw match an' seet 'em deawn nice an' comfortable. Aw wud ha' liked to ha' bin at Barnsley misel, an' I

141

shud ha' bin iv aw cud ha' raised any fare; aw raised a row istid when aw toud eawr Sarah Ellen awd like to go. 'Aw daresay tha' would,' hoo said, 'but tha' gets no brass off me to goo watchin' bigger foos nor thisel kickin' a baw abeawt. Tha can stop in an' clean th' childers' shoan and peel th' taters for Sunday. Aw mun get th' dinner o'er i' good time, awm gooin to th' meetin' at Queen's Park i'th' afternoon.'

'What meeting,' aw axed her, 'It's a Labour meeting,' hoo says, 'Th' "High Helpers," or summut o' that sooart, they're caed as are gettin' it up, an' Johnny Clynes an a tooathree mooar speykers ull be theer. Sum woman goin' to speyk, they say, an' aw want to see if th' Labour chaps dresses their wives anny better than yo Tories, an' iv they do awst jeign 'em.'

'Did hoo go?' asked Dick, very much interested.

'Hoo did an' aw,' said Tom, 'an' aw followed as sooin as awd washed th' dinner pots, fur aw thawt therd be ructions if aw left 'em. Aw were a bit late, an' when aw geet to th' park ther were a good ruck o' folk gethered reawn a platform, an' a chap wi' a rum-looking hat an' th' queerest twang aw ever yerd, in his speech, were tawking abeaut th' Budget; an' after a bit he seet deawn an' Johnny Clynes geet up an' said as he were a "High Helper," an' awlus had been, an' aw could mak nowt on it, for aw awlus theawt he were a Labour chap. He's a fairish speyker, but he tawked tae much abeawt Socialism for my liking; iv that's what th' "High Helpers" are eawt for, I mak neawt on it. Then a woman geet up, an' aw wer' very fain to see as hoo were noan varry smartly drest. Eawr Sarah Ellen'll noan want a coat like that, aw thought to misel. Hoo weren't mich of a speyker, to my mind, an' hoo favoured one o' them Suffragettes as used to go reawnd market greawnds a tooathree year sin. Aw theawt Lloyd George had got shut on 'em, but awm sure that woman were one on 'em. Th' last speyker were a youngish chap as tawked varry fast an' waved his arms abeawt a lot. He said he'd give us a good tip, but aw durn't think as he knowed mich abeawt th' horses, for he nobbut give us "Emerson" and "Shelley," an noather on 'em run, for aw took particular notice. Aw assed eawr Sarah Ellen if hoo'd jeigned 'em an' hoo said hoo should do if hoo liked, an' by gum aw think hoo will, but none o' yer "High Helpers" for me.'

'Aye, Tom,' Dick said, laughing, 'Tha art a bawster yed; it's th' I.L.P. tha meeans, an' th' young chap wer' noan tawkin' abeawt horses. But sitha, aw'll give thee one o' these *Northern Voices*, and tha can tell me heaw that likes it next week.'

'Aw reet, but awst noan beigh one, tha knows; my money's noan goin' to Russia.'

James C. Welsh   The Meeting

A short distance along the street Rennie met Barney Blades, whom he had not seen for two days, owing to the fact that the former had been busy attending to the Sneddon family in their trouble.

'Hello,' said Barney in a cheery whisper. 'I thought you were either in jail or had got chicken-pox an' had gane hame. Keep walkin', my boy,' he added, looking round as he turned to walk with Rennie. 'We're watched at every turn noo, an' I'm beginning tae think they've got on oor track. Hoo hae you been gettin' on?'

'I've had a miserable time,' was Rennie's reply. 'I hardly kent what tae dae,' and he proceeded to recount to Blades the disasters that had befallen the Sneddon family.

'Imphim,' grunted Blades, his lips closing in a snap, while a hard steely look came into his eyes. 'It's a damnable business, an' I doot there is nothing for it but oot an' oot revolution. If only we could rouse the country tae revolt.'

'Hoo has matters been gaun wi' you, since I saw you last?' asked Rennie soberly.

'Frae bad tae worse,' answered Blades, somewhat despairingly. 'But speak low,' he cautioned, 'an' keep on walkin'. The hale place is hotchin' wi' spies, an' we're a' broken up meantime. The police hae gotten on oor track, I think, aboot the blawin' up o' the engine-sheds. Halliday an' twa three ithers hae been arrested, an' the rest o' us are meetin' again the nicht in the auld mine, tae see what we're gaun tae dae. It's a hell o' a business, an' we may be nabbed at ony minute. Can you come the nicht at ten o'clock?'

'I'll try,' answered Rennie uneasily, taking a swift look round. 'But hoo is the fight gaun? What are the leaders sayin' aboot the fight noo?'

'Naething. What can they say?' was the answer. 'Even though we a' agreed tae gang back tae work noo, we canna; for the pits are nearly a' ruined. Ha, ha,' he laughed sardonically. 'If it wasna for the sufferin' o' the folk, I wadna care. I could enjoy the sicht o' the coal-owners bein' ruined. But their ruin means the starvation o' the folk on this occasion.'

For a while they walked on in silence, and it was noticeable that a great change had come over the demeanour of the people in the streets. At the beginning of the fight the men had carried themselves with jaunty confidence; but now, after ten weeks of terrible suffering, they slouched along with a disheartened look in their eyes, and a furtive expression on their faces.

'I see a meetin' advertised for the nicht in the picture-hoose,' observed Blades after a time. 'It starts at seven o'clock. I dinna ken wha arranged it; but nane o' the pit committees ken ought aboot it. I wonder what's ahint it.'

'Are you gaun?' asked Rennie, wondering what was behind Blades' statement.

'Yes,' was the reply. 'So are the rest o' them wha are still free. Are you sure you hinna seen the police since we saw you last?' he asked significantly, looking sideways at Rennie as he spoke.

'Good God, Barney,' replied Rennie, with an injured look, 'you don't mean to think I would go an' give the crowd away, do you?'

'I don't think you are the type that wad dae that,' was Blades' reply. 'But somebody has done it.'

'Why, then, do you put that question to me?' pursued Rennie.

'You are a newcomer among us, an' naebody kens very much aboot you, an' you hadna been seen for twa three days,' was the reply. 'But never mind. I believe you're genuine. We'll gang tae the meetin', an' see what is ahint it a'. It will likely be infested wi' spies, but that's in the game.'

'It wad be interestin' tae ken what is ahint,' said Rennie after a pause. 'I wonder what the purpose o' it will be.'

'Heaven knows,' was Blades' comment, 'unless it is tae get the men tae decide tae return tae work.'

'But hoo can they, if the pits are a' destroyed?' questioned Rennie.

'They'll hae tae start sometime,' was the answer. 'I hear that the Government is gaun tae supply machinery, an' sodgers are provided for protectin' them wha want tae work. They've done that already at some pits, I believe. But it'll be a lang time before there is work for many men. They're gettin' coal frae Germany tae keep the railways workin'.'

'But if the coal-owners are ruined they'll be unable tae start,' said Rennie.

'Nae fear,' was the reply. 'You an' I, an' the rest o' us will hae tae pay for it. It'll be charged tae the industry, an' oor weans will a' be grannies an' grandfathers before it is paid off, and enslavement will be complete. But I'll see you at the meetin' if we are baith free by that time,' he broke off suddenly, and turned into a side street. 'So long an' good luck,' and he left Rennie to walk on alone.

Rennie walked on for some distance, his thoughts busy, and his mind uneasy. It was a terrible prospect, and nothing but ruin seemed in front. He turned back after a time, so as to get back to the meeting, and he debated the point as to whether he should do so or go home.

He decided for the meeting, and walked along leisurely, taking stock of the people he met on the street as he proceeded.

He was obsessed by the feeling of despair all around, and the silence of the people. There was little or no traffic, and this accentuated the silence.

There were no cheery salutations between men as they met. No talk of any kind. Only that disheartened look, as if their whole spirit were crushed and broken. Poverty and hunger seemed rampant everywhere, and the coldness of the approaching winter was adding to the miseries of all.

But the look upon the faces of the women he met was the most poignant of all, and went to his heart like a knife – a look of cold, inevitable death seemed to lurk behind their eyes. They passed along with shawls over their bowed heads, and drawn tightly round their shivering bodies.

Occasionally he met a couple of men carrying a coffin, containing some victim of the epidemic, trudging with heavy feet towards the cemetery, or sometimes a woman carrying a rude little coffin towards her home, and all this seemed to deepen the tragedy of the times more and more.

The disheartening spectacle of the streets oppressed Rennie, and his heart was heavy.

Would it have been better if the men had worked away, and accepted the coal-owners' terms, he wondered?

Perhaps the position had not been examined carefully enough before the fight was entered into. Would it be better to end it all now, or go on? Thus the questions leapt in his mind, with always the doubt whether sufficient care had been taken to foresee the probable result of the policy they had pursued.

Then his mind went back over the history of the past hundred years, and the wrongs which had roused him in the past.

But in the light of the present state of things, with the sight of the women's faces before him, he asked himself, had the right time and the right methods been selected? Revolutions need organization, and must not be entered upon in a haphazard way.

This was a tragedy before which all the past paled into insignificance, and if it could be ended by any effort, would it not be better to do it? But could it be ended now? Even though the strike were called off, that would not end it. Long years of suffering must now be borne before any easing of the burden could come. The streets were more thickly populated than he had seen them for many days past, and most of the men seemed to be bent for the meeting place. But it was a silent crowd which shuffled along, like a procession of phantoms. There was no eager discussion, such as used to characterize such crowds on former occasions. No examination of the pros and cons of the case that was agitating their minds. Not even a controversy regarding the relative merits or fault of the leaders.

When Rennie reached the hall he found it packed; but what a dull, spiritless, silent crowd it was; not a single pipe was being smoked!

Men sat merely looking dully before them, or stood as if undecided what to say or do. There was no life about them, and they did not seem even to have the spirit to resent a clumsy intruder.

Prompt to time, two men emerged from an ante-room, both of them well-known colliery managers in the district, and men who had been closely identified with the public life of the town for years.

Barney Blades, as soon as he saw who the two men were, was on his feet in an instant. 'Who is responsible for calling this meeting?' he asked.

'We are,' answered one of the men from the platform. 'We felt that it was impossible to allow things to go on as they are any longer. We feel that a settlement, so far as this district is concerned, might be arrived at, and those for whom work could be provided might return.'

'If you have ony offer tae mak', why dae you no' mak' it tae the men's leaders?' questioned Blades.

'Because we feel that leaders don't matter now,' was the reply. 'And this tragedy must be ended as soon as possible.'

'Wha are you acting for?' persisted the hunchback, his eyes becoming hard.

'The coal-owners in the district,' was the answer.

'Well, the owners don't matter noo, either,' rejoined Blades, and just the faintest shuffle of feet was heard from the audience to greet his remark. 'Look here, men,' cried Blades, encouraged by this slight sign of life and spirit, as he turned to address the men, 'this is a miners' meeting. Are we sure that only miners are present? We are not, and we should mak' sure that only miners are here.'

Another faint rattle of feet greeted his remarks, and gathering still more encouragement, Blades went on to appeal to them not to be too ready to listen to outsiders, as he called the managers. If the owners had a reasonable offer to make, they could make it through the recognized channel.

'It'll be a bad day for us,' he cried, now fully warmed up, 'when we canna decide oor ain affairs. Even though it may be surrender, let us dae it like men, wi' colours flyin' – even though they fly above the grave o' oor hopes. We've still oor manhood left!'

'Hear, hear,' cried one man in the front row, roused by Blades' passionate words. 'We'll decide oorsels.'

This was soon agreed to, and Blades asked all who were not miners to retire at once. But he was not satisfied with the two managers going out.

'I want every man in this hall tae mak' sure that his neighbour sittin' aside him is a miner,' he cried, and soon began an excited altercation here and there, followed by the ejectment of about a score of individuals who could not be identified as miners. After the doors were again closed, Blades ascended the platform amid applause, and beckoning to Rennie to come up beside him, faced the men.

'Let it never be said,' he began, in his warm, musical voice, 'that the men o' Blantyre, even wi' starvation and death starin' them in the face, ratted on their comrades. We're gaun through tae the end – nae maitter what the end is – thegether. Men wha are men die wi' their faces tae the enemy, or they trample their enemies beneath their feet.'

Then breaking out into a fiery lyrical flow of words, he recounted incidents of the past, stories of the time when women and children toiled in the mines. He recalled every injustice he had ever heard of or experienced, and soon had his hearers under the spell of his magic voice.

Rennie sat trying to keep his mental balance. He was amazed at the transformation in the face and figure of Blades, as the speech rolled from the lips like a hot torrent of passion. He moved his audience just as he willed, and no one was conscious of his defective, mis-shapen form, or unpleasing features.

The magic and beauty, the unbreakable spirit, and dominant will, crying their wrongs down the ages, and the appeal to the smouldering self-respect, that even hunger could not kill, kept the audience spellbound.

Hungry faces lit up, and sunken eyes flashed with the fire of revolt once again. Rennie could see in the rows of seats lips parted and gasping, as Blades' voice soared or sank.

'If you dare gang back noo,' concluded the dwarf, his voice ringing through the hearts of his hearers, 'all the bitter tears that ever were shed shall never wash oot the shame of your surrender – the waters o' the seven seas could never obliterate it. Langer than time it shall last tae mock you. When eternity begins it will be there tae taunt you. If yin among you is prepared tae surrender noo, may God in heaven an' the devil in hell curse you forever an' ever!'

It was certainly lurid oratory, but Rennie felt that he had never listened to anything more moving, and when Blades sat down, the audience rose as one man and yelled themselves hoarse.

They had been broken and spiritless when they entered the building; but here they were now, hungry and emaciated, yet ready to storm the Bastille of tyranny at the bidding of the hunchback, who by the magic of his voice and the power of his personality, swayed them to his mood.

They were wild with excitement and enthusiasm. Hunger gnawed at every stomach, every heart was tortured by the suffering at their fireside, every mind had been dulled by privation and lack of food; but they still had their manhood, and like men they knew how to die, even though they had never known what it was to live fully.

Many speeches were made after Blades had sat down, all professing determination to fight to the end. A new fire burned in their famished bodies, and the light of it filled their hungry eyes.

'We hinna got much tae be happy on, men,' cried Blades, again taking the floor, not a little proud of his triumph as he saw the lighted eyes of the men in front of him.

'We are a' hungry for bread,' he went on, 'but we are hungrier for beauty. I'll gie you a sang, if you like. I was born tae be a singer. I ken that; but the cursed Capitalist system denied me the richt tae be yin. Listen tae this. It was written by a Blantyre miner; but it has the fire o' genius in it,' and clearing his throat, he broke into a song – a song which held them spell-bound.

I ken a road, a bonnie road, a lanesome road that's dear tae me;
It winds an' turns like mountain brook, the lovely road tae Netherlea;
For there the nicht fa's saft an' still, an' tirls the heart wi' wanton glee –
The fair road – the rare road – the lovely road tae Netherlea!

Fou' mony a bonnie laddie gangs alang that bonnie windin' way,
An' mony a lassie gangs wi' him tae hear what he has got tae say;
The merry stars look doon – the moon keeks oot frae hint a cloud
    tae see
The rare sichts, the fair sichts, upon the road tae Netherlea.

For mony a secret there is told, an' mony a tale o' grief an' pain,
The merry skies ne'er heed the sighs that wring the hearts o' maids
  or men;
An' pitiless the nicht gaes by, on fleetin' hurried wing sae free –
The sere road – the drear road – the tragic road tae Netherlea.

An' yet, for a' the pain, I lo'e that bonnie, wanderin', lanesome way,
For what it gave me, an' I'll lo'e it dearly till my hinmost day;
An' when the end comes, in my heart, you'll fin' inscribed in letters
  free –
The fair name – the rare name – the lovely name o' Netherlea!

Blades had certainly a wonderful voice. A short gasp came from an old
man in the front row, who strove to swallow something that had risen
in his throat, and Rennie saw many eyes glisten among the hungry,
famished faces, as if they had looked upon the face of beauty, and had
been awed by the glory of it.

'There is but yae thing, men, on God's earth that I care aboot,' said
Blades with emotion, 'an' that is music. I'd sell my sowl for it. I feel that
I hae a gift in that direction, but I'm prevented by the rotten system frae
makin' the maist o't. But thank God,' he went on, his voice becoming
again vibrant with passion, 'we'll change that,' and he was off again in
a tirade against 'the System,' as he called it, until it seemed as if all the
wrongs and degradations of the past, in the long evolution of human
society, were crying through his blood for redress.

A loud knocking at the door brought the meeting to a panic, and in
stepped four policemen, and a half a dozen soldiers.

The men were angry, and the policemen and soldiers were immediately driven out into the street, followed by the now infuriated mob.
But once on the street the crowd was soon broken up, a few of them
receiving broken heads, and driven along the streets till they were
dispersed, and about a dozen of them were taken prisoners.

When the soldiers and police had burst into the hall, Blades, by an
adroit move, retreated behind the screen on the platform, pulling
Rennie with him; and slipping along they got to an ante-room, and
opening the door stepped out into a back street, then through a close,
and soon were in the open fields beyond.

'Come on, let us go back,' protested Rennie, 'I don't like the idea
o' rinnin' awa' an' leaving the rest tae face thae brutes. A wise general
disna dae that.'

'A wise general,' returned Blades carelessly, 'never gets caught. He
escapes, an' has aye anither chance tae rally his men. A livin' general,

even though a rotten yin, is better than ten deid yins. Sae come on an' dinna blether.'

Rennie followed without further protest, through fields, and over ditches, scrambling through hedges, and finally, after nearly an hour's running, they reached the Cadder Glen.

'That was a dam'd narrow squeak,' said Blades, in a panting whisper, as they sat down at the mouth of the old mine to await the arrival of some others they expected to turn up. 'I suppose we are noo finished,' he went on solemnly after a pause. 'That's the end o' the game we've been playin', an' "The Morlocks" will hae tae adopt new tactics noo.'

'Ay. I'm dootin' you're richt,' agreed Rennie grimly. 'It's us noo for jail or glory, if ever they put hands on us.'

'Ay,' grunted Blades still gloomily, 'but if we are tae gang doon, by Heavens! we'll gang doon fightin' every inch o' the way. We'll either end it, or mak' it worse,' and a star or two peeped out from the thick mantle of clouds in the sky, as if to witness his vow.

H.R. *Barbor*   Sabotage

Benjamin Thatcher tended his garden during the long days of inactivity. It was fine in these lovely spring days to have nothing to do but turn the spade, tie up the tender cabbages, and inspect the blossom on the dozen fruit trees that ran down from his cottage to the railway siding.

Two Sundays had come and gone since the last signal had fallen before an oncoming train. Days ago, the young men, the shunters and the single porter among them, had marched off to join the rebel army; all except young Bert Lomas had gone, and Bert had sided with Thomas Davis, landlord of the Cross Keys, declaring himself opposed to the wild talk of the majority. What with a broken arm sustained in the final argument with a departing farm-hand, and the sneers of the village women, Benjamin reckoned that young Bert must be having a poor time of it. In a way he felt sorry for the lad, but no doubt his mother was a-fossicking of him up.

Mind you, it wasn't all so gay. You didn't know what had become of your own kith and kin, and a villageful of womenfolk wasn't likely to take things quietly, the way he had learned to. How could they, with all these rumours about?

Only the day before yesterday, Mrs Brindle had come down to his garden gate with a tale of her daughter-in-law dreaming that the little troop of Wickworth men had been ambushed by a party of cavalry in the Lisley woods ... 'and she seed the soldiers a-pricking of them with long lances, and Sid Motherwell a-running away from a corporal on a big white horse, and him with his game leg not going so fast as you might think and the soldier spurrin' and spurrin' and not catching Siddie, which howsomdever he'd nearly done, and going to run him through the back when our Mabel wakes up a-screechin' fire an' murder as you might say, and wakin' me. And that's a nice goin'-on for a young woman expecting her first at the end of May or thereabouts, Mr Thatcher!'

Then there was Cissie Cramp, who'd walked every inch of the road from Lyntham, where she'd been in service. And she'd come back with that to tell as no woman should know, and half distraught.

151

It was useless to try to keep it from the others that a whole pack of rebels caught by the troops had been finished off in the market-place like so many sheep. The other tales which passed from mouth to mouth might, he knew, be twisted and twirled till you couldn't tell one end from t'other. All the same, these were rum days and the less said the better. For his part he'd never meddled in politics. The railway company paid him enough and they knew he could do his job. There was a pension coming soon. What more did a man want? So he reasoned to himself as daily and day-long he worked on the half-acre of land that was wife, child and chapel to the lonely old man.

Beneath this egocentric philosophy, as a matter of fact he was seriously perturbed. Not his was the questing intelligence that seeks the roots of change; long years of a narrow occupational round, untempered by the common vicissitudes of family life, had made him indifferent to the happenings that went on round him in the tiny village, but his indifference was static, and he had never hardened as might a more imaginative man. The villagers regarded him as a 'rare stick-in-the-mud,' but knew him for a kindly listener, easy-going and 'proper.' They respected him by reason of his uniform and of his garden. In truth he was singularly detached from the vices and virtues of his fellows – a Diogenes who made out of a village his tub, across which the black shadow of tyranny had never fallen. And for forty years, since the death of his bride within a few weeks of their marriage, he had been content with the strait confines of that tub, had indeed still further narrowed his domain by the exclusion of chapel, which forms a large part of the life of such small communities. 'I worship the Lord as I've a mind,' he often said in explanation, 'and bein' so, I don't see what the minister has got to offer me.'

It needed, therefore, constant self-persuasion to banish the restlessness that had affected him during the last week and which threatened his sleep at night. It would have been a simple matter to account for this unease by the cessation of his official duties, and his freedom from the necessity of attending to the trucks of sand which lay neglected up the siding near the deserted sand-buoy. This would not have provided a true explanation, but it would have sufficed him, perhaps. However, he did not try to diagnose this unusual emotion. He simply denied it categorically. Nevertheless that did not allay it.

While he worked in his garden tending the familiar beds of vegetables and young plants, he was at peace. Busied with these pursuits, the days of revolution passed him by. The telephone bell, the only voice of command that ever spoke to him, was silent. When it spoke again he would be at his post; meanwhile it was fine weather for a gardener. That was all.

One afternoon the telephone bell did ring again. Benjamin Thatcher laid his hoe down gently and went to his box. A strange voice spoke from a down-line station, a hard, domineering voice which Thatcher resented vaguely. It asked him abrupt questions which seemed quite outside the range of his duties and the import of which he did not grasp. Also it told him that in a few hours a party of troops would come to the Wickworth halt. He was advised to keep a still tongue in his head. It was very strange, and when he returned to his gardening he found little zest in the work and soon gave it up, gathered together his tools and went into his cottage. He pottered about for some time, and then set about putting everything straight in the little signal-box as if for inspection. Soon he heard a train approaching.

It consisted of an old express steam-engine, the *Pegasus*, which Thatcher remembered as the one-time pride of the line which he worked. Behind the engine were half a dozen coaches, and a few open trucks covered with tarpaulins. Thatcher was still at a loss to understand the meaning of it all when the train drew up alongside the primitive platform of sleepers that served the Wickworthians as a station. From the train a number of troops disembarked with jostling hilarity. The majority were lined up on the road that ran alongside the platform. Others threw back the tarpaulins from some of the trucks and got the guns and munitions. Several officers ran hither and thither, ordering and surveying the busy troops; others stood in groups on the platform. Thatcher waited diffidently until they should notice him or require his help. He was impressed by the precision of the assembled troops and the quick business-like movements of the artillery men. The whole situation made its definite impact on his turgid mentality, exciting him. To the villagers this extraordinary descent had its news value. But underneath his interest there was that restlessness, that sense of something impending which had not left him since the youth of the village responded to the speeches of that socialist fellow and marched away.

The trouble was growing now; he felt the increasing pressure of an unknown need: something became clamant within him. He had denied, denied – but it would not be stifled.

An officer questioned him concerning the life of the village during the last few days. Thatcher told him in his own garrulous fashion the progress of events. Next, the troops were quartered upon the cottagers, in barns, in the church and the chapel. Two transport officers were apportioned to his hospitality; the rest found accommodation with the eager Welshman, the proprietor of the Cross Keys.

The military had taken control of the tiny station, but he hung about aimlessly, thinking to be of service to the indifferent officers. As the day waned parties of troops filed out of the village, 'pickets' the officers called them. They would be on the watch, he thought for ... for federals, bands of fellows like Nat Sayer, Jimmy Algood, Geoffry Field and young Chris Wrigley, and others who had gone from Wickworth. It wasn't pleasant to think of their being shot down by these crisp soldiers. Somehow they seemed too much alike, the troops and the rebel villagers. But it was no business of his, Ben Thatcher's: he was a loyal subject – never got himself mixed up with politics.

At dusk he went home and prepared a simple meal for his two uninvited and awesome guests, – eggs, ample supplies of bread and butter and jam, and a huge enamel pot of tea. The two young men ate plentifully and talked of the campaign without reserve. Obviously the villager did not impress them as a potential adversary. A good enough sort of chap, and dull.

Thatcher learned that this horde of soldiers which had descended upon the comatose village was only an advance party feeling its way up to a great company of the federal force to northward. After midnight the main body, two big trains full of troops and equipment, would arrive at Wickworth. In the morning these troops would advance to outflank the oncoming red army, and by breaking this extremity of their front would reduce the pressure of the western rebel advance on London. The railway man did not understand much about military tactics, and the terminology and the expressive campaign slang which the young men used mystified him. But one thing he did realise clearly was that by their use of this side line the goverment forces had stolen a march on the revolutionists, and that the advent of those detachments due at midnight might quite conceivably be a determining factor in this war which had been taking its fratricidal toll these two weeks while he had tended his cabbages and admired the pink and white splendour of his orchard trees.

The new facts of the situation intensified the trouble of his spirit but did not rouse him fully. When the two officers had eaten their meal they went out together, and Thatcher found the silent house too much for his nerves, excited by the surprises and revelations of the last few hours. He went to the Cross Keys. The inn was full of noisy soldiery and soon he was fain to leave their boisterous company and to escape from their excrementitious wit and their braggart talk of the approaching conflict.

Down the road he was stopped at her cottage by Jessie Tighe, who asked him hysterically what was going to happen to them all.

'Don't you be feart, Mrs Tighe. The more's the smoke the less the fire. It's no use upsettin' yourself when there's nothin' to be done. Jest take it easy and tell the others to do the same, and whatever you do don't have no big talk with the soldiers. Tomorrow they'll be gone; best let them go in peace and wait patient.'

'Bless you, Mr Thatcher,' the girl said morosely but with more composure. 'I was that worried, what with these strange tommies about and Fred away and me not knowin' how he's farin'!'

'It's a main terror and no mistake, Mrs Tighe. But nothin's to be got by worritin'. Patience, patience!'

Nothing to be done, absolutely nothing. Poor young woman – there must be a number like her, too. It didn't seem fair that these women should have to feed and house the very men who were out to kill their husbands. But then the whole thing wasn't fair. It wasn't fair that strangers should be in command at the halt, his own particular province. But there was nothing to be done. Nothing?

He had reached the field path that skirted Maxon's orchard and ran down to his own land. As he came near to the gate of his own garden he heard a masculine voice insinuatingly lowered and answering giggles of mollified reproach. Against the sky he recognised the shape of a service cap – 'Some damned soldier messin' about with Draycott's eldest,' he told himself. He was coming to hate khaki.

If only – .

Dejected and overstrung he went to bed early but not to sleep. For an hour or more he turned about on the uncomfortable mattress, listening to the unusual sounds of footsteps on the roadway, and wondering how it all would end. Soon after eleven a quick step on the flags outside was followed by a knock at his door. He slipped some clothes on and opened the door to a corporal.

'You're the station-master, ain't you?'

'Yes.'

'Major Yeo wants yer dahn at the r'ilw'y. Sed would yer come sharp?'

In a few minutes he was dressed and hurrying down to the platform where the officers were assembled. The corporal took him past a sentry and brought him to the Major.

'O, good! Sorry to fetch you out of bed, Thatcher,' said the cheerful Major with easy patronage.

'Not at all, sir. Anything I can do, you may rely –.' The formula of officialdom came heavily from his rustic tongue.

'Thanks. We want to shift this train into the siding. My men aren't quite used to your points here, so I thought we'd better apply to the expert, ha! ha! Working in the dark, y' know, isn't any too easy, and I want everything shipshape for the arrival of the regiment.'

'Just so, sir.'

'Lieutenant Sowerby might explain just what we want from Mr – er – Thatcher.'

The Major turned to other business, leaving Thatcher and the lieutenant to arrange for the removal of the train from the siding. This was soon accomplished and Thatcher was free to return to his bed or otherwise dispose of himself as inclination might dictate. Drifting out into the open space betwixt road and station, he found a corporal and sergeant whose acquaintance he had made at the tavern earlier in the evening. They were cheerfully communicative and chatted with the railway man for a few moments.

The permeating unrest was translating itself into a vague plan. He asked the two noncoms. to have a hot drink at his cottage over the way, a suggestion they were eager to follow. Soon he had between them a jug of hot milk stiffly laced with rum, and the two tired warriors were drinking his very good health in cordial style. With a skill which surprised him, so uncertain was he of his own intention, he soon had them talking of their own part in the country-wide revolt.

They had, he gathered, seen no actual fighting – 'on'y seen the dust flyin' as they sheered orf once; that's the nighest we've bin, ain't it, Sergeant?' remarked the man with two stripes.

'You wait, though. We're in for it this time, if I know a bee from a bull's foot,' the beefy sergeant replied. 'If I can't see when old man Yeo's getting the wind up, I'll swaller my puttees.'

Thatcher moved to fill the corporal's emptied glass. 'No more and thanking you,' said that worthy. 'Enough's as good as a feast. I gotta go on duty, you know.'

'Gawd's truth, 'ave it while you can drink it, my lad, with all doo respec' to the station-master 'ere. ''Andsome of you and all, it is,' the sergeant added turning to Thatcher and raising his brimming glass in silent toast.

'Jest so, Sergeant. That's the idea, I take it. Who knows where you'll be tomorrow, eh?' Thatcher replied cheerfully.

''R, that's true. Might be pushin' up the daisies, eh? Though that's not my luck just yet. I didn't go through Cambrai for nothink, nor

Ireland. No, sir, when I'm for it I reckon I shall know it,' he ended with the cocksure philosophy of the campaigner.

'Do you now?' prompted the curious Thatcher.

''R.' was the sergeant's *non sequitur.*

'I suppose you'll be movin' on tommorrer?'

''Spose so. P'r'aps tonight. Everything depends on orders, y' know. And we don't 'ave the makin' of them.'

''M. Will you be going on by train, do you think?'

'No, that's def'nit. There's no chance of that. *They*'ve got us taped.' The stressed pronoun was an uncertain quantity to Thatcher. He asked:

'*They* bein' the rebels?'

''R. Poor silly fools.'

'Bloody 'ounds I call 'em,' averred the corporal. 'Murderin' lot of swine.'

'Gawd, Corporal. They ain't so bad as what Jerry was, anyhow. Put 'em at worst, they're British.'

'I'd british 'em , if I 'ad my way. Hang 'em every man jack of em, I would, an' no bloody error.'

'Well, you won't, any'ow. There won't be such a many left for hangin' when we've got goin' on 'em tomorrow. I heard young Lieutenant Smithers sayin' as they was bringing up heavy supports of armoured cars. They'll be here soon, by Jove. One o'clock, Sergeant Matthews said, didn't he?'

''M, and it's ar' pas' twelve,' said the corporal with a yawn. Soon afterwards they bade their host goodnight and departed.

Three times Benjamin, sitting alone by the remnants of the fire, began to unlace his boots, and three times he retied the lace. A wild plan was maturing — had matured — in his slow-moving mind. He knew all the improbability of achievement, and the unforced obedience of a lifetime was inert against the new dynamism which was driving him out to strike for — Wickworth? ... the federals? ... revolution? Inward conflict frustrated clear recognition of the boundaries of his intention. The issues near at hand were harassment enough, and they would not be denied. He went down to the siding skirting the groups of military, and, keeping a line of trucks between him and the platform, walked steadily to the signal box. A single hand-lamp burned inside. He crept up the wooden stairway: no one there. Bending double lest his dark silhouette against the faint-lit windows should arouse the suspicions of the soldiery, he slipped into the box. To move the cross-over points was an affair of moments only, but the subsequent pause, while he waited to see if the noise of moving metal had told its tale to the enemy, was torment

– growing with the continued silence to exultation almost as painful. The way was open for him now.

Once out of the box and down behind the trucks again, he laughed to himself. A new mood possessed him: he had become the automaton of his scheme now, and an intensely subjective enjoyment of the doings of the automaton's other Benjamin Thatcher possessed him as he made his way to the pit siding. In his breast pocket he had a short-handled hammer which the signalman used to break up coal.

It was very quiet, but the faint mist made it difficult to ascertain if anyone were guarding the train. He knew that steam was up and guessed that there would be an engineer, if not two, in the cab of the engine. One thing at a time. An hour ago he had supervised the shunting of the train right back on to a row of trucks that had been filled only the day before the general strike had begun with that famous red sand which carried Wickworth's name through the eastern-midland counties. Those trucks must be attached to the empty carriages in order to give the momentum he required. Surely and with cat-like watchfulness he examined the couplings of the hindmost trucks, and then linked the first of them to the rear carriage of the train. Next he slipped into the brake-van and took off the brake.

These engrossing preliminaries ended, the more difficult task only remained – that of getting control of the engine. For ten precious minutes he revolved in his mind how this might be accomplished but without getting any nearer the solution. At last, grown desperate with the passing minutes, he walked noisily up to the red-lit cab.

Wonderful! Only one chap aboard!

The young engineer recognised and greeted the villager, glad of a companion to break the tedium of his vigil. For a few minutes they chatted. Thatcher was growing distracted, but still he had no plan. In open fight this young Titan would crush him, and even if he could beat him there was no time for a struggle – the platform was only a hundred and fifty yards away. They would be on him before he could master the fellow. Suddenly through the dark night came the sound of a sharp challenge followed by a nervous cry – some villager, startling or startled by a watchful sentry.

The engineer rose with a yawn and swung half out of the cab, listening. In a moment Thatcher had smashed the hammer home just above his occiput. The flexed arms straightened as the hands relaxed their grip of the rail, and soundlessly the senseless body fell forward to the ground. Then Thatcher opened up the steam, a thud of compression shook the giant engine, it moved, lurched, took the weight. Clink-clank–clank–clank, clink, the couplings of the trucks rattled together. They were off.

Elated, the railwayman thrust the lever right over; his Pegasus drank the new force eagerly and tugged at the bridle. He was now level with the platform, but between it and him ran a triple track of lines. Over these half a dozen soldiers were scampering in a vain endeavour to outdistance fatality.

The thundering engine, now rushing down the gradient under full steam, roared happily out and away through the mist. Thatcher, passenger and crew in one, fed the well-stocked entrails as he might and watched the gauges as if the fortune of his mad venture depended upon them. He was happy now; the uncertainty and self-suppression of the last days had gone. Gone too had every other thought save the immediate promise of turning, crushing in final combat the reactionary army that was coming along the line to meet him. He did not think of the results of this act; the horror of his deed, of his own position even, never once touched him. Enough that he would succeed. Glancing out through the oval windows he could see nothing ahead but the ruddy glow of the fires imprisoned by the thickening mist, for they were reaching the lower level now. 'Good old Peggie!' he muttered cheerfully.

Then it was all over. He was lying at the bottom of the embankment. Quite conscious and quite happy. He did not know that his leg was crushed into a triangle under his back, because his back also, was broken. But he knew he had succeeded because he could see the broken train on the sky-line, a piled-up mass that straggled down the side of the lofty bank.

While he watched, one or two figures, against the sky too, seemed to shift about anxiously. Then the vagrant wind drove the mist up between him and his achievement. He never saw a third train rush through that mist on to the dismembered wreckage of the other two, and pile itself also in desperate confusion along with the rest. If he had heard or seen that, he would perhaps have laughed outright. As it was, he only continued to smile, and that was because he was dead.

James Leslie Mitchell   One Man with a Dream

I

BOOM!

Hardly had the distant reverberations ceased before the sunset wind blew in the greenery of the city palms. It was as if Cairo sighed audibly. Day was officially dead. Crowned in red, squatting in the colours of the west, the Moqattam Hills peered down, perhaps to glimpse a miraculous moment on the surface of the Nile.

The Nile flowed red like a river of blood.

Rejeb ibn Saud, squatting in the Bulaq hut by the Nile bank, looked at his wrist-watch, at the face of the unconscious boy on the string-bed, at the fall of light on Gezireh across the river. But for one insistent whisper, the startling sunset was now a thing woven of silence.

'The sea! The sea!'

Song of the homing Nile! Gathering, hastening to fulfilment and freedom, joining its thousand voices, all the yearnings of its leagues of desert wandering, in that passionately whispered under-cry: 'The sea!'

All that afternoon the cry had haunted him. Now, as the boy on the bed tossed and moaned, Ibn Saud shook himself, stood up, and bent over the bed.

'Son Hassan ...'

The hut door opened of a sudden. Out of the sunset glare, into the dimness of the hut, Sayyiya, Ibn Saud's sister-in-law, entered. She was a Sudanese, young, full-faced, thick-lipped. At the tall figure of Ibn Saud she glanced inquiringly, then also went to the bed and bent over it. The boy Hassan seemed scarce to breathe.

'In an hour we shall know, master.'

'In an hour I shall not be here.' The man looked away from the string-bed. The chill on his heart had chilled his voice. Even in that moment, only by an effort could he keep from listening to the insistent whisper of the river.

'You go to the Khan Khalil to lead the Jihad? It is to-night?'

Ibn Saud nodded. It was to-night. An hour after the fall of darkness the Warren hordes, poured into the Khan il Khalil, were to be mustered and armed. Police and gendarmes, half of them active adherents of the insurrection, would have withdrawn from all western and central Cairo. The two native regiments had been seduced from allegiance to the puppet Nationalist Government: were enthusiastically for the rising: themselves awaited only the signal from the Khan il Khalil, the lighting of the torch.

And it would be lit. That was to be Rejeb ibn Saud's part. Golden-tongued, first in popularity of the rising's masters, he was to be the last to address the brown battalions in the Khan. For them he was to strike fire to the torch that would, ere another morning, light the flames of vengeance and revolution across the European city from Bulaq to Heliopolis.

The song of the Nile – of a sudden he knew why it had so haunted. Such the cry – of fulfilment, of freedom attained – that would to-night rise on the welling tide of the Black Warrens, from thousands of throats, from all the pitiful Cohorts of the Lost, the Cheated of the Sunlight ...

'Master, if you come not back –'

Ibn Saud started. In his cold ecstasy he had forgotten the hut, Sayyiya, even Hassan.

'That is with God. But if Hassan – Listen, woman. You will come to me at the Khan. When the change, one way or another, has passed upon my son, come to the Shoemakers' Bazaar, by the south side of the Khan, and send word to me. You will find your way?'

'I will come.'

Something in her glance touched him, stirred him from his abstraction.

'The time has been weary for you since Edei died, Sayyiya. If I live through this night – '

Suddenly the woman was crouching at his feet on the mud floor. Passionately, scaredly, she caught at the long cloak he had wrapped about him.

'Master – Rejeb ... Those English whom you lead against to-night – they are ever strong, ever wary. If you die, what will happen to Hassan and to me? Master –'

Ibn Saud's cold eyes blazed. He flung the woman from him, flung open the hut door. Beyond, seen from the elevation of the Bulaq bank, the Cairene roofs lay chequered in shadows.

'And what of the folk – our bothers, our sisters – who die out there in their hovels and hunger? Thousands every year.' He blazed with the sudden, white-hot anger of the fanatic. 'What matters your miserable life – Hassan's – mine – if we can show the sun to those who rot their lives away in the kennels of the Warrens? We miserable "natives" – unclean things with unclean souls – to-night we shall light such a candle in Eygpt as no man –'

He halted abruptly. The fire fell from him. Speaking in Arabic, he had yet thought in a famous alien phrase. Under his dark skin spread a slow flush. Without further speech he bent and kissed his son, and then walked out of the hut into the wine-red gloaming.

Sayyiya crouched dazed upon the floor. Then a sound disturbed her. From the throat of the boy Hassan came a strange, strangled moan.

The small, wasted body tossed for a little, then lay very still.

II

Darkness was still an hour distant. European Cairo thronged her streets, cried her wares, wore her gayest frocks, set forth on evening excursions to Saqqara and the Sphinx. John Caldon, seated on the terrace of the Continental, awoke from a sunset dream and turned towards his brother-in-law, Robert Sidgwick.

'Eh?'

'... the edge of a volcano.'

'Where?'

'There.' Sidgwick waved his hand to the brown driftage in the street below them. 'The political situation's the worst it has been for months. The Cairenes have been propaganda'ed for months by Nationalist extremists. Trade and employment are bad. The native quarters are seething.'

'Very proper of them.'

Caldon smiled into the lighting of a cigarette. An artist, he was making a westward world-tour from England. Together with his wife and daughter, he had arrived from India, via Suez, only the day before. Sidgwick's statement left him unimpressed. He had never yet encountered a white man, settled amongst brown, who was not living on the edge of a volcano. It was the correct place to live, just as it was the correct thing for a volcano to seethe pleasingly upon occasion.

Sidgwick had the monologue habit. Through the quiet air and the blue cloud from his own cigarette Caldon caught at a number of phrases.

'This damn self-government foolishness began it all ... Treat a native as a native.'

'Why not as a human being?'

'That's what we've done here. Look at the result.'

Caldon was boredly ironical. 'Self-government – with an army of occupation! An alarum-clock with the alarum taken away!'

'It's advisable – if you give it to a native ... Take it my sister's never told you about young Thomas O'Donnell?'

Caldon shook his head. Sidgwick nodded, without pleasantness.

'Well, the telling won't hurt you. He was a half-caste – an Irish-Sudanese, of all grotesque mixtures. His father had had him sent to a school in Alexandria; some kind of irrigation engineer out here the father was, and pious to boot. He died when his son was seventeen, leaving instructions for the latter to be sent to a theological college in England to train as a missionary. All very right and proper. To England young Thomas O'Donnell came. To Bleckingham.'

Caldon, with some little show of interest, nodded. Sidgwick resumed.

'You know – though your people didn't settle in Bleckingham till about a year after the time of O'Donnell – the lost tribes the Theological College spates over the countryside to tea and tennis on spare afternoons? One of these tennis-do's I met O'Donnell. He was a tall, personable nigger – not black, of course. Cream-colour. But it wouldn't have worried me in those days if charcoal had made a white mark on him. He was interesting. I liked him, invited him to tea. Clare Lily was young also, in those days, you'll have to remember.'

'Why?' A tinge of red had come on the artist's cheekbones.

'Oh, Caesar's wife is stainless enough,' hastily. 'But a young girl hardly knows herself – or the stuff she handles. Had it been a white man, of course ...

Yes, Clare Lily became fairly intimate with O'Donnell. Flirted with him, no doubt. Mother was then the same invalid as you knew; I was supposed to be my sister's protector. But I suffered from attempting the assimilation of indigestible theories on the brotherhood of man. I admired O'Donnell. Oh, he fascinated.'

The light all down the Sharia Kamil had softened. Caldon sat rigid. It was Sidgwick who dreamt now.

'The outcome of it all was what I'd expect now. O'Donnell and Clare Lily went picnicking on Bewlay Tor ... The nigger attempted to act according to his nature. Clare Lily's screams saved her – attracted some students mountaineering. O'Donnell went berserk amongst them. You see, he wasn't a white man.'

'What happened to him?'

'God knows. He didn't wait to be hoofed out of the College. They traced him as far as Southampton, where it was supposed he'd managed to get a job on board some ship ... Hallo, here's Clare. Good Lord, what's the —'

A woman was running up the steps from the taxi which had stopped below the terrace — a woman with a white, scared face. Behind her, weeping, came trailing the ayah of Caldon's daughter.

'Jack, Jack! Oh, my God ... Clare Lily — we lost her down in the bazaars, in the horrible Warrens. Jack — they stoned us when we tried to find her ...'

III

Never had it all seemed so secure.

But Rejeb ibn Saud, far out of the direct route from Bulaq to the Khan il Khalil, and striding down the Maghrabi with his '*aba* pulled close about his face, saw signs enough that were not of the olden times. Few native vendors were about; no desert folk, sightseers of the sightseers from foreign lands, lingered by the hotels. Here and there, making way for the strolling foreigner, some dark Arab face would grow the darker.

Ibn Saud had a sudden vision: Fire in the Maghrabi, massacre and loot; the screamings of rape, crackle of rifle fire, knives in brown hands ...

In three hours — at the most.

Ibn Saud half stopped in his stride; the Maghrabi blurred before his eyes. Slave of the faith which had bound him these many years, he was yet compounded of so many warring hopes and pities that his imagination could suddenly sway him, to gladness or to despair, from a long mapped-out path ... The Green Republic of Islam — attained through murder most foul and bloody — was it justified?

A stout Frenchman and his wife moved off the sidewalk in order to pass the crazed native who had suddenly stopped in their path, muttering. Looking curiously back at him, they saw him move on slowly, dully, with bent head.

So, with none of his former pace and purposefulness, he went, in a little turning northwards into the deeper dusk of the Sharia Kamil. The whimsical intent that had originally led him to diverge through the European quarter still drew him on, but he followed it in a brooding daze. At the entrance to the bookshop of Zarkeilo he was jarred with realisation of his quest.

Nevertheless, he entered, and, disregarding the assistant's question, passed down into the interior of the shop to the section that housed Continental editions of English fiction and verse. With an almost feverish eagerness he began to scan the titles. About, the walls were here and there decorated with sham antiques – bronzes, paintings of Coptic Virgins, and the like. To a small red volume Ibn Saud at length outreached an unsteady hand.

Remembering he turned the leaves. Ten years since this book had lain in his hands, but he had remembered it – remembered because of those lines which haunted him, which had inspired him since, a homeless vagrant, he had landed at Suez to his dream of Egyptian Renaissance, to the years of toil and persecution in which he had built up this night's insurrection .... With their music and their magic, undimmed from of olden time, the words leapt at him from the printed page:

> 'One man with a dream, at pleasure
>   Shall go forth and conquer a crown;
> And three with a new song's measure
>   Shall trample a kingdom down.'

Rejeb ibn Saud replaced the book, straightened, stood upright with shining eyes. Doubts fell from him. Outside, in the night, his dream went forth to conquer ...

His eyes fell on a sham antique crucifix. Last of the gloaming light upon it, the tortured Christ fell forward from the cross. Upon his head, each carven point a-glitter, shone the crown of thorns.

IV

'Stone her! Stone her!'

Nightfall; in the fastnesses of the native quarter – the maze of the streets that radiate around the eastern sector of the Sharia el Muski; a girl running – a child of nine, English, with a flushed, scared face; behind, peltingly, laughingly, dirt and stone hurling, a horde of native children.

Such adults as were about turned amused glances to follow the chase. The hunt was up!

Ibn Saud halted and watched. Nearer drew the child, casting terrified glances to right and left. Then she caught his eye. Straight as an arrow towards him she came, clutching his cloak, and clung to him, panting.

The pursuing children surrounded them. One, a ragged hunchback, caught at the girl's dress. Ibn Saud spoke.

'Let be.'

'Why? She is English. We are to kill them all to-night.'

Hate and curiosity in their eyes, the children drew closer. Two loafers joined them, and one addressed Ibn Saud.

'It is so, brother. Let the children have their sport. Who are you to stop it?'

'I am Ibn Saud.'

At that name the children, cruel no longer, but shy and worshipping, drew away. The loafers, whose hatred of the English had apparently not induced in them any desire to join the army of the insurrection in the Khan il Khalil, slunk aside. Ibn Saud touched the girl's head. She had lost her hat.

'How did this happen?' He asked in English.

'Mother and nurse took me to the bazaars. I saw a shop I liked, and went into it. It had lots of doors. Perhaps I came out at the wrong one. When I did I couldn't see either mother or nurse. Then I walked and walked. And those children struck me and cried things and chased me. I ran. Then I saw you.'

Thus, succinctly, the little maid. Ibn Saud stared down at her, a wonder in his eyes.

'But why did you think I would help you?'

The girl raised clear, confident eyes. 'Oh, I knew you would because – because you are different.'

An odd flush came on the face of the insurrectionist. He stood thoughtful. Folly, in any case. He was only saving the child for –

Oh, inevitable. He glanced impatiently round the dusking street. Then:

'What is your name?'

'Clare Lily.'

He stood very still and then bent and stared into her face. For so long did he remain in that posture that the child's lips began to quiver. As in a dream Ibn Saud heard himself question her.

'Where is your mother staying in Cairo?'

'At the Continental. If I could get a taxi – ' She was calm and methodical and very grown up now. Ibn Saud took her hand.

'Come.'

He hurried. Through a maze of odoriferous alleys and walled-in corridors – the kennels of the Cheated of the Sunlight – he led her till on the dusk blazed a long sword of light. It was the Sharia el Muski, strangely bereft of traffic. With difficulty Ibn Saud found an *arabiyeh*. When directed to take the child to the Continental, the driver blankly refused. Not to-night. Then Ibn Saud drew aside the folds of his head-dress, and spoke his name, and the driver saluted to head and heart. In Cairo that night that name was more powerful than the Prophet's.

What would it be by dawn?

'Thank you very much.' The earnest eyes of the child looked up into Ibn Saud's dark face. With a sudden thought: 'Please, what is your name? – so that I can tell mother.'

Child though she was, she was never to forget him, standing there in the lamplight as he answered her:

'I am Thomas O'Donnell.'

V

Brugh! Boom! Brugh!

In a great square space, ringed about by the bulking of the bazaar's three bonfires burned, shedding a red light on the massing hundreds of the Black Warrens. Against the Khalil wall was upraised a giant platform. At the other side of the square, curious, antique, a thing of the ages and with the passion of all Man's sweated travail in its beat, was mounted a gigantic drum. Out into the night and the lowe, over the heads of the massing insurrectionists, over the hastening chains of Cairenes converging on the Khan from alley and gutter, its challenge boomed, menacing, stifled, a gathering frenzy.

Already, eastwards and northwards, curtains of scouting insurrectionists, awaiting the final word, hung as self-deputed guards upon the heart of the revolt. But there was little need of guard. The gendarme had laid aside his uniform, kept his rifle, and was now mingling with the mobs of the Khan il Khalil. The petty official, long European-clad, was in burnous and kuftan, uplifting his voice in the wail of chanting which ever and anon rose to drown even the clamour of the drum. Spearhead of the revolt, the Cairene Labour Union massed its scores of rail and tramway strikers.

The hour was at hand.

'Brothers –'

From amidst the notables on the platform, one had stepped forth. High and dim above the Cheated of the Sunlight he upraised his hand.

Es-Saif of El Azhar. An echo and an interpretation of the savage drumming, his voice beat over the silenced square. He had the marvellous elocutionary powers of the trained native, the passion of the fanatic, the gift of welding a mob into a Jihad.

Presently, as the words rained upon them, long Eastern wails of approbation began to arise. Other speakers followed Es-Saif. The great bonfires, heaped anew, splashed the throngs and the grisly walls with ruddy colour. Quicker began to beat the blood in heart and head. Clearer and louder arose the pack bayings of applause.

Jammed in the midst of the vast concourse below the platform, Rejeb ibn Saud stood listening to the voices of his lieutenants. As if deafness had crept upon him, they sounded incredibly remote ...

Clare Lily! Dream-child, clear-eyed and unspoilt. By now she would be safe. And to-morrow, somewhere amidst charred beams and smoking rafters, he might stumble over her bones ...

Surely the square and the bodies around him steamed with heat? What was Es-Saif saying? 'Our starved children who have died, who have cried in the darkness and held out their dying hands –'

Children crying in the darkness ... What was all history but a record of that? Hundreds, this night. Clare Lily weeping in terror, the terror-filled mites of the Warrens, Hassan ...

'Ibn Saud!'

In a long lane that was closing behind him, a man had forced his way from the foot of the giant platform.

'We thought you lost or captured. We would have torn down your prison with our bare hands. Come, it is near your time to speak.'

He spoke in the commanding voice of a worshipping disciple, and then turned back towards the platform. Through the opening throng Ibn Saud followed him ... Near his time. In a few minutes now he would stand forth on that platform and fire the blood-lust in the maddened horde whose lusts he had trained and nourished all these years.

He found himself climbing to the platform. Dim hands guided him on either side, faces, red-lit, grotesque, profiled and vanished in the bonfires' glare. Abayyad was speaking now. At sight of Ibn Saud, Es-Saif leapt up, and kissed him and led him to a seat, wondering a little at his lack of greeting, and the brooding intentness of the dark, still face.

Wave upon wave, a sea of faces below him. As one looking out upon his kingdom Ibn Saud stood a moment, and suddenly his eyes blazed, aweing to silence the murmured questionings of Es-Saif.

Clare-Lily – Hassan – all the children of the Warrens and of all the warring races of men – *With them lay the world.* Not with his generation – white and brown alike, they had failed. Yet he and his faith – a faith builded on an ancient wrong in the long-dead years – had sown hatred in the hearts of the Warren children against Clare Lily and her kind. He had sought to poison the unguessable future that was not his: he sought to murder it now in death for the hearts and hands that might save the world, might win a wide path through all the tangles of breed and creed and race, reach even to that dream that might yet be no dream – the Brotherhood of Man ...

Below him the mist that was the mustering insurrection quivered. What was that?

He stared across to the far side of the Khan. Through the throngs, from the direction of the Shoemakers' Bazaar, a Sudanese was slowly forcing his way towards the platform. With the force of an utter certainty, Rejeb ibn Saud knew him for what he was.

He was Sayyiya's messenger.

VI

Abayyad's voice rose and fell in penultimate peroration. Behind him, Ibn Saud, watching the approach of the messenger, stood with a sudden fire alight in his chilled heart.

For the sake of that his vision of the World of Youth, he would stake all on Chance and the mercy of God. If Sayyiya's note told of Hassan's recovery, he would violate every enthusiasm of his life in the Warrens, would speak peace to the mobs, cry on them to desist, preach to them the vision of the world that had arisen before his eyes. So, if there was a God, if he had but spared Hassan, he would speak ...

The lights in the Khan il Khalil flung a glow upon the heavens. Ibn Saud looked up. Beyond the glow, clear and cold, shone the stars. Infinitely remote, infinitely impersonal ...

Clare Lily – Hassan – the saving of the near and dear to one – how pitiful!

'Ibn Saud! Ibn Saud!'

The shouting of his name beat in his ears. Urgently upon his sleeve he felt the hand of Es-Saif. Abayyad had finished. Following the shout, upon the Khan fell a vast hush, broken only by the sound of a throaty breathing as Sayyiya's messenger reached the platform.

Ibn Saud took the note that was handed to him, unfolded it, and read.

VII

Then a strange thing happened. About him, on the platform of the insurrectionists, they heard him. Ibn Saud laughed – a low, clear laugh, and glanced up again at the stars.

Infinitely remote.

The note slipped from his hand. To the edge of the platform he stepped forward and spoke. For a full minute, sonorous, golden, the voice beloved of the dim brown multitudes of the Warrens rang clear. Then, obscuring it, began to rise murmurs of astonishment, counter-murmurs for silence. The stillness that had held the massed insurrection vanished. The crowds wavered and shook.

'Traitor!'

A single voice spoke from the heart of the mob. A hundred voices took it up, a hundred others – those of Ibn Saud's personal following – shouted to drown the word. Pandemonium broke loose. Men screamed and argued, and over the whole Khan swung and wavered the hand of an incredible fear.

'Infidel! Englishman!'

Face distorted, Abayyad sprang forward upon Ibn Saud. As at the touch of frost, the hand of that fear stilled for a moment the tumult below.

In that moment Abayyad, with gleaming knife, struck home.

Ibn Saud shook him off. Crowned and infinitely humble, he outreached both arms in a benediction, ancient and immemorial ...

With a roar as of the sea, the hordes rose in a wave and poured upon the platform.

VIII

Es-Saif wanders an exile in the land of the Senussi. The secret history of that night in the Cairene Warrens – that night which saw the insurrection fall like a house of cards in the wreckage of the stormed platform of the Khan, which saw the rebel battalions, heart-broken and in despair, break up and scatter to hut and hovel – is as dim to him as to any who heard the traitorous speech for which Rejeb ibn Saud paid with his life.

Yet from the platform Es-Saif salved a curious relic – the crumpled note sent by Sayyiya to the leader of the insurrection. Reading it, who can guess the dream for which Ibn Saud cheated himself of his bargain with God, or what crown he went forth to conquer?

'To my master, Rejeb ibn Saud. The mercy of God the Compassionate be with you. Thy son Hassan died at the fall of darkness. – SAYYIYA.'

Sources

Liam O'Flaherty, 'The Tramp' from his *Spring Sowing* (London, 1924) pp. 40–59

R.M. Fox, 'Casuals of the City' from his *Drifting Men* (London, 1930), pp. 1–9

Alfred Holdsworth, 'The Jungle' (unpublished)

Stacey W. Hyde, 'The Turner' from his *Shopmates* (London, 1924), pp. 1–13

Norman Venner, 'Give and Take' from *Woodworkers' Monthly Journal* (November 1928), pp. 640–1 [first published in the *Passing Show*, 26 May 1928]

Arthur Siffleet, 'Joe Crabbe's Christmas Dinner' from the *Sunday Worker*, 26 December 1926

Joe Corrie, 'The Day Before the Pay' from his *The Last Day and Other Stories* (Glasgow, n. d. [1928]), pp. 19–21 [first published in the *Forward*, 28 January 1928]

Harold Heslop, 'Compensation' from the *Worker*, 24 August 1928

Dick Beech, 'A Home from Home' from the *Worker*, 17 August 1928

James Hanley, 'The Last Voyage' from his *Aria & Finale* (London, 1931)

Walter Greenwood, 'Joe Goes Home' from his *The Cleft Stick, or, 'It's the same the whole world over'* (London, 1937), pp. 107–9

Ethel Carnie Holdsworth, 'The Sheep' from the *Sunday Worker*, 30 May 1926

Katherine Mansfield, 'Life of Ma Parker' from her *The Garden Party and Other Stories* (London, 1928), pp. 154–65 (first published 1922)

D.H. Lawrence, 'Fanny and Annie' from *The Collected Short Stories of D.H. Lawrence* (London, 1955), vol. 2, pp. 458–72 [first published in *Hutchinson's Magazine*, 21 November 1921]

Rhys Davies, 'A Bed of Feathers' from the *London Aphrodite*, no. 2 (October 1928), pp. 129–50

Teddy Ashton, 'The Great Chowbent Football Match' from *Teddy Ashton's Lancashire Annual*, vol. 35 (1925–6), pp. 98–104

Hannah Mitchell (under the pseudonym of 'Daisy Nook'), 'May Day' from (*Labour's*) *Northern Voice*, vol. 1, no. 3, 15 May 1925

James C. Welsh, 'The Meeting' (title by the editor) from his *The Morlocks* (London, 1924), pp. 236–46

H.R. Barbor, 'Sabotage' from his *Against the Red Sky: Silhouettes of Revolution* (London, 1922), pp. 137–49

James Leslie Mitchell, 'One Man with a Dream' from the *Cornhill Magazine*, vol. 66 (1929), pp. 589–600

Biographical Notes

TEDDY ASHTON (1863–1935)

Teddy Ashton was one of the pseudonyms of Charles Allen Clarke, who was born in Bolton and became one of the most popular Lancashire writers of all time. At the age of eleven he started work in a mill, but soon trained as a pupil teacher, eventually turning to office work and journalism. Clarke wrote over twenty novels (mostly serialised), numerous dialect sketches and poems as well as historical, political and topographical works. He edited several newspapers and journals including the *Northern Weekly* (1896–1908) and *Teddy Ashton's Lancashire Annual* (1890–1935). He was a member of the Social Democratic Federation from 1887, later he joined the ILP and at one time formed a Piecers' Union. In 1900 he stood as joint SDF and ILP candidate for Rochdale. Among his most memorable works are the early strike novel *The Knobstick* (1893), a frequently reprinted enquiry into *The Effects of the Factory System** (1899), which is an indictment of the cotton industry, and the later novel *The Red Flag* (1908).

Biography: Paul Salveson, 'Introduction' to *Teddy Ashton's Lancashire Scrapbook** (Farnworth, 1985), pp. 2–4

Criticism: Paul Salveson, 'Allen Clarke and the Lancashire School of Working-Class Novelists' in H. Gustav Klaus ed., *The Rise of Socialist Fiction 1880–1914** (Brighton, 1987), pp. 172–202

H.R. BARBOR (1893–1933)

Herbert Reginald Barbor was born in Lowestoft, Suffolk. His life-long interest was the theatre. At one time he was the drama critic of A.R. Orage's *The New Age*. From 1919 to 1923 he edited *The Actor*, the official organ of the Actors' Association, of which he was a fierce proponent. His publications include a novel, *Against the Red Sky* (1922), a play, *Jezebel* (1924), and a pamphlet, *The Theatre: an Art and an Industry* (1924).

Criticism: H. Gustav Klaus ed., *The Socialist Novel in Britain** (Brighton, 1982), pp. 97–100

DICK BEECH (c.1895–19?)

Beech was a native of Hull. As a seaman, hobo and casual worker he
saw many parts of the world, including the United States and Australia.
He used this rich experience early in 1919 to hike from Murmansk to
beleaguered Petrograd where he attended the founding congress of the
Communist International. On his return to Britain he settled with
Moira, the daughter of James Connolly. During the 1920s he worked
for a Soviet company, but was later sacked when he refused to work
during a pay dispute. After a long period of 'odd' jobbing he opened
a junk shop. When it prospered, he started a paper of adverts, the *Small
Trader*. Like Heslop, in whose mother-in-law's house the Beechs lived
at one time, he contributed occasional short stories to the *Worker*.
Beech was later expelled from the Communist Party.

ETHEL CARNIE (HOLDSWORTH) (1886–1962)

Ethel Carnie, one of several Lancashire authors in this volume, began
working as a half-timer in a cotton mill at the age of nine. As an active
and able trade-union campaigner she became adept at articulating her
views not only in speech but also in print. Her first book was a small
volume of poetry, *Rhymes from the Factory* (1907). Thereafter she left the
mill and at Robert Blatchford's instigation served on the editorial board
of the *Woman Worker*. She now became a prolific writer of poems and
journalism, novels and children's stories. Following her marriage in 1915
she added Holdsworth to her name. Her best novels – *Miss Nobody*
(1913), *General Belinda* (1920) and *The Slavery* (1925) – are studies of
working women who display a sturdy independence and strength of
character. *Helen of the Four Gates* (1917) was made into a film. Ethel
Carnie stopped writing in the late thirties and disappeared from the labour
movement.

Biography: Edmund and Ruth Frow, 'Ethel Carnie: Writer, Feminist and
Socialist' in H. Gustav Klaus ed., *The Rise of Socialist Fiction 1880–1914**
(Brighton, 1987), pp. 251–66

Criticism: P.M. Ashraf, *Introduction to Working Class Literature in Great
Britain, Part II: Prose* (Berlin, 1979), pp. 176–95

JOE CORRIE (1896–1968)

Joe Corrie was born in Slamannan (Lanarkshire) but grew up in
Cardenden (Fife). He worked in the coalmines for some eighteen
years, then turned to fulltime writing. After writing verse (first collected

in *The Image o' God*, c.1927) and short stories (collected in *The Last Day*, 1928), he found his true vocation in drama. He began with one-act sketches and plays like *Hogmanay** (1926), written for the Bowhill Players, a group of miners and their wives, who in the late twenties and early thirties toured Scotland with Corrie's productions. Like *In Time o' Strife** (1927), his first and best-received full-length play, these early works were severe social criticism, exploring the domestic minutiae of the miners' struggle against poverty and exploitation. Altogether Corrie wrote some sixty plays, mainly for amateur companies. He also published a novel, *Black Earth* (1939), and briefly returned to verse with his *Poems* (1955).

Biography: Linda Mackenney, 'Introduction' to Joe Corrie, *Plays, Poems and Theatre Writings** (Edinburgh, 1985), pp. 7–18

RHYS DAVIES (1903–1978)

He was born the son of a grocer in the mining village of Clydach Vale in the Rhondda, which was also Lewis Jones's birthplace. Davies left South Wales in the 1920s and moved into the Bohemian world of Bloomsbury, struggling to become a professional writer. He also went to Germany and France and was befriended by D.H. Lawrence. Davies was the author of over a dozen short-story volumes and about as many novels, of which the early ones like *The Withered Root* (1927) explore the relationship between religious faith and sensual passion among the inhabitants of a Welsh mining valley. There are several collections of his short stories, among them *The Collected Stories of Rhys Davies* (1955), but none is complete.

Autobiography: *Print of a Hare's Foot* (London, 1969)

Criticism: David Rees, *Rhys Davies** (Cardiff, 1975)

R.M. FOX (1891–1969)

Richard Michael Fox was born in London and began work in an engineering plant at the age of fourteen. He became involved in trade unionism and syndicalism and joined the editorial board of the *Industrial Worker*. In 1914 he won a scholarship to Ruskin College but could not take it up as a result of the outbreak of war. He was a champion of the emancipation of women and a staunch anti-militarist for which he suffered two years of solitary confinement and hard labour. After the war he finally went to Ruskin College, followed by travels to revolutionary Russia and France. His first book, *Factory Echoes* (1919), was a collection of sketches. In the twenties Fox took to free-lance writing and settled in Ireland. Among his books are a critique of the factory system, *The Triumphant Machine* (1928), and a study of *Rebel Irishwomen* (1935). Fox always retained his commitment to, and interest in, the development of Socialism. In old age he visited Communist China and published his *China Diary* (1959).

Autobiography: *Smoky Crusade* (London, 1937)

WALTER GREENWOOD (1903–1974)

Greenwood spent his childhood in the 'Hanky Park' area of Salford, which is the setting of the work that made his name, *Love on the Dole*★ (1933). Even before leaving school at the age of thirteen he worked part-time on a milk round and with a pawnbroker. After that he went through a variety of jobs and periods of unemployment before turning to full-time writing after the success of his first novel. In the mid-thirties Greenwood joined the short-lived Socialist League and was elected to Salford City Council. He wrote ten more novels, among them *His Worship the Mayor* (1934) and *What Everybody Wants* (1954), none of which, however, was to enjoy the success of *Love on the Dole*. He was also the author of several plays and film scripts including *The Cure for Love*★ (1945) and *Saturday Night at the Crown* (1958).

Autobiography: *There Was a Time* (London, 1967)

Criticism: Roger Webster. 'Love on the Dole and the Aesthetic of Contradiction' in Jeremy Hawthorn ed., *The British Working-Class Novel in the Twentieth Century* (London, 1984), pp. 49–62

JAMES HANLEY (1901–1985)

Hanley was born in Dublin but grew up on Merseyside. At the age of fourteen he went to sea, there finding the subject to which he was to return time and again, the work and lives of sailors and dockers. Several of his early works were prosecuted and banned, among them the war tale *The German Prisoner* (1930) and his second novel *Boy*★ (1931), which is the story of the miseries and indignities suffered by a boy first in the slums, then on his first voyage. Hanley published approximately fifty books in which he continually explored the dilemmas of the common people. At the same time, he was always open to experiments in style. Apart from the early fiction, his most memorable works are the four novels that constitute the *Furys Chronicle* and, in addition, *Hollow Sea* (1938), *The Closed Harbour* (1952) and *A Woman in the Sky* (1973). The *Collected Stories* (1953) are not complete.

Autobiography: *Broken Water* (London, 1937)

Criticism: Ken Worpole, *Dockers and Detectives** (London, 1983), pp. 78–93

HAROLD HESLOP (1898–1983)

Heslop was born in the Durham coalfield and went down the mine himself at the age of fourteen. In 1924 he won a two-year scholarship to the Central Labour College in London. After the General Strike he was made redundant and suffered prolonged spells of unemployment until he secured a job at the London Intourist Office. He made his literary debut with a novel first published in the Soviet Union, *Pod Vlastu Uglya* (1926), later issued in Britain as *Goaf* (1934). Five more novels followed: *The Gate of a Strange Field* (1929), *Journey Beyond* (1930), the thriller *The Crime of Peter Ropner* (1934), *Last Cage Down** (1935) and *The Earth Beneath* (1946), an historical fiction. He also co-authored *The Abdication of Edward VIII* (1937), published under the pseudonym J. Lincoln White. In 1930 he was one of two British delegates at the Second International Conference of Revolutionary and Proletarian Writers in Kharkov. Heslop was a member of the Labour Party, and under its banner stood for Parliament in the 1950s.

Biography: H. Gustav Klaus, *The Literature of Labour* (Brighton, 1985), pp. 89–105

Criticism: Valentine Cunningham, *British Writers of the Thirties** (Oxford, 1988), passim.

ALFRED HOLDSWORTH (1885–1963)

Alfred Holdsworth was born in the West Riding of Yorkshire. After a stint of clerical work he went on the tramp in North America, on one occasion meeting Jack London. This was followed by a journey to New Zealand. On his return to Britain he became active in the labour movement. Shortly after his marriage with Ethel Carnie in 1915, he was called up, seeing the end of the war in a German prisoner-of-war compound. From 1923 to 1925 he edited and wrote most of *The Clear Light*, a non-sectarian, early anti-fascist monthly. In the latter half of the twenties he briefly joined the Communist Party. After separating from his wife he lived a solitary life in a cottage on the West Riding-Lancashire border, a noted country chiropodist and moorland lover. Some of his poems were published posthumously, *A Poet Passed* ... (1968), ed. Ian Dewhirst.

Biography: William Holt, *I Haven't Unpacked* (London, 1942 [1939]), pp. 223–35

STACEY W. HYDE (1897–19?)

Hyde was born in London, but grew up in Kent. Here, after a formal education which ended at the age of fourteen, he became an engineering draughtsman in a big industrial plant. His first publication was *Shopmates* (1924), a collection of stories. This was followed by several novels including *Simple Annals* (1925), *The Blank Wall* (1928), *The Blackleg* (1930) and *That One Talent* (1939).

Criticism: S. Dynamov, 'Stacey Hyde an Artist of English Social Fascism', *International Literature*, no. 2–3 (1932), pp. 116–21

D.H. LAWRENCE (1885–1930)

David Herbert Lawrence was born in Eastwood, Nottinghamshire, the son of a working miner. At the age of sixteen he worked briefly as a clerk in a surgical goods factory, then became a pupil teacher, and after gaining a teacher's certificate, a schoolmaster in Croydon. He gave up his post after the publication of his first novel, *The White Peacock*★ (1911), and henceforth lived by his writings. He travelled to Germany and Italy, and in 1919 left England permanently in a search for an ideal living place. The early chapters of *Sons and Lovers*★ (1913) and several items from his first short-story collection *The Prussian Officer*★ (1914) enact many aspects of the day-to-day experience of an East Midlands mining community at the turn of the century. *The Rainbow*★ (1915), his second major novel, was suppressed shortly after its publication, while *Woman in Love*★ (1920) and *Lady Chatterley's Lover*★ (1928) were at first only privately printed outside Britain. After a visit to his native district during the long miners' strike of 1926, Lawrence became once again interested in the fortunes of the mining communities, as the first two versions of the latter novel demonstrate.

Biography: Harry T. Moore, *The Priest of Love* (London, 1974)

Criticism: Graham Holderness, *D.H. Lawrence: History, Ideology, and Fiction* (Dublin, 1982)

KATHERINE MANSFIELD (1888–1923)

This was the pen-name of Kathleen Mansfield Beauchamp, who was born into a well-to-do business family in Wellington, New Zealand. At the age of fourteen she was sent to London for a higher education. She returned to New Zealand in 1907, but left again for Europe during the following year, leading a restless life in England, Germany and France which ended in a premature death from tuberculosis. A small allowance from her father had enabled her to embark on a literary career, and she became one of the few writers whose reputation rests entirely on her short stories. These were published in five volumes, of which the last four – *Prelude** (1918), *Bliss** (1920), *The Garden Party** (1922) and *The Dove's Nest** (1923) – contain much her best work. Her second husband, John Middleton Murry, later edited her *Letters** (1928) and her *Journal** (1931, 1954).

Biography: Antony Alpers, *The Life of Katherine Mansfield** (London, 1980)

Criticism: Clare Hanson and Andrew Gurr, *Katherine Mansfield* (London, 1981)

HANNAH MITCHELL (1871–1956)

Hannah Webster was born on a farm in the Peak District, Derbyshire. With practically no formal schooling, she educated herself and, after leaving the country, went into domestic service, then worked as a dressmaker and shop assistant. With her future husband she fervently embraced the socialist cause, joining the ILP and the Clarion Movement. She also campaigned for the Women's Social and Political Union and the Suffragette Movement. Hannah Mitchell spent most of her life in Lancashire. She was for many years a Manchester City Councillor, served on the magistrate's bench and on the Public Assistance Relief Committee. She published dialect sketches in *Labour's Northern Voice* and articles in various other periodicals.

Autobiography: *The Hard Way Up. The Autobiography of Hannah Mitchell Suffragette and Rebel* (London, 1968)

JAMES LESLIE MITCHELL (1901–1935)

Mitchell is probably better known as Lewis Grassic Gibbon, the author of the trilogy *A Scots Quair** (1932–4). But before he published under this pseudonym, which was reserved for his Scottish stories and novels, Mitchell wrote several novels, story cycles and ethnographical works under his real name. Among these the novels *Stained Radiance* (1930), *Thirteenth Disciple* (1931) and *Spartacus* (1933), and the non-fictional *Conquest of the Maya* (1934) deserve special mention.

Mitchell was of peasant origin and grew up on a little croft near Arbuthnott (Kincardineshire). At the age of sixteen he became a junior reporter. He was an early convert to Marxism, joining the first Aberdeen Soviet and supporting the Glasgow shop stewards movement in 1918–9. After a spell of unemployment he was constrained to seek a livelihood in the armed forces, in which he served for almost ten years. He was stationed in Egypt, Persia and India, which suited his wide-ranging historical, archeological and ethnographic interests. On his discharge from the RAF in 1929 he became a full-time writer for the remainder of his short life. *A Scots Hairst* (1967) contains a number of his short stories.

Biography: Ian S. Munro, *Leslie Mitchell: Lewis Grassic Gibbon* (Edinburgh, 1966)

Criticism: Ian Campbell, *Lewis Grassic Gibbon** (Edinburgh, 1985)

LIAM O'FLAHERTY (1896–1984)

Liam O'Flaherty was born on Inishmore, one of the poverty-stricken Aran Islands, into a large and destitute family. He won a scholarship to University College, Dublin, but after a year joined the British Army and saw active service in France, where he was seriously wounded. After being discharged O'Flaherty went to sea. In 1922 he seized the Rotunda in Dublin with some unemployed docker-comrades, hoisting the red flag. During the twenties he moved frequently between Dublin and London, eventually turning to full-time writing. In his principal novels he dealt with lower-class, civil-war Ireland (*The Informer**, 1925; *The Assassin**, 1928) or the Irish past (*Famine**, 1937; *Insurrection**, 1950). The themes of most of his short stories, of which he wrote more than a hundred and fifty, are taken from rural and animal life. O'Flaherty also wrote in Gaelic.

Biography: Patrick F. Sheeran, *The Novels of Liam O'Flaherty** (Dublin, 1976), Part I

Criticism: A.A. Kelly, *Liam O'Flaherty the Storyteller* (London, 1976)

ARTHUR SIFFLEET

Siffleet lived in South London. He served on the editorial board of *The Call* (1916–20), the organ of the British Socialist Party. Elected to Tooting Council (Greater London) in 1919, he joined the Communist

Party on its foundation. He regularly wrote for *The Call*, both articles and short stories, and later contributed sporadically to *The Sunday Worker*.

NORMAN VENNER (1863–193?)

Norman Venner (i.e. George Alfred Wade) was a journalist and short story writer. In 1889 he took a B.A. from London University. One of his first book publications was the manual *Writing for the Magazines* (1901). The author wrote for very many different journals and newspapers using his real name as well as the pseudonyms The Scholar Gipsy and Norman Venner. Under the latter he published five novels between 1925 and 1929, the most successful of which was *The Imperfect Imposter* (1925).

JAMES C. WELSH (1880–1954)

James Welsh was born in the mining village of Haywood, Lanarkshire, which is also the setting of his first novel, *The Underworld* (1920). He went down the mine at the age of twelve, working in the pit for the next twenty-four years. As an active trade unionist and a member of the ILP, he was elected vice-president of the Lanarkshire Miners' Union in 1919. From 1922 to 1931 he was MP for Coatbridge, and from 1935 to 1945 for the Bothwell division. Welsh's first book was a volume of poems, *Songs of a Miner* (1917), but his real breakthrough came with *The Underworld*, of which some 80,000 copies were sold during the twenties and which was translated into several languages. This was followed by *The Morlocks* (1924) and a third, highly autobiographical novel, *Norman Dale, M.P.* (1928).

Biography: Joyce Bellamy and John Saville, 'James C. Welsh' in *Dictionary of Labour Biography**, vol. 2 (1974), pp. 399–401

Criticism: H. Gustav Klaus, 'James C. Welsh: Major Miner Novelist', *Scottish Literary Journal**, XIII,2 (1986), pp. 65–86

N.B.

The editor would be grateful for any additional information on H.R. Barbor, Dick Beech, Stacey W. Hyde, Arthur Siffleet and Norman Venner.

Suggestions for Further Reading

The preceding biographical notes include information on other works by the authors represented in this anthology as well as listing one (auto)biographical and one critical study where available. Titles marked with an asterisk* were in print at the time of going to press.

These suggestions can be usefully supplemented by consulting the following historical works:

Noreen Branson, *Britain in the Nineteen Twenties* (London, 1975)

Allen Hutt, *The Condition of the Working Class in Britain* (London, 1933)

Stuart Macintyre, *A Proletarian Science: Marxism in Britain 1917–1933*★ (Cambridge, 1980)

Charles Loch Mowat, *Britain Between the Wars 1918–1940*★ (London, 1955)

A.J.P. Taylor, *English History 1914–1945*★ (Oxford, 1965)

Two critical books of related interest are:

Walter Allen, *The Short Stories in English*★ (Oxford, 1981)

Andy Croft, *Red Letter Days: British Fiction in the 1930s*★ (London, 1990)